Changing
Political Economies

Emerging Global Issues
Thomas G. Weiss, Series Editor

Published in association with the
Thomas J. Watson Jr. Institute for International Studies,
Brown University

Changing Political Economies

Privatization in Post-Communist and Reforming Communist States

■

edited by

Vedat Milor

Lynne Rienner Publishers ■ Boulder & London

Published in the United States of America in 1994 by
Lynne Rienner Publishers, Inc.
1800 30th Street, Boulder, Colorado 80301

and in the United Kingdom by
Lynne Rienner Publishers, Inc.
3 Henrietta Street, Covent Garden, London WC2E 8LU

Library of Congress Cataloging-in-Publication Data
Changing political economies : privatization in post-communist and
  reforming communist states / edited by Vedat Milor.
     p. cm.—(Emerging global issues)
  Includes bibliographical references and index.
  ISBN 1-55587-405-3 (alk. paper)
     1. Privatization—Europe, Eastern. 2. Privatization—Central
Europe. 3. Privatization—Asia, Central. I. Milor, Vedat.
II. Series.
HD4140.7.C48 1994
338.947—dc20   93-34548
                                                              CIP

British Cataloguing in Publication Data
A Cataloguing in Publication record for this book
is available from the British Library.

Printed and bound in the United States of America

The paper used in this publication meets the requirements
of the American National Standard for Permanence of
Paper for Printed Library Materials Z39.48-1984.

Contents

List of Tables and Figures   vii
List of Abbreviations   ix

1   Changing Political Economies: An Introduction
      Vedat Milor   1

Part 1   Privatization and Public Enterprise Reforms in Asia

2   Progress Without Privatization:
      The Reform of China's State Industries
      Thomas G. Rawski   27

3   Corporate Organization and Local Government
      Property Rights in China
      Andrew G. Walder   53

4   Mongolia: Privatization and System Transformation
      in an Isolated Economy
      Cevdet Denizer and Alan Gelb   67

**Part 2   Privatization and Private Sector Reform
in Central and Eastern Europe**

5   Rethinking Reform: Lessons from Polish Privatization
      Anthony Levitas   99

6   Path Dependence and Privatization Strategies
      in East-Central Europe
      David Stark   115

7 Strategy, Structure, and Spontaneous Privatization
   in Russia and Ukraine
   Simon Johnson, Heidi Kroll, and Santiago Eder   147

8 Private Sector Manufacturing in Eastern Europe:
   Some Cross-Country Comparisons
   Leila Webster   175

Part 3 Restructuring and Soft Budget Constraints
in Post-Communist States

9 Restructuring Programs in Transitional Economies
   Izak Atiyas   195

10 Can Privatization Solve the Problems of
   Soft Budget Constraints?
   Zhiyuan Cui   213

About the Authors   229
Index   231
About the Book   237
Books in the Series   238

Tables and Figures

Tables

2.1 Basic Data on State and Collective Industry, 1978 and 1988   30
2.2 Gross Value of Industrial Output, 1980 and 1990   31
2.3 Industrial Profits and Losses for 1989 by Industrial Branch   34
2.4 Industrial Profits and Losses for 1989 by Province   36
2.5 Links Between Profits and Retained Earnings
      for State Firms, Sample Data, 1980–1989   45
2.6 Links Between Profits and Retained Earnings
      by Industrial Branch, Sample Data for 1986   45
2.7 Links Between Per Capita Retained Earnings
      and Bonuses, Sample Data for State Enterprises
      in Selected Industrial Branches, 1986–1989   46
2.8 Links Between Access to Funds and Current or Lagged
      Retained Earnings, EI Sample Results for 1985 and 1986   49
4.1 Mongolia: Structural Indicators   70
4.2 Key Economic and Structural Reforms   72
4.3 Trading Data on Ulaanbaatar Hotel, Inc., Shares as
      of June 7, 1992   81
4.4 Model Equations and Base Values   88
4.5 Responses to External Shocks   90
4.6 Reverse Migration and Rural Taxation   91
4.7 Cushioning Adjustment Through Aid   92
7.1 Distribution of Firms in Kiev by Sector and
      Number of Employees   149
8.1 Numbers of Enterprises   178
8.2 History of Firms   183
8.3 Source of Factory Buildings   184
8.4 Strong and Weak Firms   188

Figures

4.1 Number of Shares   80
4.2 Stock Trading Volume   80
4.3 Share Price of Ulaanbaatar Hotel   81
4.4 Resource Envelope and Reforms   86
6.1 A Typology of Privatization Strategies in East-Central Europe   121

Abbreviations

AO	*Aktsionernye Obshchestva* (Joint Stock Companies)
CES	Constant Elasticity of Substitution
CGE	Computable General Equilibrium
CMEA	Council for Mutual Economic Assistance
EI	Institute for Economic Research of the Chinese Academy of Social Sciences
FDIC	Federal Deposit Insurance Corporation
GAAP	Generally Accepted Accounting Principles
GDP	Gross Domestic Product
GDR	German Democratic Republic
GMK	Economic Work Partnership
GNP	Gross National Product
IDA	Industrial Development Agency
IMF	International Monetary Fund
KFTs	Limited Liability Companies
m-c-m	money-commodity-money
MGOs	*Mezhotraslevye Gosudarstvennye Ob"edineniya* (Interbranch State Associations)
MP	*Maloe Predpriyatie* (Small Enterprise)
MPRP	Mongolian People's Revolutionary Party
RE	Retained Earnings
RTs	Joint Stock Companies
SBC	Soft Budget Constraint
SOE	State-Owned Enterprises
SPA	State Property Agency
TGS	Institute for Economic System Reform
UK	United Kingdom
US	United States
USSR	Soviet Union
VGMK	Enterprise Economic Work Partnership
VKFT	Enterprise Limited Liability Company

■ 1 ■

Changing Political Economies:
An Introduction

VEDAT MILOR

The economic architects of the post-Communist governments of East European and former Soviet Union republics, who are engaged in the heroic search for how to transform their backward economies into efficient and competitive ones, have turned to Western experts for help and advice. Interestingly, as Thomas Rawski argues in Chapter 2 of this volume, the advice given by some economists to these governments often sidesteps the basic rules of economic science in favor of quasi-theological dogma. This dogma, which finds a receptive audience in some university economic departments and powerful international organizations, is quite straightforward: introduce free prices, remove subsidies, open your economies to international trade, make your currencies freely convertible, tighten fiscal and monetary policy, quickly privatize state-owned enterprises, close inefficient plants, and lay off redundant workers.

The reform package offered to East European reformers required two unmistakable elements that were said to be necessary for success: coherence and optimal pace. Coherence implies that to be successful in the historic transition from centrally planned to market-driven economic systems, reformers "have little choice but to move on all fronts at once—or not move at all."[1] In other words, implementing some aspects of the reform program, such as price liberalization, while avoiding the pursuit of others, such as the privatization of state-owned enterprises (SOEs), would destroy the logic of the whole package and result in perverse forms of economic behavior. This idea is why reformers believe the optimal pace of the reforms is the fastest one—the so-called "shock-therapy" or "cold-turkey" approach.

The radical experts who advocate this approach are aware of the immediate implications of the program, and they acknowledge that the radical reform program would involve costs such as higher prices, unemployment, lost income, and more foreign debt. Yet they claim that these are short-term effects that will be offset by the longer-term benefits bound to accrue from

1

far-reaching marketization of all aspects of economic life in Eastern Europe. In addition, a political motive underlies the plea for the fastest possible pace of all reforms, especially speedy privatization of SOEs. According to advocates of the radical approach, it is important that organized political parties and lobbying groups barely existed in Eastern Europe when post-Communist governments took office. This absence provided a window of opportunity to implement a radical program guided by technical solutions rather than partisan considerations. In a similar vein, they argue that the privatization of the large industrial SOEs has to be accomplished quickly to avoid the risk that political parties may soon try to wrap their tentacles around these enterprises, which "can be a seemingly bottomless gold mine for patronage and party financing."[2]

It is interesting that, although immediate and complete privatization of state-owned industrial assets is central to the shock-therapy strategy, there is no support in theory or in Western experience for such a lopsided focus on privatization. The proponents of the radical approach invoke the notion of property rights to claim that only unrestricted and indivisible ownership rights lodged in the hands of private individuals will motivate economic agents to enhance the value of the productive assets they own. Yet Western experience suggests that property rights may be broken down in a variety of ways, including "the right to use, to derive income from the use of, to exclude others from, and the right to exchange the goods (or services) in one's possession."[3] This breakdown indicates that the notion of property rights is a plural one, in the sense of a number of rights that are neither indivisible nor unrestricted. Similarly, there is no a priori reason to believe that property rights in private hands lead necessarily to higher efficiency in the use of productive assets than property rights in the hands of public agencies. In fact, economic efficiency depends less on the nature of ownership than on the successful resolution of the monitoring problem, which is in fact a good deal more complicated than the question of private ownership. More will be said on the issue of private ownership in the discussion of "institutional economics," which addresses the ownership problem in a nonsimplistic way.

These theoretical considerations aside, there exist good empirical reasons to be skeptical about the merits of the shock-therapy approach. Almost three years have passed since the radical shock-therapy approach was the major inspiration behind economic reforms in Eastern Europe, but hopes for a rapid transition to prosperous market economies have faded. The problem is, contrary to the expectations of advocates of shock therapy, that all of the countries in Central and Eastern Europe are in the grip of a severe and extended recession.[4] Even in relatively successful countries such as the former Czechoslovakia, Hungary, and Poland, industrial output at the end of 1991 stood at about 65 percent of levels in 1989, when the reforms began.[5] Moreover, not only do prospects of a rapid recovery look dim but economists now estimate that it may take another decade before the real per capita output returns to prereform levels across the region.

The current decline in GDP and the contraction of industrial output in Eastern Europe may not cause alarm if one believes, as do proponents of shock therapy, that the dismal statistics reveal an inevitable adjustment process that will eventually lead toward a new pattern of production more in line with Eastern Europe's comparative and competitive advantages. There are elements of truth in this argument. For example, economists estimate that about a third of the fall in industrial output across the region was due to the enormous trade shock created by dismantling CMEA trade, which, in the past, guaranteed easy outlets for uncompetitive products, especially for the heavy industries.[6] Perhaps more important is the fact that in all East European countries and the former Soviet Union before transition, the share of industry in the GDP was more than 50 percent. This share is much higher than in capitalist countries at an analogous level of development. Inevitably, as post-Communist countries attempt to become more fully integrated into the international capitalist economy, they will need to downsize inefficient industrial enterprises and create new ones, especially in the service sector and in light manufacturing, in order to meet the higher standards of Western markets.[7]

However, the collapse in output hardly indicates a healthy structural adjustment to new markets. On the contrary, it reflects low-capacity utilization of capital and labor in public industries because of monetary and fiscal austerity measures, not redeployment to more productive ventures. In Poland, for instance, branches of industry such as electronics, ship building, textiles, and agricultural machinery are particularly hard-hit because of a virtual cessation of business with the former Soviet Union and a sharp decline in domestic demand. Yet not a single large enterprise in these industries has gone out of business in Poland so far, indicating that the state-owned industrial sector is in decline but not adjusting.

The ubiquity of this lack of adjustment, not only in Poland but throughout the region, has prompted research in enterprise behavior. The dominant form of explanation widely shared by neoclassical economists, the World Bank, and the IMF emphasizes that state managers still do not strive to maximize profits. Instead, the incentive structure they face motivates them to preserve employment and maintain wages at levels higher than those that would maximize the value of the enterprise.[8] There are three interrelated reasons for this situation, which smacks of market socialism. First, in countries such as Poland and Russia, organized labor is strong and is endowed with the legal and/or de facto power to fire managers who want to undertake effective restructuring of the enterprises. Second, the slow progress in institutional aspects of reform, such as the breakup of monopolies or the implementation of liquidation and bankruptcy procedures, has made managers unaccountable for their firms' performances by insulating them from market forces. Third, the slow progress of privatization has exacerbated this situation, which will not change until managers are controlled by shareholders exercising their voting rights and the associated threat of takeovers.

Advocates of shock therapy and radical market reform use some or all of the above arguments to justify early disappointment in their schemes. On closer inspection, however, a number of questions and paradoxes are left unanswered by a simplistic "free market" approach. In Chapter 5 of this book, for example, Anthony Levitas raises the question of how accurate it is to treat the employee councils or workers' councils as the chief culprit in preventing industrial adjustment. Before pointing fingers, one should consider the desperate economic plight and deteriorating industrial relations of the 250 Polish firms in which the state forced employees to scrap the employee councils and become commercialized properties of the Polish treasury. The 250 SOEs were commercialized to follow the advice of economists from international development organizations, who suggested corporatizing industrial enterprises from the top down as a prelude to eventual privatization. Is it not ironic that the defenders of this position, such as the European Bank for Reconstruction and Development, the IMF, and the World Bank, which are supposed to be proponents of market forces, are actually recommending that the transition from command to market economies start with a substantial legal enlargement of the role of the state? By the same token, slow progress in institutional reform can be accelerated only if the states further enhance their role and involve themselves in preprivatization restructuring of some large firms. Why is this prospect condemned by radical promarket reformers, who do not see a contradiction in banning the state from preprivatization restructuring of enterprises but at the same time advocate wholesale corporatization?[9]

In addition to these questions, some admittedly "free market" governments in Central Europe, such as in the former Czechoslovakia, followed the advice of radical reformers by adopting a "hands-off" approach to industrial restructuring. In essence, these governments were wishing away the question of sound management and regulation of the public sector, while relying on macroeconomic anchors and instruments (such as convertible exchange rate, tight credit, and high interest rates) and hoping that the complete privatization of large-scale SOEs would solve the thorny issue of structural adjustment. How realistic is it to pin so much hope on quick privatization when technical, practical, and sociopolitical impediments make it nearly impossible to find private owners for tens of thousands of enterprises in only two to three years, a goal that has been declared by many post-Communist governments?[10] If economic liberalization is implemented (which is easier than rapid privatization), and privatization and institutional reforms are slowed by the inevitable obstacles overlooked by radical privatizers, would not the radicals end up in the uncomfortable position of promoting a variant of self-management, even if their aims are to do just the opposite by demolishing the remnants of market socialism in post-Communist societies?

In addition to these theoretical musings about the drawbacks of the dominant paradigm, there is an unmistakable fact that brings radical views into question. The countries that adopted a more gradual and phased approach to economic reform seem to be doing better than those experimenting with the cold-turkey method. Hungary, for example, which adopted a less radical approach and retained controls on prices, foreign trade, and interest rates, seems to be economically outperforming Poland, which was a testing ground for the transition theories of neoclassical free-marketers.[11] In this context, it is also interesting to note that the first signs of a turnaround appeared in Poland at the end of 1992, after "a brilliant technocratic team under the leadership of Deputy Prime Minister [Leszek] Balcerowicz"[12] had been ousted from power and replaced by two successive governments that were more cautious in following radical precepts.[13]

Most impressive, however, is the economic record of China (elaborated by Andrew Walder, Chapter 3, and Thomas Rawski, Chapter 2, in this book), which is pursuing a middle-of-the-road approach between comprehensive planning and private initiative and has an impressive economic record. Conversely, as one eloquent advocate of gradualism reminded us, "no normative model is ever implemented cleanly, but in East Germany, the radical model came as close to complete implementation as one is likely to see. . . . That implementation resulted in the largest economic disaster in Europe in the postwar period."[14]

Ironically, despite theoretical and empirical evidence to the contrary, the radical free-market approach still remains the dominant paradigm in academic and policy circles and continues to set the parameters of ongoing public debate. Thus, the burden of proof lies with shock-therapy opponents, who should investigate the failures of this approach and search for alternatives. The authors of this volume, including distinguished academic and World Bank economists and social scientists, while differing in their themes and priorities, without exception resist the orthodox views of reform unless these views are first subjected to careful theoretical and empirical scrutiny. Hence, this book should be seen as a first step toward formulating an alternative approach by undertaking a sustained critical analysis of various elements of reform programs, especially privatization attempts, in reforming and post-Communist states in Eastern Europe and the former Soviet Union and in China.[15]

The chapters of the book grew out of a conference sponsored by Brown University's Center for the Comparative Study of Development and the Thomas J. Watson, Jr., Institute for International Studies at Brown University. Distinguished academicians and policymakers provided detailed comments on the papers presented at the conference, with the difficult goal of initiating a fruitful dialogue across disciplinary boundaries.[16]

The book is divided into three parts that are linked by the overarching theme of privatization. The three chapters in the first part tackle the systemic transformation of former socialist economies in Asia, namely China and Mongolia, by focusing on the privatization of industrial state enterprises and economic alternatives to privatization. The four chapters in the second part discuss similar issues for selected post-Communist economies in Central and Eastern Europe and the former Soviet Union. The third part consists of two chapters that question some of the neoclassical dogma about the role of states versus markets in industrial restructuring. It also analyzes the link between ownership and the soft budget constraints that face industrial enterprises.[17] Before highlighting the salient features of these chapters, it is necessary to discuss briefly the significance of privatization of state-owned assets in the new economics literature, which has informed many of the contributions to this book.

Institutional Economics and Privatization

One of the most exciting intellectual developments in economics in recent years was the resurgence of so-called institutional economics as a respected subdiscipline. This resurgence occurred many years after the teachings of such economists as F. List and T. Veblen had been relegated to the footnotes of scholarly treatises on the history of economics.[18] Like other new paradigms, the relevance of institutional economics stems less from its ability to discover new facts than from its pertinence in shedding new light on well-known phenomena and in generating a research program to address puzzles left unanswered by competing paradigms.[19] One feature of the new paradigm that is relevant for the privatization debate is its capability to distinguish between different types of capitalist and/or state-socialist economies on the basis of institutionalized ownership and control mechanisms. This capability makes it possible to go beyond the simple dichotomy of plan versus market theoretical constructs, with crucial implications for shaping the concept of reform in post-Communist societies.[20]

To simplify the discussion, institutional economists begin with the observation that in both state-socialist and modern capitalist economies, most productive resources are controlled directly by managers whose interests generally differ from those of owners.[21] A "principal-agent" problem arises because managers (agents) have more knowledge than owners (principals) of the technology and operating environment of the firm. It is plausible that managers, while pursuing their immediate interests, can hide crucial information from owners by painting a glorious but false picture of a company's future prospects in order to draw handsome salaries and bonuses. Of course, no rational "owner" will let a manager decapitalize a firm.

To prevent this problem, owners must directly monitor the behavior of managers, obtain information about performance indicators other than dividends and stock appreciation—which are often very misleading, and evaluate the quality of the strategies chosen by the manager.

However, directly monitoring a firm's performance is costly, and owners will weigh benefits and costs to determine the extent to which they will engage in direct monitoring. From this vantage point, there are distinctions not only between the capitalist and state-socialist economic systems but also among the categories of different subsystems, with crucial implications for economic efficiency and development. If in a particular capitalist economy ownership is so diluted that no owner has a controlling share of the firm, then it might be optimal for all owners to "free ride" and leave the task of managing to others. This is what happened to a great extent in the US economy during the 1980s, when, according to *The Economist,* a myriad of "punter capitalists"—institutional investors in mutual, pension, and money market funds—bought and sold equity in companies without even bothering to find out where these companies were located and what they produced.[22] This behavior was normal for these punter capitalists because, since they owned only a fraction of equity in a given firm, they lacked the incentive to monitor performance.

In contrast, other capitalist countries such as Japan and Germany outperformed the United States because they were able to institute ownership mechanisms that successfully addressed the principal-agent problem. Structural differences between these two countries notwithstanding, the existence of an easily identifiable set of corporate owners—such as large banks and industrial enterprises—helped to impose market discipline on managers. Consequently, not only was self-destructive behavior prevented but managers found it rewarding to adapt a long-term horizon in deciding on future investment and research strategies.

Of course, US capitalism is not entirely devoid of self-corrective mechanisms to reform the incentive structure for managers. One obvious mechanism that can motivate managers to pursue objectives compatible with the requirements of long-term growth is to give a share of the firm to the manager. Another less palatable and more unpopular choice is to discipline managers by the threat of hostile takeovers. Both of these mechanisms have been used in the United States in recent years, which—to some extent—counteracted the built-in self-destructive tendencies of the ownership structure in that country.[23]

In the post–state socialist bloc, except China, we can differentiate analytically between two variants of changing property regimes and the organizational structure of the economy. First, countries such as Poland in 1990 and some former Yugoslav republics, as Anthony Levitas remarks in Chapter 5, seem to resemble "the theoretical model of market socialism." That is, the historical legacy of the struggle against communism by organized workers in these countries created an economic order in which firms are self-managed by workers' collectives that have the authority to fire managers. Another key feature of this system is that, because the hierarchical links between the state and these firms have been completely broken during the reform process, enterprises are not accountable to any "owner" for their performance. In other words, it is a situation of all agents and no principal!

The other type of property system in Eastern Europe, which seems to be the dominant one (and even Poland may be evolving in this direction, to the extent that corporatization of the state-owned enterprises is accomplished), differs from the theoretical model of market socialism in two ways. First, the balance of power between managers and workers favors the managers, who are now much less constrained by the threat of their removal by workers. Second, after the breakup of hierarchical links with the central authority, enterprises have attempted to form or consolidate lateral links among themselves by creating "new vertical organizations [of their own] from below, and by consolidating or even extending their monopolistic patterns."[24]

Naturally, there are serious problems with both systems concerning the incentive structure facing enterprise directors. State managers are not motivated to achieve maximum profits in either system. In the first system, market socialism, decapitalization of existing firms can occur in three ways. First, existing machinery may not be maintained properly in an effort to lower maintenance costs and swell the surplus of resources immediately available. Second, replacement investments may amount to less than depreciation. Third, "reckless" wage setting may raise payments to workers at the expense of the long-term health of the company. The information collected in six major industrial sectors of Poland in 1990 proves that the second and third forms of decapitalization have been most common.[25]

The second system is a modified form of market socialism. It is not immune to the decapitalization problem, although the beneficiaries may be different from those in classical market socialism. In classical market socialism, workers are the beneficiaries because wages are maintained at higher levels than would maximize the value of the enterprise. In modified market socialism, however, the prime beneficiaries are the managers, who maximize their own salaries and perks. Another concrete danger of this second system is the effective suppression of economic competition and the resulting monopolistic behavior of the conglomerates that dominate the economy. It is as if all the negative features of command-style economic planning are reproduced except the one positive feature, which was the centrally planned system's ability to counteract monopolies' unproductive expansionist tendencies through myriad fiscal and monetary controls. The most alarming development under this second model is that, as in Russia's Vorkuta Coal Industry, the huge conglomerates that control almost all stages of commodity production and distribution may find it profitable to subordinate production to trade, primarily through a system of barter exchange that seems to have proliferated after the onset of shock therapy.[26]

Given all of the negative features of the property regimes in post-Communist societies summarized above, the obvious question revolves around the nature and speed of reforming them. To many, and above all to the advocates of the radical "big-bang" strategy, the answer is straightforward: immediate and complete privatization. The reassignment of ownership or property rights from governments to private entities is considered the major institutional reform that is the "only real hope" for Eastern Europe.[27] The skeptic may dare to qualify this statement by arguing that the priority for Eastern Europe should be the establishment of market-supportive institutions such as banking supervision, stock markets, regulatory agencies, and ownership organizations, controlled by the state treasury, that are necessary to exercise the state's property rights in the enterprises. One can also add that the state may be the sole force powerful enough to create these market-supportive institutions.[28] The skeptic will add that only after this process is underway can the privatization of large firms bring beneficial results. However, radical reformers, as epitomized in the following quotation from the liberal weekly, *The Economist,* hold no ambiguous views: "The idea that Eastern Europe's thousands of state-owned firms can be whipped into shape while still in government hands is a dangerous delusion."[29]

Privatization and Public Enterprise Reforms in Asia

A dangerous delusion? Perhaps, but China's success in improving the performance of productive enterprises without divesting the government of ownership rights in these enterprises renders such categorical statements suspect. In Chapters 2 and 3 of this book, various aspects of Chinese economic reforms are discussed. In "Progress Without Privatization: The Reform of China's State Industries," Thomas Rawski argues that gradual and partial introduction of market forces has substantially altered the managerial culture in a way favorable to risk-taking and innovation in the absence of privatization. In this well-documented chapter, Rawski highlights the role of competition, which is orchestrated carefully by the state, as the major factor responsible for the growing responsiveness of state enterprises to market signals. One can extrapolate that if a government opts for comprehensive privatization without tackling the thornier issues of de-verticalization of existing monopolies and antitrust reforms, privatization may do no more than replace public with private monopolies. Contrary to the practice in many East European countries, Chinese authorities do not conceive of privatization as the sole means of hardening budget constraints. Instead, reformers in China are trying to make the environment for enterprises much more competitive, while at the same time trying to provide incentives for the incumbents (both managers and workers) through profit sharing and bonus plans. The early results are encouraging and suggest that it may be feasible for state enterprises to move considerably toward market-oriented behavior, even in an economy in which 56 percent of industry is in state hands.

Although the Chinese government does not intend to privatize the bulk of the productive enterprises, the state is not adverse to undertaking comprehensive property rights reform as an inseparable part of the general reform program. Andrew Walder's chapter, "Corporate Organization and Local Government Property Rights in China: An Alternative to Privatization," makes a good case for the claim that it is feasible to alter the incentive structure in a socialist economy. This reform is done by reassigning the rights to use a productive asset in different ways and the rights to the income flows from these assets downward within government hierarchies, while imposing restrictions on the outright sale of government property. In fact, this reassignment is what the Chinese government has done with great success, in the sense that the reassignment of property rights from higher to lower levels of government administration, or from government administration to enterprises and households, had favorable effects on productivity in publicly owned industry.

Another interesting facet of Walder's chapter is the suggestion that the so-called budget constraints may be hardened within the context of quasi-hierarchical bargaining relations between the central authority and the firms. This suggestion contrasts with the assertion of many authors who, following János Kornai's lead, saw a distinct dichotomy between market versus bureaucratic regulation and therefore ruled out the possibility of tightening soft budget constraints in a nonmarket environment.[30] Walder also highlights the nature and the content of "regime of bargaining" between industry and government rather than its presence or absence as the key determinant of productivity growth. Indeed, in China, behind the facade of continuous bargaining, important changes have been happening to the very issues over which the two sides bargain, altering the nature of the underlying constraints and incentives that institutionalized patterns of bargaining between government and firms are thought to symbolize. Specifically, although the terms of taxation and finance are still subject to bargaining, and because "traditional" concerns such as output and investment targets are no longer on the table, budget constraints are now much harder than they were previously. This important observation, which prompts Walder to adopt the notion of "flexible bargaining," is also supported by Rawski's findings of a positive relationship between profitability and access to bank credit in China.

In contrast to China, Mongolia, a newly independent country in Asia, has undergone an intriguing reform process. This country is of special interest because, although Mongolia has been insulated from the rest of the world both intellectually and in terms of economic interaction, a coalition post-Communist government that came to power in July 1990 announced in less than six months its full commitment to a radical big-bang strategy. Which factors encouraged the big bang reform strategy, especially the for- mulation of a privatization program that was extremely ambitious in scope and speed? Was the radical program successfully implemented, and, if not, what were the factors responsible for slowing it down? These are some of the questions discussed in "Mongolia: Privatization and System Transformation in an Isolated Economy," by Cevdet Denizer and Alan Gelb of the World Bank. One interesting finding of the chapter is that (in total contrast to Poland, for instance) the privatization of small and large enterprises, which is being done through a virtually free distribution scheme to citizens, is proceeding very quickly, whereas macroreforms such as the freeing of controlled prices are lagging behind. This finding does not mean that the privatization process will end up with the complete reassign- ment of rights from the government to core private investor groups and the accompanying legal guarantees of ownership rights to these groups instead of the state. Indeed, as Walder reminds us, ownership is a bundle of enforceable rights, but it is not clear in the Mongolian context how many rights regarding the use of or derivation of income from assets are actually granted to the new owners of privatized enterprises.

A tacit understanding drawn from the Latin American experience dom- inates the thinking in academic and policy circles concerning the propensi- ties of various countries to adopt radical reform programs. According to this view, the reform process is likely to be accelerated by economic stag- nation and decline because, like drug addicts, interest groups and political actors become more ready for reform and adjustment the more they approach the pain threshold. Denizer and Gelb question the general applic- ability of this metaphor by using a computable general equilibrium model calibrated to conform to the structural characteristics of the Mongolian economy. The model suggests that, as the domestic resource envelope tightens sharply after a radical aid cutoff and subsequent trade disruption and squeezes away the margin above subsistence, especially in the urban sector, it will become more difficult to stay on the course of radical reform beyond a certain point. In an extreme case, a country like Mongolia could be forced to shift from state socialism to a rationed "wartime economy," despite intentions to carry out economic liberalization and to create a Western-style capitalist system.[31]

Privatization and Private Sector Reform in Central and Eastern Europe

Officials of successive Polish governments have declared their intentions to accomplish quick privatization in the large-scale, state-owned industrial sector both through public offerings and mass privatization. However, so far the major advance in privatization has been employee buyouts, a method that advocates of radical reform have refused to countenance as a feasible method of privatization. Anthony Levitas, in his chapter, "Rethinking Reform: Lessons from Polish Privatization," calls attention to unfortunate parallels between radical communism and radical liberalism. As mirror images, both experiments attempted to sever the past from the future by trying to substitute unilateral resolutions imposed by the state for more decentralized and participative forms of decision-making. Ironically, mass privatization and public offerings required the renationalization of publicly owned assets because the historical legacy of the struggle in Poland had created an industrial order similar to market socialism, in which firms were managed by so-called employee councils. Levitas notes the painful economic consequences of self-management but does not advocate its preservation. However, he disagrees with Polish government officials and their foreign advisors and/or lenders who single out the existence of employee councils as the chief obstacle to industrial adjustment and privatization. Neither top-down renationalization or commercialization of firms through the elimination of employee councils nor privatization through public offerings has led yet to successful restructuring and overhauling of loss-making firms. Instead, as Levitas reminds us, privatization has been most successful in those places where the Polish state has allowed the existing asset holders—the managers and workers—to negotiate property settlements among themselves and with outside buyers under the supervision of state authorities. After all, only the insiders can judge which settlement best allows them to survive and prosper in a market economy.

While Levitas looks at the adverse economic and social consequences of imposing top-down solutions to property reform problems, David Stark's chapter, "Path Dependence and Privatization Strategies in East-Central Europe," launches a scathing theoretical attack on blueprints that purport to solve the problems of economic transition by relying on radical marketization as a sharp sword to cleave through the economic etatism and political legacies of the past. Such radical perspectives underestimate the institutional legacies of the past that set limits on the applicability of hastily drawn-up recipes to create capitalism in x steps or y days. Furthermore, according to the designers of such plans, the only obstacle in the way of the speedy enactment of "sound" economic reforms consists of the actions and preferences of subordinate social groups that may succumb to populist appeals. In contrast, Stark takes the position that economic transformations currently attempted in Eastern Europe will be marked by "path dependency." This idea means that results will depend less on conscious designs than on the outcomes of multiple interactions in which "the designs of transformation are themselves transformed, shaped, and modified in response to and even in anticipation of the actions of subordinate social groups."[32]

Stark's chapter applies the path dependency framework to a comparative analysis of the strategies of privatization in Poland, Hungary, the former Czechoslovakia, and Germany. He develops a comprehensive typology that portrays the three major dimensions along which privatization strategies in these countries differ. In other words, Stark adopts an analytic comparative framework in which the specificity of each privatization strategy is revealed through its simultaneous, mutual contrast with the others. In the final part of the chapter, which marks his most original contribution to economics literature, he goes beyond the description of "how" to the analysis of "why" privatization experiments differ from each other. Highlighted in this context is the bearing of distinct "paths of extrication" from state socialism. The paths signify "reunification" in Germany, "capitulation" in the former Czechoslovakia, "compromise" in Poland, and "electoral competition" in Hungary. Specifically, these paths, combined with the differences in preceding patterns of interest intermediation between the state and society and the preexisting forms of political institutions, hold the clue to the differences in the types of privatization reforms that the four countries adopted to spearhead economic transformation.

In general, researchers who look at the transition problem in post-Soviet countries underestimate the resilience of preexisting economic institutions to reproduce themselves, albeit in mutated forms.[33] However, in "Strategy, Structure, and Spontaneous Privatization in Russia and Ukraine," Simon Johnson, Heidi Kroll, and Santiago Eder go beyond the identification of legal changes in the ownership structure of industrial enterprises to investigate the corresponding transformations in the internal organization and external links of these enterprises. Viewed from this angle, so-called spontaneous privatization, defined as the allocation to enterprise managers of residual control rights in enterprises that once belonged to the state, becomes just one part of a broader set of strategies used by managers (and workers) to ensure the survival of their enterprises. Indeed, the results of the authors' comprehensive survey of large-scale industrial enterprises in Kiev indicate that only in a limited number of enterprises, those that began the transition with a strong market position, has a genuine market-oriented search been underway, aimed at cutting off the hierarchical links between the enterprise and state authorities. Otherwise, enterprises have responded to the disruption in the centralized distribution of inputs and outputs, caused by the collapse of the former Soviet Union, by either attempting to reconstruct former hierarchies on a more local plane or by building new hierarchies. The latter strategy seems to be the most common, with managers protecting their supply channels by joining newly created concerns and associations and by converting state enterprises into closed joint stock companies in which shares are not tradable outside the firm. A local potentate in Vorkuta reportedly said of the transformation, "The more things change, the more they stay the same!"[34] The authors of this chapter are not so pessimistic, and they suggest that, albeit in painful, drawn-out ways, state firms are beginning to make the adjustments necessary to survive in a market economy. They caution policymakers, however, not to attempt to impose uniform privatization plans drawn from Western textbooks on all enterprises, because these plans are likely to be met with insiders' resistance. Hence, Levitas's and Stark's warnings of the dangers of imposing rationalistic schemes on actors for the sake of creating a true market economy in Eastern Europe seem to be equally relevant for the former USSR.

Normally, as Stark states in Chapter 6, one cannot expect that a simple transfer of ownership rights from state to private hands would be the sole condition for creating a dynamic private market economy. It may be more opportune and less costly to create a private sector by stimulating the start-up of new ventures rather than by increasing the speed and scope of privatization. Furthermore, given the enormous intellectual, social, and political capital that is consumed in the privatization process, there may be "a trade-off between efforts to create a new private sector and the speed and scope of privatization"[35] in the early stages of reform. Yet, the investigation of how and under what conditions a nascent private sector can flourish in Eastern Europe is a relatively neglected phenomenon.

Leila Webster, in "Private Sector Manufacturing in Eastern Europe: Some Cross-Country Comparisons," attempts to shed light on some aspects of these questions using representative firm-level surveys of private manufacturers in five preselected industries. The surveys were conducted in 1991 and early 1992 in Poland, Hungary, and the former Czechoslovakia. Among the findings of her study are three thought-provoking conclusions.

First, the revival of entrepreneurial ambitions in Poland, Hungary, and the former Czechoslovakia, which is a necessary ingredient of successful transitions, is a nonissue given the enthusiastic response by Poles, Hungarians, Czechs, and Slovaks to starting their own firms when the governments created a suitable economic environment. Second, the relative failure of Polish entrepreneurs compared to their counterparts in Hungary and the former Czechoslovakia is partially explained by the design of shock therapy, which was supposed to create the foundations for a truly functioning market economy. Instead, premature trade liberalization and currency convertibility, combined with the pent-up consumer demand for foreign goods and the appreciation of Polish currency in the early stages of reform, led to a flood of imports into the country with which the budding entrepreneurs could not compete. An unintended effect of the big bang in Poland was the promotion of commercial over industrial activity, in contrast to Hungary, where domestic producers were accorded some respite from intense foreign competition. Finally, a tight monetary policy, propagated in Poland by shock-therapy advocates and the International Monetary Fund (IMF), seems to have contributed to the chronic shortage of working capital, which is a major obstacle in the expansion of existing units in the emerging private sector. In fact, interest rates reached about 40 percent real in the second quarter of 1991 in Poland. These high rates were the result of a tight monetary policy and deterred entrepreneurs in all of the countries from raising capital in financial markets. The experience of these East European countries supports the argument that even if a tight monetary policy needs to be pursued in the early stages of reform to bring inflation under control, government intervention to subsidize credits in certain industries, preferably exports, may be an important ingredient in the development of a domestic private sector in post-Communist economics.

Restructuring and Soft Budget Constraints in Post-Communist States

The last two chapters in the book do not deal with a specific country but instead attempt to reexamine the theoretical case for privatization and a hands-off approach by the state to industrial restructuring from the vantage points of different theoretical traditions. Izak Atiyas, in his "Restructuring Programs in Transitional Economies," closely scrutinizes the case for quick privatization in Eastern Europe by adopting a perspective inspired by the literature on agency problems and neoinstitutionalist economics. One of the important messages of his chapter is that privatization, although a crucial step, is not a sufficient solution to the problems faced by the state-owned enterprise sector in East European economies. Moreover, governments in these countries will need to undertake at least some of the necessary financial, organizational, and technological restructuring of state-owned enterprises, especially in cases where privatization is slow because of administrative constraints or in cases of large loss-makers whose closure would have serious regional implications. Conversely, in the cases of enterprises that may be immediately privatized, and especially through the mass privatization method discussed in detail in the chapters by Levitas and Stark, it is not clear that privatization will provide enough incentives for management to undertake efficient restructuring. If privatization leads to a diffuse ownership structure, it may fail to address the so-called ownership problem because it will not solve the conflict of interest between the managers who exercise effective control over assets and the owners who are the holders of residual claims. In other words, the ills of US-style punter capitalism, in which a great deal of discrepancy exists between the objectives of the principal and its agents, may be imposed on the East European industrial arena. But even if we make the optimistic assumption that privatization will adequately address the ownership problem, a second equally serious issue remains that may hinder the flow of finance necessary for successful industrial adjustment in postprivatized enterprises. This problem is rooted in the conflict of interest between insiders of an enterprise and (actual and potential) providers of outside finance, or what has been called in finance literature "agency costs" of external finance. Atiyas's chapter reviews institutional responses to the agency problem in different countries, which all require more intelligent, if not decentralized, state involvement in the affairs of the privatized companies than advocates of the liberal "hands-off" approach are willing to admit.

Zhiyuan Cui's chapter, "Can Privatization Solve the Problem of Soft Budget Constraints?", provides an unambiguous and compelling answer: No! Cui incorporates what he calls a monetary perspective, which should not be confused with Milton Friedman's theory of "monetarism." Contrary to neoclassical economics' assumptions about the neutrality of money, Cui emphasizes that money and credit markets and institutions have real effects on the functioning of an economic system. From such a novel perspective, it is possible to claim that, contrary to conventional wisdom, the so-called soft budget constraints afflicting industrial enterprises in many countries are caused primarily not by state ownership per se but by many dilemmas caused by the existence of credit money, incomplete capital markets, and a modern bankruptcy code, which are among the essential features of advanced capitalist economies. From this observation, which is painstakingly elaborated in this chapter with examples from the US experience, two important policy recommendations can be made. First, especially in view of the region's current recession, dogmatic insistence on continued tight monetary policies will add fuel to the fire and worsen the recession by forcing even some potentially profitable industrial firms to fold. The only way firms can protect themselves against an unwarranted credit crunch is to barter and avoid paying their debts to other enterprises, which results in a huge increase in interenterprise debt. The snowballing of interenterprise debt hampers the privatization effort by making the valuation of firms extremely difficult and unreliable. Second, a headlong rush into privatization may be counterproductive in the absence of a myriad of institutions and regulations that are necessary for the smooth functioning of a market economy based on credit money. Substitution of private for public ownership may amount to no more than the creation of opportunities for private "rent seeking."[36]

Conclusion

Not long ago, the proponents of a radical shock-therapy approach hailed their program as the only means to ensure a rapid transition of former command economies to advanced capitalist systems. In their eyes, the major obstacle to rapid transition was the willingness of the populace to bear the necessary transition costs of the great transformation. Furthermore, the advocates of a radical program viewed the wholesale transfer of productive assets from the state into private hands as the fundamental step in the creation of a modern market economy. In retrospect, it is now clear that the radical reform program faces major implementation problems in post-Communist societies, which cannot simply be explained by the resistance of this or that social group, or by the populistic competition caused by the creation of many new political parties.[37] It may still be premature to condemn the whole radical project, but the emerging consensus from the chapters in this book by authors who have looked at the different aspects of the transition problem is unmistakable. It is doubtful that the overall radical approach and privatization experiments, based on either textbook approaches or utopian plans, are adequate to accomplish the goal of systemic transformation of former state socialist economies to efficient, competitive capitalist systems.

The major problem, as Levitas and Stark argue, is that the property structure and the market-determined coordination and resource allocation mechanisms of modern capitalism should be viewed as the products of socially embedded and historically determined evolutionary processes rather than the result of teleological, rationalistic designs driven by hypothetical end-states. There are, in fact, numerous varieties of the capitalist model in the West, and there is no a priori reason to assume that the same situation will not happen in Eastern Europe. Furthermore, it is not clear that a headlong rush into the marketization of all aspects of life will enhance economic efficiency, aside from the moral issue of the desirability of this approach. A host of new studies in political economy have indicated that there are sectors in modern capitalist economies in which the most competitive forms of economic coordination are based on "network forms of organization," which are distinct from either market or bureaucratic-hierarchical forms of coordination.[38] Moreover, a tradition in development economics that includes diverse authors, such as Albert Hirschman, Gunnar Myrdal, Paul Streeten, and Lance Taylor, suggests that at its best "the market maximizes economic efficiency under given conditions; whether it also fosters growth and structural transformation is—even with ideal assumptions—open to further questions."[39]

This problem does not mean that the key message of this book is the rejection of all designs based on an irrational perspective. On the contrary, the challenge faced by decisionmakers may be simply stated. The destruction of state socialism's existing control institutions, such as central planning and bureaucratic provision of inputs and allocation of outputs, is hardly enough to lead to a viable capitalist economy. Instead, it is necessary to create market-supporting institutions beyond the provision of legal guarantees to the private sector against government confiscation of private property. The problem is in fact in the "public good" nature of these institutions such as effective banking and stock market regulation, commercial and civil codes, bankruptcy legislation to ensure firms' orderly exit and restructuring when possible, modern accounting and auditing systems, and the organization of a planning system to supply businesspeople with an adequate informational and educational network.[40] In addition, as Atiyas emphasizes, in cases in which privatization is not an immediate option, governments in Eastern Europe will need to establish corporate governance mechanisms that will create incentives for the restructuring of public enterprises to stem losses and prevent environmental damage.

Even ardent advocates of a laissez-faire market economy in Eastern Europe admit that "market failures" in the region are not confined solely to well-known issues such as national defense and pollution.[41] A well-informed skeptic may make an even stronger statement, pointing out that it may be futile to identify sources of market failure in an environment in which the old control mechanisms and incentive structures are being dismantled but have not yet been replaced by more efficient ones. Certainly, as Stark insists, the collapse of communism has not left an institutional vacuum. Countries in the region will need to rely on their different traditions and historical legacies to create and consolidate the economic institutions of an advanced industrial economy. What is common to all of these countries is that the monumental task of building institutions—unprecedented in recent history—only can be achieved as a result of a long-term reform process.[42] Some shortcuts, such as rapid privatization, may be difficult to implement, and such measures may also be counterproductive if they generate the incentives in the bureaucracy that encourage rent-seeking behavior, to the detriment of the growth of a distinctive "esprit de corps" without which capitalist states degenerate into "predatory states."[43]

If capitalist development is the goal, no country can do without effective state intervention predicated on the existence of a coherent bureaucratic apparatus and well-developed links to the private sector. The immediate issue in Eastern Europe is to determine the best ways to use existing state institutions by selectively strengthening and streamlining them to exert control over state enterprises and to channel private sector activity into productive areas before privatization and creation of market-supportive institutions takes place.[44] If this tactic fails, we fear that, as Eastern Europe and most of the former Soviet Union continue on a downward slope, we will witness a resurgence of a new version of modernization theory in social sciences—the natural if unconscious bedfellow of neoclassical economics—that will attribute the failure of industrial modernization in the region to the persistence of antientrepreneurial values.[45] We hope that the chapters in this book, which are the product of exemplary collaboration between academic and policy circles, will contribute to a more thoughtful, nuanced, and empirically based assessment of reform issues than what we see in the first wave of radical reform proposals.

Notes

Earlier drafts of this chapter were read by Michael Burawoy, John Freeman, Anthony Levitas, Peter Murrell, Thomas Rawski, Dietrich Rueschemeyer, and Andrew Walder. I thank them for their comments.

Many academicians and policymakers participated in the April 1992 workshop and served as discussants, in addition to the authors of this book. The editor would like to thank the following individuals for their contributions to the discussions and consequently to the composition of this volume: Gerald McDermott, John Freeman, Barbara Lee, Janos Lukacs, Peter Murrell, Branko Milanovic, Louis Putterman, Dietrich Rueschemeyer, Svava Salameh, Charles Sabel, Cathy Schneider, Thomas Skidmore, Michael Spagat, and Eric Olin Wright.

The editor also wishes to express his gratitude for the intellectual, moral, and financial help he received while conducting the workshop and working toward the publication of this volume from Dietrich Rueschemeyer, director of the Center for the Comparative Study of Development; Thomas Weiss, associate director of the Watson Institute; Fred Fullerton, who copyedited the manuscript; and Melissa Phillips, who was a most able conference coordinator. Special thanks are due to Artemis Joukowsky, vice-chancellor of Brown University, who kindly accepted an invitation to attend this conference and shared his views with the participants in a keynote address. Finally, I would like to acknowledge a German Marshall Fund of the United States research fellowship that provided me with the opportunity to devote myself fully to the preparation of this book.

1. Olivier Blanchard, Rudiger Dornbusch, Paul Krugman, Richard Layard, and Lawrence Summers, *Reform in Eastern Europe* (Cambridge, Mass.: MIT Press, 1991), p. vii.

2. Jeffrey D. Sachs, "Accelerating Privatization in Eastern Europe," paper prepared for the World Bank's *Annual Conference on Development Economics,* Washington, D.C., April 25–26, 1991, p. 4.

3. Ellen Comisso, "Property Rights, Liberalism, and the Transition from 'Actually Existing' Socialism," *East European Politics and Societies* 5, 1 (Winter 1991).

4. According to the World Bank statistics in Poland, for instance, GDP fell by about 12 percent in 1990 and 8 percent in 1991. Hungary fared slightly better, with a GDP decline of 4 percent in 1990 and 8 percent in 1991. Other countries fared worse, with GDP declining in CSFR by 9 percent in 1990 and 16 percent in 1991, in Romania by 7 percent in 1990 and 12 percent in 1991, and in Bulgaria by 12 percent in 1990 and 26 percent in 1991.

5. See Mario I. Blejer and Alan Gelb, "Persistent Economic Decline in Central and Eastern Europe: What Are the Lessons?" *Transition* 3, 7 (July–August 1992): 1–3.

6. Ibid.

7. See Peter Murrell, "An Antidote to Shock Therapy: An Evolutionary Approach to the East European Economic Transition," East European Studies Occasional Paper no. 37, The Woodrow Wilson Center (March 1992), p. 16. Murrell writes: "On the basis of very crude calculations, I estimate that the East European economies would have to shut down half of the manufacturing capacity of large plants (and create a similar amount of capacity in small plants) in order to obtain a distribution of plant sizes that is roughly comparable to that in Western Europe. In individual industries, such as textiles, the figure could be as large as 70 percent."

8. See Domenico Mario Nuti, "How to Contain Economic Inertia in the Transitional Economies," *Transition* 3, 11 (December 1992–January 1993): 1–3.

9. A group of leading Massachusetts Institute of Technology economists states that privatization should take place before firms are restructured. See Blanchard et al., *Reform in Eastern Europe*. Jeffrey D. Sachs, on the other hand, is even more adamant that preprivatization restructuring should be avoided at all costs. He writes: "The operating guidepost of the World Bank should be that privatization is urgent—and politically vulnerable—and that privatization should almost always precede restructuring, at least for industrial enterprises." See Sachs, "Accelerating Privatization in Eastern Europe," p. 1.

10. The major problem encountered in privatization is the absence of *domestic savings*. Sales of assets are limited by the absence of an organized private sector and functioning capital markets. Some governments are attempting to avoid this problem by offering the free distribution of vouchers. However, this strategy does not solve the more basic problem of how to create effective control (ownership) of enterprises. That is, effective shareholder control requires at least some degree of concentration of share ownership, but fairness and political wisdom call for a wide degree of dispersion for any free distribution scheme.

11. See Kemal Dervis and Timothy Condon, "Hungary: An Emerging Gradualist Success Story?", paper presented at the National Bureau of Economic Research Conference, Cambridge, Massachusetts, February 26–29, 1992.

12. See Sachs, "Accelerating Privatization in Eastern Europe," p. 6.

13. It is also interesting to note that in the late summer of 1991, following the demise of the Tadeusz Mazowiecki and Jan Krzysztof Bielecki governments for which Balcerowicz was the deputy prime minister, the International Monetary Fund suspended its endorsement of Polish economic policy. The government of Prime Minister Olszewski, which came to power following the October 1991 parliamentary elections, adopted a much more gradualistic approach to economic policy. That is, fiscal and monetary policy were gradually loosened, credits to state enterprises began to grow, tariff rates in foreign trade were increased, and a more cautious approach to privatization was adopted. Consequently, contrary to the expectations of the "big bangers," the first signs of economic recovery began to surface at the end of 1992. Relations with the IMF were restored in 1993 following the formation of the radical reformist Suchocka government, which came to power in July 1992.

14. Murrell, "An Antidote to Shock Therapy," p. 2.

15. A crucial research area that is not addressed in this volume is the examination of the connections between democratization on one hand and the requirements of radical reform on the other. Is democratic politics, in fact, compatible with market-oriented reforms? Or, viewed from a different angle, can a democratic state create market-supportive institutions as readily as a nondemocratic one?

16. The conference was held April 24–25, 1992.

17. The term *soft budget constraints* was coined by the Hungarian economist János Kornai. Soft budget constraints exist when the link between an enterprise's earnings and expenditures is broken in the sense that the excess of expenditures over earnings is automatically compensated for by an outside agency, most likely the state. For an analytic account, see Sadao Nagaoka and Izak Atiyas, "Tightening the Soft Budget Constraint in Reforming Socialist Economies," Industry Development Division, Industry Series Paper no. 35, The World Bank, Washington, D.C. (May 1990).

18. O. Williamson, D. North, H. Demsetz, and A. Alchian, among others, have been instrumental in the development of institutional economics. For an illuminating survey, see Thrainn Eggertsson, *Economic Behavior and Institutions*

(Cambridge: Cambridge University Press, 1990). For an application of the theory to the transition debate in Eastern Europe, see Ellen Comisso, "Property Rights, Liberalism, and the Transition from 'Actually Existing' Socialism."

19. It is interesting that A. Berle and G. Means, writing in 1932 (*The Modern Corporation and Private Property,* New York: Macmillan, 1932), drew attention to the high cost to shareholders of monitoring corporate managers in modern corporations. Yet the implications of their work for economic behavior were not incorporated into neoclassical analysis until the 1970s. In the meantime, during the 1950s and 1960s, a number of sociologists such as D. Bell and R. Dahrendorf, writing polemically against Marxist and radical sociologists, argued that "class struggle" had ceased to exist in modern society. This cessation occurred because, thanks to the dilution of ownership, modern corporations were run by professional managers who, unlike the owner-capitalists of the nineteenth century, put a higher premium on public than private interest and sought industrial peace rather than confrontation with labor. Radical sociologists retorted by claiming that the dispersion of ownership did not end capitalist control because, given the pyramidal structure of modern holding companies, a mere 5 percent or so of equity was more than enough to exert control. In other words, the ruling elite was alive and well, and the source of its power still lay in the ownership of the means of production. It is also interesting that the work of A. Berle and G. Means was a source of inspiration for the empirical research of radical sociologists such as M. Zeitlin and R. Ratcliff (in their monumental book on the nature of the Chilean ruling class), as it is now inspiring the work of neoinstitutional economists. Yet institutional economists, armed with the "rational choice" theory, drew very different conclusions from the book by Berle and Means and cast the old debate in a new light. In fact, what for radical sociologists was a problem, specifically the existence of "big shares" that enabled a single capitalist (either a person or an institution) to exert control over managers in modern corporations, was to institutional economists a blessing, preventing managers from being derailed in the search for efficiency. In fact, some economists who adopt the agency approach, such as M. Jensen, argued that the troubles of large corporations such as IBM in the 1980s were attributable to the extreme dilution of ownership, which rendered managers effectively unaccountable for the performance of their firms.

This whole debate is relevant for the choice of privatization strategies in Eastern Europe. Governments such as those in Poland and the former Czechoslovakia, which are experimenting with the free distribution of shares to citizens, are concerned about the control problem that can emerge if the stock of an enterprise is dispersed too much. For more details, see Denizer and Gelb, Chapter 4, and Stark, Chapter 6, in this book. See also M. Zeitlin and R. Ratcliff, *Landlords and Capitalists: The Dominant Class in Chile* (Princeton: Princeton University Press, 1988).

20. The concept of reform went through several mutations in the past decade in Eastern Europe. Concerning Hungary, see David Stark, "Privatization in Hungary: From Plan to Market or From Plan to Clan?", *East European Politics and Societies* 4, 3 (Fall 1990): 351–392.

21. The two following paragraphs rely on Fernando Saldanha, "Agency Problems in Market Socialism," mimeo (February 1989).

22. See the survey "Capitalism: In Triumph, In Flux," *The Economist,* May 5, 1990.

23. See Michael Jensen, "Takeovers, Their Causes, and Consequences," *Journal of Economic Perspectives* 2, 1 (Winter 1988): 21–48.

24. Michael Burawoy and Pavel Krotov, "The Rise of Merchant Capital:

Monopoly, Barter, and Enterprise Politics in the Vorkuta Coal Industry," *Harriman Institute Forum* 6, 4 (1992). See also Simon Johnson and Heidi Kroll, "Managerial Strategies for Spontaneous Privatization," *Soviet Economy* 7, 4 (1991).

25. See "Microeconomic Response to the Economic Transformation Program: Evidence from the Largest SOEs," report prepared by the World Bank Resident Mission, Poland (1991).

26. See Michael Burawoy and Pavel Krotov, "The Soviet Transition from Socialism to Capitalism: Worker Control and Economic Bargaining in the Wood Industry," *American Sociological Review* 57, 1 (February 1992): 16–18. See also Burawoy and Krotov, "The Rise of Merchant Capital."

27. This statement was made by Harold Demsetz, one of the founders of the "property rights" school in neoinstitutional economics. See his review of János Kornai's *The Road to a Free Economy, Journal of Economic Literature* 29, 3 (1991): 1213–1214.

28. This quote is taken from Louis Putterman and Dietrich Rueschemeyer, "State and Market in Development: An Introduction" in Putterman and Rueschemeyer (eds.), *State and Market in Development: Synergy or Rivalry?* (Boulder: Lynne Rienner Publishers, 1992).

Roman Frydman and Andrzej Rapaczynski wrote: "We have . . . the makings of a genuine paradox which constitutes the most fundamental systemic obstacle to the economic transformation in Eastern Europe. The most important aspect of the transition to a spontaneously functioning market economy cannot be initiated by market forces themselves. Indeed, the only force powerful enough to set the market forces in motion is the very state which is supposed to remove itself from the economy." Roman Frydman and Andrzej Rapaczynski, "Privatization and Corporate Governance in Eastern Europe: Can a Market Economy be Designed?" C.V. Starr Center for Applied Economics, Research Report no. 91-52, New York University (September 1991).

29. This comment is quoted from an article in *The Economist* in "Quotation of the Month: Big Bangers in Retreat," *Transition* 3, 5 (May 1992): 8.

30. See János Kornai, "The Affinity Between Ownership Forms and Coordination Mechanisms: The Common Experience of Reform in Socialist Countries," *Journal of Economic Perspectives* 4, 3 (Summer 1990): 131–149.

31. See Peter Murrell, Karen Turner Dunn, and George Krosun, "The Culture of Policy Making in the Transition from Socialism: Price Policy in Mongolia," IRIS Working Paper Series no. 32, University of Maryland at College Park (1992).

32. See Chapter 6 by David Stark in this volume.

33. See Burawoy and Krotov, "The Rise of Merchant Capital": 5.

34. Ibid.: 1.

35. Murrell, "An Antidote to Shock Therapy," p. 17.

36. Paul P. Streeten reminds us of the simple fact that rent seeking does not result exclusively from public action but is equally common in the private sector. See his chapter titled "State Minimalism" in Putterman and Rueschemeyer, *State and Market in Development,* pp. 15–39.

37. See Marek Dabrowski, "Interventionist Pressures on a Policymaker During the Transition to Economic Freedom," *Communist Economies and Economic Transformation* 4, 1 (1991): 59–73.

38. For references to this literature, see note 65 to Chapter 6 by David Stark in this volume.

39. Dietrich Rueschemeyer and Louis Putterman, "Synergy or Rivalry?" in Putterman and Rueschemeyer (eds.), *State and Market in Development,* p. 243.

40. For the role of indicative planning in successful capitalist development,

see Vedat Milor, *The Comparative Study of Planning and Economic Development in Turkey and France* (Madison: University of Wisconsin Press, forthcoming).

41. See Marek Dabrowski, "The Role of the Government in Post-Communist Societies," unpublished manuscript presented at the think tank Public Sector Management in Eastern Europe, organized by the Economic Development Institute of the World Bank, June 17–21, 1992, Washington, D.C.

42. See Dietrich Rueschemeyer and Peter Evans, "The State and Economic Transformation: Toward an Analysis of the Conditions Underlying Effective Intervention," in Dietrich Rueschemeyer, Peter Evans, and Theda Skoopol (eds.), *Bringing the State Back In* (Cambridge: Cambridge University Press, 1985), pp. 44–79.

43. See Peter Evans, "Predatory, Developmental, and Other Apparatuses: A Comparative Political Economy Perspective on the Third World State," Center for Comparative Study of Development at Brown University, Working Paper no. 11 (1989).

44. See Murrell, "An Antidote to Shock Therapy," p. 21.

45. Indeed, Chapter 8, by Leila Webster, in this volume indicates that the revival of entrepreneurial traditions in Eastern Europe seems to be almost automatic once an enabling environment to pursue private activity is created by the state.

■ Part 1 ■
Privatization and Public Enterprise Reforms in Asia

■ 2 ■

Progress Without Privatization: The Reform of China's State Industries

THOMAS G. RAWSKI

The idea of rapid transition to a private market economy dominates proposals for economic reform in the former USSR and in Eastern Europe. Respected international organizations propose radical change as the sole feasible reform strategy for these nations. However, the same organizations counsel gradualism in China, where business enterprises display a growing responsiveness to market forces despite the absence of privatization, effective bankruptcy procedures, and other features widely regarded as key components of economic reform. Furthermore, the vision of free trade, flexible prices, and minimal government that suffuses much of the reform literature clashes with the current reality in Western Europe, North America, and, most particularly, the East Asian states whose economic accomplishments reform seeks to emulate.

These divergences signal our present inability to answer fundamental questions about reform. How extensively must market forces penetrate to elicit the beneficial consequences of a "market economy"? How can we measure the strength of market forces or the progress of economic reform in transitional economies? Do semimarket economies face a choice among reform paths, or can we identify a narrow set of reform prerequisites?

This chapter focuses on a subset of these issues that deals with privatization; more specifically, the progress of China's state-owned industries in the absence of privatization. I begin with a critical examination of the idea that transferring state enterprises to private hands is an essential ingredient for successful reform. I then outline the dynamics of recent industrial development in China's economy by describing the process through which partial and uneven reforms that exclude privatization have expanded the role of market forces and financial pressures in state industry. I reinforce this controversial interpretation by introducing statistical evidence that tests the proposition that gradual and partial introduction of market forces has substantially reshaped the behavior of China's state industries in the absence of privatization.

Privatization and Reform: A Skeptical Perspective

Reformers generally aim to elevate individual income and material welfare by raising the trend rate of productivity growth. We can think of reform as an investment process in which governments select a menu of reform policies, such as privatization or subsidy reduction, as well as the intensity of implementation (e.g., how many state enterprises to auction off during the first year). From this perspective, which is elaborated by Jefferson and Rawski,[1] the significance of including a specific policy instrument or magnifying its intensity within a particular reform program depends on several factors. These include a variety of initial conditions, such as the government's managerial capacity and the intensity of competition, as well as the degree to which other policies can usefully substitute for the instrument in question.

The experience of China as well as that of other states demonstrates that, in comparison with feasible private alternatives, state enterprise often performs dismally in terms of productivity, cost control, technical development, customer satisfaction, and even (but not in China) output growth. Many economies could benefit from the transfer of state firms to private ownership. What is not clear, however, is whether such transfers should come early or late in the reform process or whether they should be partial and gradual or total and immediate.

Unfortunately, discussions of reform policy often lead to hasty and extreme judgments on privatization that seem unrelated to any coherent theoretical perspective or empirical evidence. Some international agencies, for example, advised reformers in the former USSR that "the ultimate goal of ownership reform is to privatize almost all enterprises."[2] Another theorist announces that "privatization is necessary because only private owners can establish an enduring basis for self-financing and managerial independence."[3] A third insists that privatization is "urgent" but justifies this judgment by political rather than economic arguments.[4]

I read these statements and many like them as excursions into what Harold Demsetz has called "the *nirvana* approach,"[5] in which the nonoptimality of arrangements observed in actual economies is considered sufficient reason to invoke the superiority of an unexamined alternative. Demsetz attacked Kenneth Arrow for recommending that government intervention could improve upon the private allocation of resources to intervention without carefully analyzing possible costs of state entry into the management and financing of research and development. Ironically, we now encounter nirvana arguments from the opposite direction as economists advocate privatization without considering the possibility that the future costs of market failure and regulatory intervention could make privatization less attractive than seeking to improve the performance of inefficient state enterprises. Demsetz himself steps forward as an exponent of nirvana, insisting that "solving the privatization problem is the only real hope" for Eastern Europe and that "long delay in this matter will inevitably [result in] continuing poverty and bureaucracy."[6]

Economic studies of privatization offer little support for this confident determinism. A recent survey observes that while "private ownership has efficiency advantages in competitive conditions," there is no evidence of its general superiority "when market power is present." If state regulatory intervention "is substantial, the differences between public and private [ownership] can become a matter of degree."[7] There is no general presumption that state-owned firms are less efficient than private firms if the latter are subject to government regulation.[8] The reality of government failure makes privatization, which is often "highly politicized," an option that "poses formidable problems."[9]

Privatization may do no more than replace public monopolies with private ones and replace soft budget constraints with the sort of regulatory protection that can enable blatantly uneconomic producers (e.g., Japanese rice farmers, US sugar growers, factories in Pakistan and elsewhere that generate negative value added at international prices, Polish producers of tropical plants, etc.) to achieve commercial viability under what only appear to be "market" conditions.

The real question, which the earlier Demsetz[10] highlights and the nirvana method ignores, is whether the *actual,* as opposed to the textbook, consequences of privatization are likely to represent a sufficient improvement over the alternative of restructuring state firms to elevate privatization to a position near the top of the reform policy agenda. The point here is not to claim that privatization is irrelevant or unnecessary but to highlight the failure of its proponents to muster a strong case for arguing that early privatization of large-scale industry is essential to the success of socialist reform efforts.

Perhaps these proponents, many of whom receive comfortable salaries from organizations that are owned or funded by the public sector, see the need for privatization as so obvious that no detailed argument is required. If so, they should consider China's recent economic experience, which revolves around two features that differ widely from recent events in Eastern Europe and the former USSR. First, China's urban reforms have remained partial and somewhat hesitant, with no significant transfer of industrial resources from state enterprises to the hands of private owners. Second, despite episodes of instability inspired by political as well as economic factors, the economy has grown rapidly, avoiding the massive uncertainties, shortages, idleness, hoarding, price gyrations, and dislocations experienced in the former USSR and Eastern Europe.

The crucial issue is to determine the extent to which these peculiarities are causally related. This issue cannot be resolved here. In the following pages I argue that, contrary to widespread belief, China's limited industrial reforms have brought about substantial and beneficial changes in the behavior of industrial enterprises, including large firms in the state sector.

An Overview of Chinese Industry

Table 2.1 provides an overview of Chinese industry for the years 1978 and 1988. Village-level industries are excluded. The following points emerge:

Table 2.1   Basic Data on State and Collective Industry, 1978 and 1988 (excluding village-level industry)

	Number of Enterprises (thousands)		Gross Output Value (Current Yuan, billions)		Year-End Employment (millions)	
	1978	1988	1978	1988	1978	1988
State (SOE)						
Independent units	N.A.	72.4[b]	317.3	994.7[b]	30.4	42.6?
Total	83.7[a]	99.1[b]	342.1[c]	1,035.1[b]	31.4[d]	42.6[e]
Collective (COE)						
Independent units	219.9	343.9[b]	72.0	422.0[b]	12.1[d]	31.4
Total	264.7[a]	1,119.2[#c]	81.6[c]	488.3[#c]	N.A.	37.7[#c]
All industry						
Independent SOE and COE units	N.A.	420.9[c]	389.3*	1,416.7*	42.6	74.0*
Total	348.4[a]	7,371.8[#b]	423.7[a]	1,652.0[#b]	60.9[f]	97.3#

Source: Except as noted, data were provided by the State Statistical Bureau.
Notes: # indicates data obtained by subtracting figures pertaining to village-level units from global total; * indicates sum of state and collective components; ? indicates an apparent inconsistency in the source materials.

a. *Zhongguo gongye jingji tongji nianjian 1988* (Statistical yearbook of China's industrial economy 1988) (Beijing: Zhongguo tongji chubanshe, 1988), pp. 15, 25.
b. *Zhongguo tongji nianjian 1989* (China statistical yearbook 1989) (Beijing: Zhongguo tongji chubanshe, 1989), pp. 268–269, 271, 272, 275, 295.
c. Calculated by applying the shares of state and collective industry in 1978 gross industrial output at 1970 prices to the total in current prices. Output shares are from *Zhongguo gongye jingji tongji ziliao 1986* (Statistical materials of China's industrial economy in 1986) (Beijing: Zhongguo tongji chubanshe, 1986), p. 128.
d. *Zhongguo tongji nianjian 1988*, pp. 163, 166.
e. *Zhongguo gongye jingji tongji nianjian 1988*, pp. 3, 353.
f. *Zhongguo gongye jingji tongji nianjian 1988*, p. 10; including village and subvillage units.

- The bulk of industrial output comes from "state" and "collective" firms. All of these firms are legally and practically tied to some level of government (although the closeness of ties varies widely, especially for "collective" firms).
- Despite extremely rapid growth during the past decade, private industry remains small, accounting for only 5.9 percent of the 1990 output and 6.9 percent of incremental output during the years 1980–1990 (Table 2.2).
- These figures confirm that privatization is not an important feature of the Chinese industrial scene. Despite the rapid expansion of private industrial output, at least 90 percent of incremental industrial production during the 1980s came from state and collective firms that have no private owners (note that the category labeled "other" includes some private and semi-private firms).

Table 2.2 Gross Value of Industrial Output, 1980 and 1990

	Total	State	Collective	Private	Other
Output Value					
(¥ billion, current prices)					
1980	515.4	391.6	121.3	0.1	2.4
1990	2,392.4	1306.4	852.3	129.0	104.8
Increase					
Amount	1,877.0	914.8	731.0	128.9	102.4
Share (percent)	100.0	48.7	38.9	6.9	5.4

Source: Zhongguo tongji nianjian 1991 (China statistical yearbook 1991) (Beijing: Zhongguo tongji chubanshe, 1991), p. 394.

The Dynamics of Industrial Change in China During the 1980s

Economic agents in any system strive to reach specific, mainly financial, objectives. Following Nelson[11] we can distinguish two major types of activity: routine and innovation. Routine activities are those for which the dispersion of anticipated outcomes is relatively narrow; alternative outcomes are tightly clustered around the mode. Innovation involves departure from routine, which entails greater risk and increases the dispersion of returns. Both routine and innovation have market and nonmarket components. One might define economic reform as a process that encourages or obliges firms, managers, and workers to tilt their activity portfolios toward market rather than nonmarket efforts and toward innovation rather than routine.

Prior to the introduction of economic reforms in the late 1970s, industrial activity in China, as in other socialist economies, was oriented primarily toward nonmarket routine. Managers concentrated on meeting plan targets and on satisfying the requirements of their superior agency (*guanli bumen*) rather than emphasizing financial results or the needs of customers. This orientation has changed dramatically. An investigation of the time that industrial managers devote to dealing with government officials, market-linked operations (sales, procurement, advertising, fund-raising, collections), and production matters (product design, enterprise layout, etc.) would undoubtedly reveal a massive postreform decline in the importance of industry-government relations (telephone records would be an ideal source for such a study). How has this shift toward the market emerged from a rather limited set of reform initiatives?

Before seeking an answer to this question, it is important to note several features of China's prereform industrial structure that differed significantly from the standard picture of a "Soviet-type" economy.

1. There was a certain degree of decentralization of industrial investment, production, pricing, and marketing. Provinces, municipalities, and counties competed to develop industries that could benefit their own economies, using mainly local resources and serving local markets. These developments sometimes included the formation of ties with large firms in the state sector.[12]

2. Investment outlays during the period of socialist planning included a substantial effort to build complete sets of industries in most provinces and, whenever possible, in many regions within the provinces. As a result, the sort of deregulation that leads to monopoly in Russia or Poland creates competition in China.

3. Efforts to socialize China's rural economy failed to extinguish the spirit of enterprise in what must surely rank as one of mankind's most entrepreneurial and business-oriented cultures.

4. The world's most dynamic economies stand at China's doorstep. These nations, with strong traditions of commercial ties to China, together with millions of business-oriented Chinese scattered around the Pacific Rim, represent a unique pool of latent resources that can magnify the impact of any reform effort.

5. Tantalizing scraps of evidence suggest the presence of marketlike forces prior to reform. Jefferson, Rawski, and Zheng find, for example, that the marginal revenue product of materials is virtually identical in state and collective industry throughout the period 1980–1988.[13]

China's reforms have taken the form of *enabling* measures that remove barriers to enterprise activity and permit new initiatives. For the most part, the Chinese have avoided *mandatory* changes such as privatization, bankruptcy, or elimination of subsidies. The principal reforms begun during the late 1970s and early 1980s included profit sharing for successful enterprises; a bonus system intended to harness latent energies within the labor force; gradual increase in enterprise autonomy in such matters as product mix, sales, and procurement; gradual creation of markets for resources; gradual expansion of price flexibility for the increasing proportion of commodities exchanged outside plan auspices; and a rapid expansion of opportunities for participation in foreign trade and investment.

A second series of reforms implemented in the mid-1980s created additional opportunities to which enterprises could respond. The key innovation was the creation of a "two-track" or "dual price" system that permitted the emergence of regulated but unplanned market exchange for nearly all commodities. These included energy, minerals, farm products, building materials, semifabricates, and equipment, as well as foreign exchange and many services, among them technical knowledge and expertise. As the scale of these semimarket transactions expanded, price information generated outside the network of officially controlled transactions gradually eroded the operation of the planning system. Producers began to seek means of removing products from the planning system to take advantage of more lucrative sales opportunities. Beneficiaries of underpriced official allocations were systematically squeezed by suppliers who knew exactly what they were losing by being forced to deliver at planned prices.[14] Bankers, themselves looking for profit, increasingly turned toward commercial lending criteria.

The impact of these developments, however, was not even. The reforms provided the greatest opportunities for and elicited the most dynamic response from urban and rural collective firms (and also from China's small private sector). Prior to these reform efforts, these firms rarely commanded the attention of planners. Their operations were constrained by the operation of a system designed to serve the needs of state firms.

On the whole, larger firms, typically state owned, that enjoyed greater access to the resources distributed through the planning system, responded less eagerly to the opportunities that arose from the reforms of the 1980s. This much is clear. But did they respond at all and, if so, how vigorously? Here, controversy arises. Chinese journals are filled with discussions of how to "energize" large- and medium-scale enterprises, suggesting that any response by these firms was slow and weak. External researchers offer similar views: James Stepanek, for example, asserts that "Ten Years of Reform Have Left China's Big State Factories Unchanged."[15] Another observer sees an economy "dominated by huge state-owned companies that specialize in inefficiency."[16]

Table 2.3 Industrial Profits and Losses for 1989 by Industrial Branch

A	B	C	D	E	F	G	H	Branch Shares (percent) of				M
								I	J	K	L	
Branch	No. of Losers	Losses (¥ mil.)	Profits (¥ mil.)	KFN (¥ mil.)	AV Loss (¥ mil.)	Losses as Percentage of Profits	Rate of Return (percent)	Losers	Losses	Profits (percent)	KFN	J/L (ratio)
1	1,622	50.55	−26.72	622.46	3.12	NA	−4.29	2.49	21.96	−2.81	7.44	2.95
2	18	43.19	−25.11	536.56	239.94	NA	−4.68	0.03	18.77	−2.64	6.41	2.93
3	120	0.42	3.38	28.10	0.35	12.43	12.03	0.18	0.18	0.36	0.34	0.54
5	1,055	0.85	7.69	51.54	0.08	11.05	14.92	1.62	0.37	0.81	0.62	0.60
6	76	0.49	3.45	25.70	0.64	14.20	13.42	0.12	0.21	0.36	0.31	0.69
8	104	0.83	10.50	101.95	0.80	7.90	10.30	0.16	0.36	1.11	1.22	0.30
9	362	1.93	4.64	103.91	0.53	41.59	4.47	0.56	0.84	0.49	1.24	0.68
10	6,166	11.36	50.43	366.08	0.18	22.53	13.78	9.47	4.94	5.31	4.38	1.13
11	3,682	7.76	8.36	104.04	0.21	92.82	8.04	5.66	3.37	0.88	1.24	2.71
12	88	7.12	1.27	59.72	8.09	560.63	2.13	0.14	3.09	0.13	0.71	4.33
13	393	0.94	4.69	22.65	0.24	20.04	20.71	0.60	0.41	0.49	0.27	1.51
14	5,106	13.00	99.45	671.04	0.25	13.07	14.82	7.84	5.65	10.47	8.02	0.70
15	3,035	2.37	15.45	70.10	0.08	15.34	22.04	4.66	1.03	1.63	0.84	1.23
16	1,546	2.55	3.99	45.58	0.16	63.91	8.75	2.38	1.11	0.42	0.54	2.03
17	1,468	1.74	4.45	49.68	0.12	39.10	8.96	2.26	0.76	0.47	0.59	1.27
18	1,630	0.95	2.75	26.54	0.06	34.55	10.36	2.50	0.41	0.29	0.32	1.30
19	2,226	3.29	21.08	139.65	0.15	15.61	15.09	3.42	1.43	2.22	1.67	0.86
20	988	0.62	14.21	66.88	0.06	4.36	21.25	1.52	0.27	1.50	0.80	0.34
21	534	0.44	5.83	21.07	0.08	7.55	27.67	0.82	0.19	0.61	0.25	0.76
22	1,501	0.90	8.59	30.87	0.06	10.48	27.83	2.31	0.39	0.90	0.37	1.06
23	1,338	13.94	67.05	1,093.51	1.04	20.79	6.13	2.06	6.06	7.06	13.07	0.46
24	54	0.16	31.68	215.79	0.30	0.51	14.68	0.08	0.07	3.33	2.58	0.03

A	B	C	D	E	F	G	H	I	J	K	L	M
25	400	5.33	-0.47	60.81	1.33	NA	-0.77	0.61	2.32	-0.05	0.73	3.19
26	3,402	9.02	102.12	611.01	0.27	8.83	16.71	5.23	3.92	10.75	7.30	0.54
27	296	0.66	28.16	85.66	0.22	2.34	32.87	0.45	0.29	2.96	1.02	0.28
28	82	0.43	26.42	149.73	0.52	1.63	17.65	0.13	0.19	2.78	1.79	0.10
29	654	1.56	10.48	66.74	0.24	14.89	15.70	1.00	0.68	1.10	0.80	0.85
30	2,698	2.60	16.97	119.05	0.10	15.32	14.25	4.15	1.13	1.79	1.42	0.79
31	10,539	13.76	50.63	534.34	0.13	27.18	9.48	16.19	5.98	5.33	6.39	0.94
32	617	2.29	106.64	696.93	0.37	2.15	15.30	0.95	0.99	11.22	8.33	0.12
33	3,938	3.28	30.04	142.42	0.08	10.92	21.09	6.05	1.43	3.16	1.70	0.84
34	5,115	13.24	116.86	746.02	0.26	11.33	15.66	7.86	5.75	12.30	8.92	0.65
35	1,279	4.94	44.15	288.28	0.39	11.19	15.31	1.97	2.15	4.65	3.45	0.62
36	1,833	3.13	55.64	204.89	0.17	5.63	27.16	2.82	1.36	5.86	2.45	0.56
37	767	3.79	34.94	154.07	0.49	10.85	22.68	1.18	1.65	3.68	1.84	0.89
38	355	0.73	10.49	52.51	0.21	6.96	19.98	0.55	0.32	1.10	0.63	0.51
Sum	65,087	230.16	950.18	8,365.88	0.35	24.23	11.36	100.00	100.00	100.00	100.0	1.00

Source: *Zhongguo gongye jingji tongji nianjian 1990*, pp. 182–307, including independent accounting units at and above the *xiang* (township) level.

Notes: A: branch of industry (note that the source omits sectors 4 [nonferrous mining], 7 [a small residual mining branch], and industries not included elsewhere).
B: Losers = number of firms making losses.
C: Losses of losing firms (¥100 million).
D: Profits = total profits (net of losses; ¥100 million).
E: KFN = net (of depreciation) year-end value of fixed assets (¥100 million).
F: Average loss per losing firm (¥ million).
G: Losses as percent of net profits: G = 100 x C/D.
H: Branch rate of return on fixed assets: H = 100 x D/E.
I, J, K, L: Branch share (percent) of loss-making firms, losses, profits, net fixed assets.
M: Branch share of losses/branch share of fixed assets. Figure for all branches = 1.

Branches of industry: 1. coal mining; 2. crude oil and gas; 3. iron ore; 4. nonferrous mining; 5. nonmetallic mineral; 6. salt; 7. other minerals; 8. lumber and bamboo; 9. water supply; 10. food processing; 11. beverages; 12. tobacco; 13. animal feed; 14. textiles; 15. apparel; 16. leather goods; 17. wood products; 18. furniture; 19. paper and paper products; 20. publishing; 21. cultural products; 22. handicrafts; 23. electricity; 24. petroleum refining; 25. coke; 26. chemicals; 27. pharmaceuticals; 28. chemical fibers; 29. rubber products; 30. plastics; 31. building materials; 32. ferrous metallurgy; 33. nonferrous metallurgy; 34. metal products; 35. machinery; 36. transport equipment; 37. electric machinery; 38. electronics.

Table 2.4 Industrial Profits and Losses for 1989 by Province

Province	A Number of Firms Making Losses	B Losses (¥100 mil.)	C Profit (¥100 mil.)	D NVIO (¥100 mil.)	Provincial Shares (percent)				Index: average = 1	
					E Loss-making Firms	F Losses	G Profit	H NVIO	F/G Loss/prof	G/H Loss/NVIO
Beijing	587	5.63	64.31	175.17	0.85	2.41	6.43	3.57	0.35	0.13
Tianjin	776	6.94	26.88	124.18	1.12	2.97	2.69	2.53	0.38	0.42
Hebei	1,840	14.63	40.42	193.63	2.65	6.26	4.04	3.95	0.42	0.66
Shanxi	1,148	8.93	22.63	121.52	1.65	3.82	2.26	2.48	0.43	0.73
Inner Mongolia	730	4.88	11.47	67.57	1.05	2.09	1.15	1.38	0.50	0.92
Liaoning	3,422	23.27	70.14	381.63	4.93	9.96	7.01	7.78	0.49	0.70
Jilin	1,648	8.23	31.08	134.83	2.37	3.52	3.11	2.75	0.67	0.76
Heilongjiang	2,035	22.43	24.64	261.50	2.93	9.60	2.46	5.33	0.31	1.19
Shanghai	1,127	5.66	128.48	371.81	1.62	2.42	12.84	7.58	0.67	0.13
Jiangsu	8,373	14.19	77.07	422.07	12.06	6.08	7.70	8.61	1.99	1.57
Zhejiang	7,382	7.80	52.48	253.41	10.63	3.34	5.25	5.17	3.18	2.03
Anhui	2,837	6.11	21.01	129.51	4.09	2.62	2.10	2.64	1.56	1.95

Fujian	1,706	2.66	24.20	108.64	2.46	1.14	2.42	2.22	2.16	1.02
Jiangxi	2,304	6.82	14.58	88.94	3.32	2.92	1.46	1.81	1.14	2.28
Shandong	2,297	15.37	67.53	366.60	3.31	6.58	6.75	7.48	0.50	0.49
Henan	2,057	11.39	37.34	191.51	2.96	4.88	3.73	3.91	0.61	0.79
Hubei	4,131	7.27	50.99	221.34	5.95	3.11	5.10	4.51	1.91	1.17
Hunan	4,180	9.37	29.24	168.92	6.02	4.01	2.92	3.44	1.50	2.06
Guangdong	4,128	13.85	50.94	311.43	5.95	5.93	5.09	6.35	1.00	1.17
Guangxi	4,198	4.51	16.74	83.51	6.05	1.93	1.67	1.70	3.13	3.61
Hainan	237	0.58	2.31	9.44	0.34	0.25	0.23	0.19	1.37	1.48
Sichuan	7,194	14.69	56.64	284.14	10.36	6.29	5.66	5.79	1.65	1.83
Guizhou	876	4.22	8.31	63.90	1.26	1.81	0.83	1.30	0.70	1.52
Yunnan	1,160	2.30	21.71	110.23	1.67	0.98	2.17	2.25	1.70	0.77
Tibet	42	0.05	0.32	1.08	0.06	0.02	0.03	0.02	2.83	1.89
Shaanxi	1,657	5.51	19.00	100.80	2.39	2.36	1.90	2.06	1.01	1.26
Gansu	444	2.99	15.13	69.77	0.64	1.28	1.51	1.42	0.50	0.42
Qinghai	211	0.60	3.44	17.69	0.30	0.26	0.34	0.36	1.18	0.88
Ningxia	184	0.60	3.26	17.06	0.27	0.26	0.33	0.35	1.03	0.81
Xinjiang	512	2.09	8.10	51.60	0.74	0.89	0.81	1.05	0.82	0.91
Sum	69,423	233.57	1,000.39	4,903.43	100.00	100.00	100.00	100.00	1.00	1.00

Source: *Zhongguo gongye jingji tongji nianjian 1990*, pp. 308–361.
Notes: B, C, D = Losses of losing firms, total profits (apparently net of losses), and net value of industrial output, all measured in ¥100 million.

I view these perceptions as considerably exaggerated. I believe that state enterprises have experienced substantial pressures to improve financial performance that have moved them a considerable distance toward market-oriented behavior patterns. I see state enterprises as gradually drifting away from their official benefactors (and regulators). What evidence can be mustered in support of these assertions?

A good place to begin is by analyzing the mounting financial losses of China's industrial sector. This monetary drain is widely cited as evidence of the general decrepitude of China's rust-belt industries. Table 2.3 contains information on profits (column D) and losses (column C) by branches of industry. Table 2.4 provides data on industrial profit and loss by province. Both data sets refer to 1989, and both include "independent accounting units," exclusive of village-level firms. Although the source gives no separate compilation for the state sector, we know that 1989 losses of independent units in state industry amounted to ¥18.02 billion, or 77.1 percent of the total losses shown in Table 2.4.[17] In 1989, state industry also accounted for 56.1 percent of industrial output;[18] independent state units accumulated profits amounting to 74 percent of the total shown in Table 2.3.[19]

Where do the losses come from?

- 40 percent of the losses come from two sectors: coal mining (branch 1 in Table 2.3) and petroleum extraction (branch 2). Losses are common in these sectors because of artificially low administered prices.
- 16 percent of the losses come from five provinces: Jiangsu, Zhejiang, Fujian, Guangdong, and Hainan, which have few large-scale state plants, one small oil field, and little coal mining. These provinces are among China's most dynamic in terms of industrial growth, structural change, and export development. The accumulation of losses in these areas reflects the intensity of competition and the rapidity of economic change rather than any sort of industrial decline.
- Another cluster of losses is attributable to defense-related industries of two types: (1) producers of military goods whose output faces declining demand following the abrupt drop in political tension between China and its neighbors, especially Russia, South Korea, and Taiwan; (2) "Third Front" producers of civilian goods established in remote areas as part of China's defense against possible attack from the United States or the USSR. Losses reported for Sichuan province amounting to 6.3 percent of the 1989 total (Table 2.4) may offer a crude approximation for this item.
- 1989 was a recession year in China; investment declined for only the second time since the start of reform,[20] creating losses in

branches such as building materials (branch 31 in Table 2.3), which accounted for one-sixth of firms earning losses and contributed 6 percent to the industry-wide loss total.

Based on these crude calculations, we find that about two-thirds of the losses reported in 1989 stem from causes that have no connection to the alleged unresponsiveness or noncompetitiveness of state industry, which accounts for a disproportionate share of profit as well as loss. Overall financial results (again for independent units exclusive of village firms) for 1989 appear rather favorable: If we focus on profits as a percentage of net fixed assets, a measure that is far from ideal,[21] we find negative returns in three branches; positive returns below 5 percent in two more; five branches reporting returns between 5 and 9.9 percent; 17 earning 10–19.9 percent; and nine obtaining returns of 20 percent or more (column H of Table 2.3). If we had separate results for state firms, they would be very similar: The 1989 rate of return for independent state firms was 10.6 percent,[22] just slightly below the figure of 11.36 percent (for state, collective, and private units) shown in Table 2.3.

If mounting losses (1990 and 1991 brought further increases) reflect the outcome of specific factors rather than fundamental weaknesses in the state sector, and if state firms, including the largest, have responded to the government's reform initiatives, how did this happen? Specifically, what prevented state firms from continuing in their traditional role as favored clients of government ministries?

Competition is the main factor responsible for the growing responsiveness of state enterprises to market forces. The explosive growth of urban and rural collective industries and the simultaneous erosion of long-standing barriers to markets for industrial inputs and outputs have undercut profit margins throughout the industrial sector. Barry Naughton persuasively argues that a wide variety of empirical observations, including a sharp drop in both the level of and interbranch differences in industrial profit rates, fall neatly into place once attention is focused on the effect of China's reform policies in reducing the monopoly power of state enterprises in markets for industrial goods.[23]

Despite the continuation of extensive regulatory intervention and regional protectionism, it seems clear that the 1980s have confronted virtually all industrial enterprises with unprecedented increases in business competition. For example:

> China's largest tractor manufacturer is trying to improve the quality of its products as well as its marketing and publicity techniques in a bid to offset . . . sluggish domestic sales . . . the sluggish market . . . provoked incessant price undercuttings by producers. . . . The Luoyang tractor complex had been forced to sacrifice more than half of its profits in trying discounts, lotteries and free delivery of goods to boost sales.[24]

China's largest cookie producer, the Shanghai Yimin No. 4 Foodstuff Factory, is launching a counter-attack to recover [Shanghai's] biscuit market [which has been] taken over by products from Guangdong Province . . . the factory . . . [is] developing well-packaged biscuits, a line now dominated by Guangdong products. . . . Sources said the high commissions and high profit for stores selling Guangdong biscuits are one of the major reasons that . . . state-run cookie producers are facing difficulties.[25]

These and many other examples demonstrate that references to "the domestic and international competition facing large and medium state enterprises"[26] in Chinese industry are not exercises in rhetoric but realistic descriptions of widely shared experience.

Competition and falling profits have sharply curtailed the growth of government revenues, which have long been heavily dependent on the profits of industrial producers.[27] Revenue growth slowed first because of declining profits but also because decentralization and the emergence of complex new commercial channels allowed enterprises to revive China's venerable tradition of tax avoidance. Because actual collection of taxes is primarily a provincial and local rather than a central government responsibility, it is no surprise to learn that the central government has found itself obliged to bear the brunt of the revenue squeeze.

The declining ratio of government revenue, especially central government revenue, to national product has increased pressures on state-owned enterprises. After paying for administration, defense, key projects, and unavoidable subsidies to industries (such as coal) suffering from policy-induced losses, discretionary resources available to the central government have declined steadily. Following a brief episode of enlarged deficits that led to a painful bout of inflation during the late 1980s, the center has returned, at least temporarily, to the traditional policy of limiting its own deficit.

The provinces and localities are more able, but less willing than the center to devote funds to subsidizing loss-making enterprises. The reason is simple: competition. China's junior governments compete among themselves for access to funds from private investors in Hong Kong, Taiwan, and elsewhere, and from various international agencies. These funds gravitate toward localities that show signs of rapid progress in developing airports, telecommunications, roads, and other expensive infrastructure facilities. Every increase in provincial or local government spending to subsidize loss-making enterprises threatens the diversion of foreign funds (and perhaps fungible domestic funds) to rival jurisdictions.

The direct and indirect consequences of China's reforms, including commercial competition as well as the reduction of public spending, have come to exert growing financial pressures on increasing numbers of state enterprises. Subsidies continue, but the long-standing tradition of soft budget constraints has developed uncomfortable lumps. We may speculate that official responses to requests for financial support, even when buttressed by the customary arguments about circumstances beyond the enterprise's control, have become less satisfactory. As more firms secure the benefits available from the successful pursuit of market opportunities, the relative attractiveness of seeking financial gains through various forms of rent-seeking has begun to decline.

At the same time, the growth of markets encouraged suppliers to divert resources from the state supply system that allocates materials to favored state-owned enterprises at concessional prices. This leakage creates additional cost pressures for state firms. The answer to these difficulties is money, and the primary source of new funds is the marketplace.

Inflation, which drew adverse comment beginning around 1980 and accelerated sharply after about 1986, heightened the pressures on state enterprises. Inflation threatened to erode the living standards of urban workers unless their employers could supplement basic wages with rising bonus payments. One of the purposes of the profit-sharing reforms implemented during the early 1980s was to "activate the enthusiasm" of workers by creating pools of funds that could be used to pay bonuses and fund the provision of housing and other nonmonetary benefits for employees. As we shall see, substantial links emerged between profits and bonuses and also between profits and housing investment. With living standards endangered and subsidies harder to come by, inflation provided one more reason for state firms to look to the market as a source of financial benefits.

The final contribution to the mounting pressures facing state firms came from the twin shocks of contractionary monetary and fiscal policies, introduced in late 1988 as an antidote to inflationary pressures, and the abrupt reduction of revenue flows from foreign investment and tourism following the violent suppression in June 1989 of popular protests in Beijing and other large cities. These shocks stripped many firms of long-standing protection against market forces. In retrospect, the contraction of 1989–1990, which is widely viewed as a hiatus in the reform process, may in fact constitute a watershed or turning point that wrenched the attentions of managers and even workers toward greater market orientation. Many state firms, faced with falling orders and growing stocks of unsold goods, "stopped production and sent their workers home with as little as 50 percent of their salaries."[28] In a step reminiscent of crisis behavior in Japanese firms,[29] "some factories have even resorted to paying employees with products, leaving it to the workers to sell the products if they need cash."[30]

I hypothesize that the pressures resulting from these changes have substantially altered the culture of management in Chinese industry, including the state sector. This is not to say that dynamic entrepreneurs lead every enterprise or that none specialize in angling for official protection or subsidy. This is certainly not true of China (or of any other economy). But the rules of the game have changed. Consider the following:

1. Profit is now the chief managerial objective in Chinese industry.

2. For more and more firms, success in the marketplace is the chief source of profit.

3. Descriptions of Soviet management, which might have applied to the Chinese realities of 10–15 years ago, now seem incongruous when matched against current Chinese conditions. Nellis writes that in the USSR, "every one of the managers [we] met saw that the rules of the game had been altered. But rather than take steps to position themselves . . . to take advantage of the changed set of rules, many were waiting to be told—by the ministry, by other central authorities, by anybody—what to do next."[31] In China, the prevalence of such managerial passivity has declined steeply.

4. Managers in the state sector who compare market opportunities with the mixed blessing of embracing leviathan are increasingly ready to choose the former. This explains the seemingly bizarre complaints from managers of state firms that have benefited for decades from an extraordinary array of preferential arrangements, who now insist that "state-run enterprises are not treated fairly but reduced to an unfair competitive position."[32] Such expressions reflect the growing belief that the cost to state enterprises of the regulations and restrictions that surround them is higher than the benefits conferred by preferential treatment.

5. These new views are reflected in statements that ten years ago could have come only from radical opponents of the regime. A 1991 conference organized by the China Association of Investment Studies, a group apparently linked with the State Planning Commission, and attended by representatives of large state enterprises, municipal planning commissions, and the State Economic Commission, expressed the following views:[33]

- "The resolution of difficulties facing the efforts of state large scale enterprises to develop technically will not come from grants provided through the state planning system."
- "The meeting called for an appropriate reduction of basic construction investment within the government budget."
- Enterprises should have the right to select their own technical development projects, to choose their own designers, and to hire construction firms and equipment suppliers. They should also "have expanded rights to sell their products freely in foreign and domestic markets" as well as "the right to enter the capital market by issuing stocks, bonds, and collecting funds from urban and rural residents."
- One postulate summarizes these views: *"In the management of investment, create a system that places the enterprise's investments at the core."* (my emphasis)

In short, we see a clarion call for "corporatization" of large firms from the very people who seemingly have the most to lose from further erosion of the planning system.

6. Along with such discussions, there is a rush for the exits by former participants in the planning process. In Shanxi province, for example, measures to "activate large and medium scale enterprises" include the following provision:[34]

> If the state is unable to purchase goods according to the time schedules specified in the contract stipulations or to provide commodities specified in mandatory plans, or if customers cannot absorb the goods according to the contract stipulations, then it is allowed for the producing enterprises to sell on their own, and this will be regarded as fulfilling the mandatory plan.

With the execution of state plans routinely behind schedule, this is a prescription for legitimizing wholesale desertion from the planning system. It is cited by proponents of parallel opportunities for "specially designated enterprises" that remain firmly tied to mandatory planning—a state of affairs that now seems exceptional.

China's partial and limited industrial reforms have initiated a process of change that exposes enterprises at all levels, including large firms in the state sector, to a growing array of market forces and increasing pressures to improve financial performance. According to one source, one-third of large and medium-sized state enterprises have responded "with rich vitality" (*fuyou huoli*) to these circumstances.[35] Competition has slashed profits. Low profits have reduced the growth of tax revenues and limited the state's capacity to subsidize unprofitable enterprises, particularly since the most severe fiscal pinch comes at the center, which is more amenable to subsidies than the provinces, where subsidies may endanger the capacity to attract external funds. Leakage from official supply channels, inflation, macroeconomic policies intended to wind down inflationary pressures, and the political shock of June 1989 have heightened these pressures. As a result, large numbers of enterprises, managers, and workers have begun to redirect their energies toward the market rather than the plan, and toward innovation rather than routine.

These impressionistic conclusions may prove controversial. In any case, they are largely qualitative. How can we begin to measure the impact of reform in a systematic fashion? The following pages offer some preliminary efforts in that direction.

Microeconomic Reflections of Industrial Reform

How has economic reform affected Chinese industrial enterprises? Although several studies have considered the consequences of reform for small groups of firms or for selected localities, researchers have only begun to probe the possibilities for large-scale investigations. Several Chinese organizations have collected large sets of panel data that are suitable for this research. I have begun to explore two such data sets. One, collected by the Institute for Economic Research of the Chinese Academy of Social Sciences (EI), provides data for 453 firms, 363 of which are in the state sector, with 278 designated as "large" or "medium," for the years 1980 and 1983–1986. The second set comes from the Institute for Economic System Reform (TGS) and covers 852 enterprises, of which 736 are in the state sector, with 617 designated as large or medium, for the years 1986–1989.

My first question concerns incentives. Have the reforms offered appropriate incentives to Chinese enterprises? Do financially successful enterprises end up in stronger positions than loss-making firms? In Hungary, Kornai and Matits found that reform failed to alter the leveling tendency of tax and subsidy policy, which extracted funds from profitable firms and compensated losers until there was virtually no correlation (and sometimes even negative correlation) between profit and retained earnings.[36] Farrell obtains similar results from Polish data for 1986.[37] What about China?

Results of initial calculations appear in Table 2.5.[38] In 1980, the situation resembled what Kornai and Matits observed in Hungary: increased profit had almost no impact on retained earnings. This changed quickly. With the exception of the TGS sample for 1986, the remaining years show strong and (almost) consistent statistical association between profit and retained earnings. It appears that firms do have a clear incentive to pursue profit and avoid loss. Financial outcomes are not equalized by "whipping the fast ox"—the Chinese term for the "ratchet principle" of impromptu exactions from successful firms.

The reforms have brought large and beneficial changes. The retention rate suggested by the regressions rises in all but two years. There is the suggestion of a regime change in 1984–1985. We find no difference in results if a small number of loss-making enterprises are excluded. Similar regressions limited to firms within a single branch of industry show very tight links between profit and retained earnings, as illustrated by the calculations in Table 2.6, using 1986 data from the EI sample (these calculations include some firms outside the state sector).

If profits affect the well-being of enterprises, what about their link with material benefits to workers? Table 2.7 gives the results of calculations that explore this issue by focusing on the relationship between retained earnings per worker and bonus payments per worker across firms in particular industries during the late 1980s. The results, based on data for state enterprises included in the TGS survey, show a clear pattern of strong, positive links between per capita retained earnings and per capita bonuses. Most of the variation in per capita bonuses across enterprises in a single industry branch can be attributed to the interenterprise variation in per capita retained earnings. In several branches, the regression results are virtually perfect, suggesting that bonus funds may actually be determined as a percentage share of retained earnings (note that the constant term in these regressions rarely displays "statistically significant" difference from zero).

Table 2.5 Links Between Profits and Retained Earnings for State Firms, Sample Data, 1980–1989

Year	All Firms			Firms with Positive Profits		
	c	b	R^2	c	b	R^2
EI sample						
1980	60.61#	.01	.21	65.93#	.01	.21
1983	34.51	.14	.64	16.94	.15	.65
1984	334.54	.22	.07	330.30	.22	.07
1985	9.50	.29	.95	−21.21	.29	.96
1986	47.81	.36	.92	−32.84	.38	.97
TGS sample						
1986	476.17#	.02*	.00	503.21	.02*	.00
1987	−86.60#	.39	.90	−107.87#	.39	.90
1988	55.78	.25	.55	29.41	.25	.56
1989	−27.89	.46	.94	−142.75#	.48	.96

Notes: Regressions take the form RE = c + b x PROF, where RE = retained earnings; PROF = pretax profits. Except as noted, t statistics attached to the constant term are less than or equal to 2.5 in absolute value. The symbol # indicates a t statistic with absolute value greater than 2.5. Except as noted, the t statistics attached to the estimate of b exceed 15.0. The symbol * indicates t values between 0 and 1.0.

Table 2.6 Links Between Profits and Retained Earnings by Industrial Branch, Sample Data for 1986

Industry	c	b	R^2	N
Metallurgy	−332.98**	0.53	0.997	24
Chemicals	24.37*	0.26	0.96	44
Machinery	25.24	0.25	0.92	124
Building Materials	−27.81*	0.41	0.98	31
Food Processing	13.03*	0.42	0.77	21
Textiles	52.36**	0.36	0.97	22

Notes: Regressions take the form specified in Table 2.5. Except as noted, absolute values of all t statistics exceed 3.0. * = absolute value of t statistic less than 2.0. ** = absolute value of t statistic within the range $2.0 \leq t \leq 3.0$.

These results are fully consistent with the view that reform has given industrial workers a strong material interest in the financial performance of their firms. When profits (or retained earnings—as noted above, the two are closely related) per worker increase, bonuses per worker increase as well.

Table 2.7　Links Between Per Capita Retained Earnings and Bonuses, Sample Data for State Enterprises in Selected Industrial Branches, 1986-1989

	Constant	Estimate for b	R^2
Food processing (N=23)			
1986–1989	−5.64	.054	.28
1989	−.25	.956	.98
Beverages (N=20)			
1986–1989	.48	1.129	.91
1989	2.80	1.137	.90
Textiles (N=63)			
1986–1989	−2.21	.204	.55
1989	−3.26	.496	.18
Apparel (N=29)			
1986–1989	−3.84	.212	.93
1989	−3.28	.476	.94
Paper and paper products (N=24)			
1986–1989	−1.44	.367	.84
1989	−2.36	.298	.88
Chemicals (N=46)			
1986–1989	−.68	.198	.82
1989	−.84	.197	.82
Chinese medicine (N=29)			
1986–1989	−4.85	.103	.35
1989	−2.86	.403	.50
Rubber products (N=25)			
1986–1989	−.54#	3.597	.83
1989	.06	.292*	.10
Plastic products (N=24)			
1986–1989	−1.82	.349	.81
1989	−2.32	.592	.69
Building materials (N=37)			
1986–1989	−.03	.523	1.00
1989	−.05	.523	1.00
Ferrous metallurgy (N=29)			
1986–1989	−1.01	.541	.67
1989	.49	.804	.86
Nonferrous metal processing (N=17)			
1986–1989	−1.15	.167	.43
1989	.04#	.114	1.00
Metal products (N=26)			
1986–1989	16.68	1.042	.83
1989	42.38	1.122	.86

(*continues*)

Table 2.7 (*continued*)

	Constant	Estimate for b	R^2
Machinery (N=73)			
1986–1989	−1.92	.147	.64
1989	.55	.556	.99
Transport equipment (N=31)			
1986–1989	−6.77	.087	.98
1989	−1.78	.087	1.00
Electrical equipment and components (N=38)			
1986–1989	.31	.813	.99
1989	1.56	.814	1.00

Source: Calculations from TGS sample data.
Notes: Regressions take the form PCBONUS = a + b x (PCRE), where PCBONUS = annual bonus payments per worker; PCRE = annual value of retained earnings per worker. Results include all branches in the TGS sample for which the number of firms with valid observations for 1989 is at least 20. Nonferrous metallurgy is included because its military links make it an interesting special case. The number of firms reporting 1989 data is shown for each branch. All regressions are limited to state-owned firms. Except as noted, t statistics attached to the constant term are less than or equal to 2.5 in absolute value. The symbol # indicates a t statistic with absolute value greater than 2.5. Except as noted, the t statistics attached to the estimate of b exceed 3.0. The symbol * indicates t values between 0 and 2.0.

What of the link between profits and access to funds? In a market economy, access to funds is closely linked with profitability. Lenders and shareholders seek to avoid committing funds to enterprises or projects with poor profit prospects. If profitability declines, creditors seek ways of accelerating the recovery of their funds, and sources of new funds rapidly disappear. In a planned economy, this link between profitability and access to funds need not exist. The state may choose to support or even expand loss-making enterprises. In Hungary, Kornai and Matits found a negative relationship between profitability and access to bank credit in which smaller profits were associated with greater access to funds.[39]

The EI data set provides extensive information about the sources of funds. I classify them into five overlapping groups as follows:

1. State funds for investment purposes B1 = D76 + D77 where D76 = central government allocations; D77 = local government allocations
2. Borrowing for investment purposes B2 = D78 + D81 + D82 + D83 where D78 = investment funds from bank loans; D81 = borrowing from other units; D82 = funds from bond issues; D83 = funds from abroad
3. Other forms of borrowing B3 = D60 + D123 + D132 + D134 where

D60 = bank loans for new product development; D123 = production turnover borrowing; D132 = special borrowing; D134 = special funds obtained from other firms
4. B4 = B1 + B2 = total funds for investment
5. B5 = B2 + B3 = total commercial borrowing

Successful reform involves the gradual commercialization of access to funds. This means an increase in the share of commercial borrowing (constructed variables B2, B3, and their sum, B5) as well as a tightening of the link between profitability and access to funds. We anticipate that funds provided by government allocations (item B1) will remain less closely linked to profitability even if the overall funding situation takes on an increasingly commercial character. In part, this reflects the commitment of the state to protect and subsidize certain enterprises and groups. Noncommercial funding also may be undertaken to promote infant industries or to offset the effect of distorted prices. In China's coal industry, for example, artificially low prices furnish little commercial incentive for investment, despite widespread reports of plant closures due to insufficient supplies of energy.

We first check the simple relationship between current retained earnings (RE) and access to funds in the current year. The regressions take the form:

$$\text{New Funds in year t (B1, B2, B3, B4, or B5)} = c + b\,(RE_t)$$

Although certain of the estimated coefficients (not shown) pass standard tests for statistical significance, the share of variation "explained" by these calculations is consistently small. There is no evidence of a strong trend toward commercialization of funding, nor do we see any sign of greater commercialization of bank loans as opposed to state allocations. Similar regressions using gross profit as the independent variable produce even weaker results. The weakness of these results may arise because lenders look at past rather than (as yet unknown) current-year profits in judging a firm's prospects. Additional regressions explore possible links between current funding (dependent variable) and current profits, along with retained earnings lagged by one or two years. The general form is:

$$\text{New Funds in year t} = c + b_1(RE_t) + b_2(RE_{t-1}) + b_3(RE_{t-2})$$

These results, shown in Table 2.8, give a much stronger impression of financial commercialization.[40] Most of the coefficients are statistically significant. The share of variation accounted for by the regressions is substantial. As expected, evidence of commercialization is more pronounced in categories of funds provided by loans (B2, B3, B5) than for state grants (B1). Commercial forces are sufficiently strong that we see a clear relationship between total investment funds (B4, which includes both grants and loans) and lagged or lagged and current profit. However, the results for 1986 seem somewhat weaker than for 1985; furthermore, the negative coefficients attached to one element of retained earnings in nearly all of the regressions are puzzling.

Table 2.8 Links Between Access to Funds and Current or Lagged Retained Earnings, EI Sample Results for 1985 and 1986

Equations	c	b_1	b_2	b_3	R^2
1985					
B1	177.60		−0.14*	0.38**	0.03
	152.41	1.36	0.04*	−0.61	0.08
B2	195.25**		3.37	−4.62	0.51
	16.96*	2.31	4.69	−4.30	0.87
B3	521.12		−0.36*	1.75	0.20
	398.88	6.50	0.54**	−2.94	0.39
B4	372.86		3.23	−4.23	0.41
	169.38**	3.68	4.74	−4.90	0.78
B5	716.38		3.00	−2.86	0.27
	415.84**	8.82	5.23	−7.24	0.62
1986					
B1	187.46**		−0.05*	0.18*	0.02
	145.18**	−0.88	1.14	0.26*	0.16
B2	102.57*		−2.32	4.08	0.46
	153.81*	1.07	−3.77	4.00	0.49
B3	953.46		−0.69**	1.67	0.13
	958.17	0.10*	−0.83*	1.66	0.13
B4	290.02*		−2.37	4.27	0.41
	298.99*	0.19*	−2.62	4.25	0.41
B5	1,056.03		−3.01	5.75	0.33
	1,111.98	1.17**	−4.59	5.66	0.34

Notes: Except as noted, the absolute value of t statistics exceeds 3.0. * = absolute value of t less than 2.0. ** = absolute value of t in the range: $2.0 \leq t \leq 3.0$.

Taken together, these results are strikingly different from the Hungarian findings of Kornai and Matits.[41] There is strong evidence that market forces are present. Although these initial results are neither uniform nor indicative of a steady shift in the direction of market controls, they are surely supportive of the view that Chinese reform has injected market forces into what was formerly a "planned economy" and that the state sector is not immune from the impact of these forces.

Conclusion

This chapter began with questions about the role of privatization in socialist reform. Privatization is widely regarded as preferable to reforming state industry. Both strategies have costs and risks as well as benefits. Given the lack of experience in this area, any marked preference must reflect intuitive judgments about possibilities and dangers that remain largely uncharted.

In this context, the experience of China is worthy of attention. The initial outcome of China's reform efforts shows that state firms burdened with all the trappings of socialist planning can be moved in the direction of market-oriented and entrepreneurial behavior. Chinese firms now face negative as well as positive incentives. Despite the continuation of subsidies, we find concrete evidence that firms with low profits fall behind in such areas as retained earnings, wages, bonuses, and access to funds. All this suggests that neglect of the reform or corporatization option in favor of ex cathedra pronouncements favoring early privatization of state enterprises may be mistaken.

The economies of Eastern Europe and the former Soviet republics are now enduring great suffering. Much of the pain is knowingly inflicted by reform-minded governments. Supporters of current policies believe that long-term economic progress is unlikely without an initial process of creative destruction. Reform proponents are encouraged to grasp the nettle of drastic adjustment with visions of a rosy future.

China's experience raises the possibility that "growing out of the plan" is a feasible alternative to creative destruction. By avoiding extremism, China may have enabled its citizens to move toward a better future without incurring large transition costs. The analysis of China offered here may be disputed. Even if it is correct, the state of China's prereform economy, polity, and society may be sufficiently different from circumstances in other socialist nations to make successful Chinese policies largely irrelevant to the choices facing those economies. Until we acquire a clearer view of these possibilities, discussions of privatization and other policy issues should consider China's experience before drawing strong conclusions about the nature of appropriate reform strategies.

Notes

The author gratefully acknowledges comments from Louis Putterman, Robert Mead, and Albert Keidel, research assistance from Kuan Chen, and financial support from the Henry Luce Foundation, the Woodrow Wilson International Center for Scholars, and the University of Pittsburgh's China Studies Endowment.

1. Gary H. Jefferson and Thomas G. Rawski, "A Theory of Economic Reform," Socialist Economies Reform Unit, Research Paper Series, The World Bank, Washington, D.C. (1992).

2. International Monetary Fund, International Bank for Reconstruction and Development, Organization for Economic Cooperation and Development, and European Bank for Reconstruction and Development, *The Economy of the USSR: Summary and Recommendations* (Washington, D.C.: The World Bank, 1990), p. 26.

3. Kimio Uno, "Privatization and the Creation of a Commercial Banking System," in Merton J. Peck and Thomas J. Richardson (eds.), *What Is To Be Done? Proposals for the Soviet Transition to the Market* (New Haven: Yale University Press, 1991), p. 150.

4. Olivier Blanchard et al., *Reform in Eastern Europe* (Cambridge, Mass.: MIT Press, 1991), pp. xiv, 32–33.

5. Harold Demsetz, "Information and Efficiency: Another Viewpoint," *Journal of Law and Economics* (1969): 1–22; reprinted in D. M. Lamberton (ed.), *Economics of Information and Knowledge* (London: Penguin, 1971), pp. 160–186.

6. Harold Demsetz, review of *The Road to a Free Economy* by János Kornai, *Journal of Economic Literature* 29, 3 (1991): 1213–1214.

7. John Vickers and George Yarrow, "Economic Perspectives on Privatization," *Journal of Economic Perspectives* 5, 2 (1991): 111–132.

8. Jean-Jacques Laffont and Jean Tirole, "Privatization and Incentives," *Journal of Law, Economics & Organization* 7 (special issue, 1991): 84–105.

9. Ira Lieberman, "Industrial Restructuring Policy and Practice," Policy and Research Series Paper no. 9, The World Bank, Washington, D.C. (1990).

10. Demsetz, "Information and Efficiency."

11. Richard R. Nelson, *Understanding Technical Change as an Evolutionary Process* (Amsterdam: North Holland, 1987), chapter 2.

12. Dwight H. Perkins et al., *Rural Small-Scale Industry in the People's Republic of China* (Berkeley: University of California Press, 1987).

13. Gary H. Jefferson, Thomas G. Rawski, and Yuxin Zheng, "Growth, Efficiency, and Convergence in Chinese Industry: A Comparative Evaluation of the State and Collective Sectors," *Economic Development and Cultural Change* 40, 2 (January 1992): 255–256.

14. Liu Zhenzhong, "Tan meitan jiage gaige wenti" (Discussing the problem of reforming coal prices), *Jiage lilun yu shijan* (Price theory and practice) 3 (1991): 16–19.

15. James B. Stepanek, "China's Enduring State Factories: Why Ten Years of Reform Have Left China's Big State Factories Unchanged," in US Congress Joint Economic Committee, *China's Economic Dilemmas of the 1990s: Problems of Reforms, Modernization, and Interdependence* (Washington D.C.: US Government Printing Office, 1991), pp. 440–454.

16. Nicholas D. Kristof, "Manchuria Shows Economic Decay," *New York Times*, February 9, 1991, p. 5.

17. *Zhongguo gongye jingji tongji nianjian 1990* (Statistical yearbook of China's industrial economy 1990) (Beijing: Zhongguo tongji chubanshe, 1990), p. 66.

18. *Zhongguo tongji nianjian 1991*, p. 26.

19. *Zhongguo gongye jingji tongji nianjian 1990*, p. 66.

20. *Zhongguo tongji nianjian 1990*, p. 147.

21. Net fixed assets, as measured by Chinese statistics, mix industrial facilities with housing and other nonindustrial assets and cumulate nominal figures from different years with no allowance for price changes. Such data cannot provide a good

measure of capital stock. Furthermore, the conceptual difference between the separate accounting categories of "profit" and "tax" is by no means clear.

22. *Zhongguo tongji nianjian 1990,* p. 410.

23. Barry Naughton, "Implications of the State Monopoly over Industry and Its Relaxation," *Modern China* 18, 1 (January 1992): 14–41.

24. Anming Gao, "Giant Tractor Maker Plagued by Slow Sales," *China Daily,* May 28, 1991, p. 4.

25. Gang Bing, "Biscuit Maker Seeks Recovery," *China Daily,* June 2, 1991, p. 2.

26. "Speed Up the Pace of Technical Reform at Large and Medium State Enterprises, Summary of a Meeting on 'Policy Toward Enterprise Technical Reform' Organized by the China Association of Investment Studies," *Touzi Yanjiu* (Investment research) 7 (1991): 45–48.

27. Naughton, "Implications of the State Monopoly."

28. Sheryl WuDunn, "Consumer Demand Drops in China," *New York Times,* March 26, 1990, p. C10.

29. Richard Pascale and Thomas P. Rohlen, "The Mazda Turnaround," *Journal of Japanese Studies* 9, 2 (1983): 219–264.

30. WuDunn, "Consumer Demand Drops in China."

31. John Nellis, *Improving the Performance of Soviet Enterprises,* Discussion Papers no. 118, The World Bank, Washington, D.C. (1991), p. 20.

32. "State Firms in Focus," *China Daily,* May 22, 1991, p. 4.

33. "Speed Up the Pace," *Touzi Yanjiu* 7 (1991).

34. Qiao Jian, Wang Houhai, and Li Yining, "Let Special Enterprises Also Open Up," *Jingji ribao* (Economic daily), July 16, 1991, p. 1.

35. Luo Zheng, "Ba guoying dazhong qiye tuixiang shichang" (Push large and medium state-owned firms toward the market), *Renmin ribao* (People's daily), March 28, 1992, p. 2.

36. János Kornai and Agnes Matits, "Softness of the Budget Constraint—An Analysis Relying on Data of Firms," *Acta Oeconomica* 32, 3–4 (1984): 223–249.

37. John P. Farrell, "Monitoring the Great Transition," *Comparative Economic Studies* 23, 2 (1991): 9–28.

38. Except as noted, all results pertain only to state firms.

39. Kornai and Matits, "Softness of the Budget Constraint."

40. These regressions include data from a small number of collective firms.

41. Kornai and Matits, "Softness of the Budget Constraint."

■ 3 ■

Corporate Organization and Local Government Property Rights in China

ANDREW G. WALDER

This chapter examines two related ideas about the transition away from a centrally planned economy. The first is that budget constraints on firms cannot be hardened and clear incentives for productivity growth cannot be provided so long as terms of taxation and finance are flexible, bargained, and (system-wide) redistributive in nature. The second is that privatization of state assets—that is, the creation of clear and legally enforceable property rights of firms versus the state—is the only way to remedy the problems associated with soft budgets and bargaining over financial terms. This examination involves a reflection upon and reinterpretation of certain aspects of China's post-Mao economic reforms. It also involves a shift in emphasis in common ways of thinking about the institutional aspects of the "market transition"—in particular, of property rights, the role of the state, and the neglected subject of industrial organization.

Reflecting upon the Chinese experience, I shall seek to establish two distinctions. The first is the distinction between property rights reform and privatization. The former term refers to the clarification and reassignment of various ownership rights among economic actors, whether they are government jurisdictions, agencies, public or private corporations, households, or individuals. The latter term, privatization, is a narrower, more specific concept of property rights reform—one that refers to the reassignment of rights from government to private firms and to accompanying legal and administrative reforms that are designed to provide guarantees of the rights of firms against state manipulation or abrogation of such rights.[1]

When one speaks of privatization, the emphasis is on stripping away ownership rights from state agencies and the protection of newly established private rights against the state. This distinction between this idea and property rights is important because Chinese reforms have involved extensive reassignment and clarification of property rights among government agencies and publicly owned firms. However, with the exception of agriculture, which we shall not examine here, the reforms have involved only a very limited role for privatization.

The second distinction is that between a "soft" and a "flexible" budget constraint.[2] Pervasive bargaining over terms of taxation and finance and extensive government redistribution among firms do not rule out the possibility that financial constraints nonetheless may increasingly influence the behavior of managers. Such bargaining and redistribution characterize relationships among plants and divisions within large corporations in market economies. The hardness of a flexible budget constraint depends ultimately on the fiscal resources of the government entity with which an enterprise bargains and on the incentives and constraints presented by fiscal mechanisms to government overseers in the bargaining process. This distinction is important because, despite continued flexibility in bargaining relations between government and state firms, there has been significant productivity growth in China's state-owned industry. Moreover, growth in output and productivity has been most striking in precisely the areas of the public sector where government intervention has been most intimate—villages and townships.

In the three sections that follow, I shall review the relevant aspects of the Chinese experience. First, I shall elaborate the distinction between property rights reassignments and privatization and illustrate ways in which Chinese reforms have widely reassigned property rights without the kinds of privatization currently being discussed, and to some extent implemented, in the former Eastern Bloc. Second, I shall review the impressive record of growth in output, income, and resulting living standards and cite emerging evidence of sustained productivity growth. Third, I shall elaborate the distinction between soft and flexible budget constraints, describe the emerging relationship between government and enterprise both in the large-scale state urban sector and the smaller-scale township and village sector, and thereby suggest that there is an important industrial organization aspect to effective departures from traditional central planning.

The Chinese Reforms in Property Rights Perspective

Reform in China has proceeded by systematically altering property rights, despite only marginal changes in the proportions of the economy that are "public" versus "private" and the marked absence of the kinds of privatization processes now associated with the transition to "post-Communism" economies in Europe.[3] Even in traditional systems of central planning, public property embodies a complex and often ill-defined pattern of property rights exercised by government agencies, organizations, households, and individuals. Moreover, these rights may be changed in consequential ways without ever altering the public-private legal distinction.[4]

Property Rights Defined

Property rights may be defined as the sanctioned relationships among people or organizations regarding the use of goods. Sanctioned by norms, customs, and laws, these rights form expectations in dealings with others: An owner of property rights has the consent of others to act in particular ways without interference by the community, provided the actions are not prohibited in the specification of rights.[5] The best-known variety of property rights pertains to ownership,[6] which includes:

1. The right to use an asset. This aspect of ownership rights is often referred to as "control"; it involves the making of decisions about the management of assets. As in a modern corporation in a capitalist economy, the control of assets in a socialist economy is often delegated by owners to agents, or professional managers. Such a separation of ownership from control is in effect a delegation of selected property rights to management.[7]

2. The right to appropriate the returns from an asset. This aspect of ownership amounts to "distribution" rights regarding the flow of income. State socialist economies are commonly referred to as "redistributive." This indicates a distinctive set of rules regarding the distribution of income flows from productive assets.

3. The right to change the form or substance of an asset by transferring rights to others and to bear the consequences from changes in value. We might refer to this aspect as "exchange" rights because it involves the decision to buy or sell assets as well as the right to proceeds from the sale (or responsibility for losses).

Ownership, and by extension contract, is the right to exclude others, but this right is always restricted by regulation or law. This is equally true in market and planned economies. What differs is not the fact of regulation but what entities are assigned the above rights and in what ways these assignments are monitored and enforced.[8] The central insight of the economics of organization is that any type of economic institution is in essence a distinctive configuration of property rights.

Viewed from this perspective, the distinctions commonly drawn between "market versus plan" or "public versus private ownership" are not always meaningful and may prove to be blunt tools to use in analyzing the organization of an economy. Capitalist and socialist economies differ in the extent to which market mechanisms allocate goods, but they differ just as surely in their methods of economic organization and planning. We could argue that planning processes within large modern corporations in market economies are far more detailed, enforceable, and effective than the crude forms of rationing, inaccurate information, and constant bargaining that characterize the planning of ministries, bureaus, and corporations in their socialist counterparts. The main differences are in the methods of planning, how performance is monitored, and what kinds of incentives are provided.

Similarly, the distinction between "private" or "public" ownership can be ambiguous. In capitalist economies assets are held by a wide variety of highly regulated and interdependent private and public institutions such as corporations, banks, investment firms, pension funds, and households. However, in socialist economies assets are held separately by a wide variety of government jurisdictions and agencies, including central ministries, provinces, cities, townships, and villages. The formal distinction between public and private provides limited insight when ownership rights in each economy are exercised by a wide spectrum of organizations.

The differences between economies and their characteristic forms of economic organization are better understood as variations among bundles of property rights in the use of assets, the distribution of income derived from them, and their sale or transfer to others. Control over the large firm in both capitalist and socialist systems is delegated by owners (shareholders or specific government agencies) to professional managers; the main differences are in the regulations and mechanisms that govern the accountability of the latter to the former. Owners of large firms in both capitalist and socialist economies retain rights to income from their assets; what differs are the ways in which these income flows are calculated and divided with professional managers. The greatest contrast between capitalist and socialist economies probably lies in rights to transfer and liquidate assets because such transfer is much more common in capitalist economies. Yet the transfer of assets is restricted in capitalist economies by public ownership and regulation of such industries as utilities, railways, port facilities, airports, and fishing rights and by laws designed to avert monopolies and trusts or the transfer of assets to foreign entities. In agriculture, the contrast between capitalist smallholding and socialist collective farms is more striking, yet the distinction between "capitalist" sharecropping and "socialist" household contracting is more subtle.

Reform as a Reassignment of Property Rights

In the literature on government regulation, "attenuation" of property rights is a key concept. Attenuation of property rights takes place when restrictions are imposed on asset uses, on the income flows from that asset, and on the freedom of an owner to transfer these rights to others. Attenuation of property rights may occur in two different ways. Many restrictions are established by the state through various legal provisions written into commercial, corporate, and tax law or in procedural regulations enforced by government agencies. Attenuation may also arise from the inherent unenforceability of laws and regulations, especially when this problem arises from influence processes within bureaucracies and firms.[9]

Although it is natural to think that government regulation attenuates property rights in market economies dominated by private sectors, the process of economic reform in a socialist economy implies the reverse: a downward devolution of property rights in political or administrative hierarchies or reassignment and clarification of property rights among institutions and households. Reform invariably devolves selected property rights over assets (especially those of use and those with claims to income distributions) from higher to lower levels of government administration or from government administration to enterprises, households, or individuals. An economic reform program therefore may be defined as a specific package of property rights reassignments. The impact of a reform package will flow directly from the effects of these specific reassignments on incentives for economic behavior, subsequent income flows, and political power and interests.

The Reassignment of Use Rights

One of the most important latent principles of economic reform in China has been the widespread downward reassignment of use rights within government hierarchies and at the grass roots, from government agencies to households and individuals. The most dramatic of these reassignments took place in the dismantling of collective agriculture. Collectively owned village land formerly cultivated under the direction of production team leaders was reassigned to households under long-term contracts. While quota contracts for staple grains were commonly retained, peasant households obtained new rights to make cropping, management, and marketing decisions on their own. The same principle has been applied widely to collectively held assets in villages, towns, and cities. Agricultural sidelines and small-scale industrial and commercial enterprises commonly have been leased to households and individuals under a wide variety of contracts that specify compensatory payments to the owners. These payments entitle the leaseholders to a right to manage the assets with considerable autonomy and in effect remove owners from the direct management of the assets. This principle has been applied also to the larger collective and state enterprises still under the planning authority of rural and urban governments, but here the reassignment of use rights to managers has been far less extensive. Efforts to expand enterprise autonomy within the scope of the plan have been restricted largely to certain areas of staff compensation, sales and supply work, and technical operations. Decisions about investment, technical renovation, changes of product lines, and finance are still closely supervised by government officials.

The Reassignment of Rights to Returns from Assets

In all of these downward transfers of use rights, the relationship between the principals (owners) and agents (their subordinates) has been altered from one of hierarchical authority, in which the principal specifies in detail the duties and methods of work of the agent, to one of contract, in which the agent gains increased autonomy in carrying out the assigned task in return for a contractually specified payment to the owner. This means that the widespread downward reassignment of use rights has been accompanied and given content by a corresponding downward transfer of rights to returns from assets. Whenever a hierarchy is replaced by a contract, there is a partial reassignment of the owner's right to returns from assets to the contracting agent.

This downward reassignment is most dramatic in the shift from collective to household agriculture. Returns, formerly funneled through production team accounts and redistributed at year's end in the form of work points, are reassigned to households that deliver obligatory crops at low state prices while retaining the right to residual income from their land and other assets. When a village or town leases an enterprise to an individual or household, it similarly reassigns part of its rights to income from it. Such contracts typically specify a reassignment that varies from a flat lease payment, which gives the agent complete rights over all residual income, to various formulae for sharing income over a specified minimum. This principle has been applied, in a more limited fashion, even in large state enterprises. Various redrawn profit contracting schemes, and the eventual replacement of profit remission by tax payments, has led to the increased retention of profit by firms rather than government. Although the reassigned rights are still vague and subject to bargaining, state managers now enjoy significantly expanded rights to appropriate and use shares of profit at their discretion.

The examples cited are self-evident, but it is less evident that the reform of China's fiscal system in the 1980s similarly reassigned these same rights to returns from assets downward *within hierarchies of government.* Keep in mind that the overwhelming majority of productive assets in China are held by clearly specified government entities. As far as property rights assignments go, the common administrative distinction between "state" and "collective" ownership is virtually without meaning. More meaningful are the signboards outside Chinese factories, where ownership of the assets is made clear: Dongguan township, Zouping county, Shandong province, or the Ministry of Metallurgy. These are the kinds of corporate entities that hold most of the productive assets in China. Property in China has never been held by "the state"—it always has been held by thousands of separate government jurisdictions, from villages right up to central ministries.

When we say that a government jurisdiction owns an asset, we mean in part that it has the right to income from it and that the asset is part of that jurisdiction's revenue base. As China's fiscal system has moved from internal transfers of profits and tax payments to new kinds of negotiated tax "responsibility contracts," the rights of localities to income from their assets has been clarified and strengthened. In many areas of the country, tax responsibility contracts have been extended down to the level of the township (just below the rural county). Responsibility for collecting taxes is delegated to the government jurisdiction, which also has earned new rights to add additional local taxes and levies of its own and is obligated to turn over a quota of tax revenues to the level of government above it. Revenues collected above that target level are shared according to a variety of formulae and in extreme cases are kept entirely by the jurisdiction that collects them. In the same way that household contracting in agriculture reassigns rights to income from assets downward to the peasant family, tax quota contracting reassigns rights to income from assets downward to local governments.

The Reassignment of Rights to Transfer Assets

The right to sell productive assets outright remains controversial and highly constrained. Land, factories, and other enterprises are not freely bought and sold, even among local governments, and generally remain under the de facto ownership of territorially defined government agencies. However, the rights to transfer assets have been reassigned in two other areas.

First, in what is commonly called the "spread of the market," enterprises and households have been assigned greatly expanded rights to transfer assets in commodity form. The proportion of crops that must be delivered directly to village purchasing stations and the proportion of industrial products to be delivered to state agencies and enterprises under mandatory plans have been reduced drastically or eliminated entirely for much of the small-scale rural sector.[10] These property rights are central to the entire reform process, and despite extensive legal restrictions on sales and prices of various commodities, such rights have become almost unrestricted because of the difficulties of monitoring such a vastly expanded volume of transactions.

Second, there have emerged a number of informal subcontracting and leasing schemes that in effect amount to a de facto right to transfer productive assets to others. This has created an extensive "secondary market" in use rights and rights to income over productive assets. In many parts of the country agricultural land contracted to households is being subcontracted by those households to specialized farmers who amass landholdings within villages and farm on a large scale, while in other areas household land is subleased to poor farmers from mountainous regions who migrate to richer regions. Individuals who lease enterprises from local governments now commonly subcontract those enterprises out to others. Government offices and institutions that had no productive assets before the reforms are now finding that their budgets can be enhanced considerably by transferring use rights over land, buildings, vehicles, and meal halls to entrepreneurs who turn them to productive use in return for rents or shares of profits. In all of these cases, there is not a transfer downward of use rights as part of the conception of reform but a lateral transfer of assets as a secondary effect. Such transfers of rights sometimes have a tenuous legal basis, but the widespread development of such a secondary market in productive assets has had important social and political consequences.

The Record of Growth:
Output, Incomes, and Productivity

The large-scale reassignment of property rights has coincided with a record of economic performance that is enviable by any standard—not solely by the standards of China's Mao-era performance or by the standards of other socialist or developing economies.[11] China's total GNP grew 2.5-fold in the decade after 1978; real GNP, which grew at an average annual rate of 6.4 percent from 1965 to 1980, grew 10.4 percent annually from 1980 through 1988. Annual growth in employment increased from 2 to 3 percent; nonagricultural employment grew at an annual rate of 6.5 percent, and urban unemployment fell from 5 to 2 percent. Foreign trade has expanded fivefold, and exports have jumped from 4.8 percent of GDP in 1978 to 13 percent in 1988. Per capita GNP doubled in real terms in the decade after 1978, leading to an average annual growth rate for real per capita income of 9.6 percent for rural residents and 6.3 percent for urban residents. Average housing space doubled for both rural and urban residents.[12] Per capita consumption of pork, beef, poultry, and eggs have all increased by two- to fourfold. Per capita ownership of such consumer items as bicycles, radios, and cameras has grown by a factor of more than three, while consumption of such items as television sets, tape players, and stereos has increased fortyfold.[13]

More directly relevant to the central concerns of this chapter is the question of productivity in publicly owned industry, where the problems of reform are recognized to be most intractable. Many theorists have thought that the gains of the 1980s coincided with relative stagnation in state-owned industry and have usually pointed to evidence of continuing soft budget constraints (see the next section of this chapter) and to deteriorating profitability in the state sector as the reason. Careful work with Chinese data has documented, however, sustained improvements in several measures of productivity. In state-owned industry, for example, the total factor of productivity grew during the 1980s at an annual average rate of 2.4 percent, while in rural (township and village) industry, the most rapidly growing sector of the economy, it improved at a rate of 4.6 percent. The productivity improvements accelerated in the last half of the decade.[14] Further evidence of increasing financial pressures and economic competition in industry is found in a marked equalization of returns to capital, labor, and intermediate inputs among sectors and enterprises,[15] in rates of profit across industrial sectors, and through time between the state (monopoly) sector and the new rural industries.[16] It is plausible that the deteriorating profit performance of state industry can be reconciled with data of increasing factor productivity if we recognize the growing competition and financial pressures represented by the equalization of returns across sectors and enterprises.[17]

Soft Versus Flexible Budget Constraints

How can we reconcile China's economic dynamism and evidence of improved industrial performance with the fact that the relationship between industry and government still can be characterized as a "regime of bargaining," the defining behaviors of which remain identical to those described in the partially reformed Hungarian economy of the 1970s?[18] Interview research has shown that the terms of taxation and finance are highly variable and subject to bargaining. Budget constraints are flexible both ex ante, as subsidized loans and tax breaks are built variably into investment projects according to a firm's perceived ability to repay, and ex post, as firms that run into difficulties may renegotiate financial terms to allow them to continue operating.[19] As in the characteristic bargaining regime described by János Kornai, local financial officials still consciously exercise discretion to level off earnings variations that often are seen as due to conditions beyond the control of firms; for instance, they may expropriate "excess profit" from more lucrative firms and use these funds to subsidize less profitable firms that supply important products.[20]

While several observers (including myself) have described such behavior as evidence of continuing soft budget constraints and as a barrier to productivity growth, the continuity of bargaining behavior may mask important changes in the underlying constraints and incentives it is thought to symbolize. That is, the terms of taxation and finance that define a firm's budget constraints may continue to be highly flexible and tailored to individual firms while the constraints that actually operate upon the behavior of managers are hardening. The productivity improvements and converging rates of return cited above suggest that this is indeed happening. It may in fact be the new *intensity* of bargaining over the terms of financial transfers between government and enterprise—not unlike the bargaining in market economies between divisions and plants on one hand and corporate headquarters on the other—that is having the greatest impact upon the behavior of managers.

The argument that budget constraints may be hardening despite continued flexibility rests on two claims. The first is that there are behavioral consequences of constant bargaining over financial terms. This rests on the crucial observation that while bargaining still characterizes relations between enterprise and government, the objects of bargaining have changed decisively over the years. Where bargaining in the "traditional" system of central planning took place over output targets, supplies, investment projects, and delivery schedules, postreform bargaining takes place primarily over financial issues: the setting of effective tax rates, the evaluation of investment proposals for feasibility and creditworthiness, and the terms on which credit is offered. Bargaining over these matters puts a firm's financial performance and productivity under much closer scrutiny than was the case in past decades. While there are surely many remaining shortcomings in this process, and while the budgetary constraint is still soft compared to constraints experienced by an independent firm in a market economy, it appears plausible that the activity of intense bargaining over financial terms is bringing increased pressure to bear upon managerial performance.

The second claim is that budget constraints on firms can be soft only to the extent that a given government jurisdiction has the fiscal resources to subsidize underperforming firms. This subsidization can vary considerably, and two features of the Chinese economy affect such variation. The first is the contractual nature of the system of revenue collection introduced in the 1980s: Each government jurisdiction collects tax revenues from enterprises under its jurisdiction and turns over a contracted amount to the next higher level of government. Residuals above that amount either are kept entirely by the collecting jurisdiction or are shared according to an explicit formula. This fiscal reform has created a heightened interest in revenue collection (and expansion of the revenue base) among local governments and has served to clarify the fiscal limits of a government's ability to be lenient toward underperforming firms.[21] The second feature is the widespread local government ownership rights over enterprises that are allocated across the whole hierarchy of the Chinese state from ministry to village.[22] The heightened fiscal constraints facing governments are most immediate and hardest at the lower levels, which have a more limited industrial (and tax) base.[23]

These new constraints and incentives have brought about interesting variations in industrial organization. At the higher levels of government—such as the ministry, provincial, and municipal levels—relations between enterprises and government bureaus involve constant bargaining over and flexible adjustment of financial terms that affect a firm's budget constraint. The relations between enterprise and government are analogous to relations between plants or divisions and the corporate headquarters of a large and loosely integrated conglomerate.[24] At the lower levels of government, especially at the rural county, township, and village levels, there is tangibly less bargaining and more unilateral decision-making by government officials. Here the local corporation is smaller, more tightly integrated, and more centralized, with village and township officials, who are interested especially in expanding their revenue base, reviewing all important plans and decisions regarding expansion, investment, and product lines and playing very active roles in marketing. In many respects, local officials in rural areas have become entrepreneurs analogous to company executives.[25]

Industrial performance has been most spectacular in this small-scale rural sector. Output in this sector grew at an average annual rate of over 20 percent from 1980–1988, and its annual rate of growth in total factor productivity (4.6 percent) was double that of urban state industry. In this sector, the fiscal constraints on local governments with inherently small industrial bases are most immediate and the incentives to growth are greatest. Also note that the reasons for this sector's success so far are completely contrary to the logic of privatization proposals: China's industrial reforms have worked best precisely where government property rights are strongest and the boundary between government and enterprise is most blurred. The logic behind privatization proposals is to divest government of ownership rights and create legally enforceable private claims for enterprises versus government regulation. It is ironic that China's most striking industrial reform successes have occurred where this is least true.

The broader question raised by this phenomenon is one of industrial organization. Where, and how, does one draw the boundary between government and enterprise? How shall rights over use and income be allocated and enforced? Privatization proposals seek to sharpen the boundaries between government and enterprise and replace hierarchies with markets wherever possible—something that immediately requires a new and elaborate regulatory and legal framework. The Chinese approach has been to alter the fiscal and market incentives for governments and firms and to alter the relations between them, while leaving intact government property rights and corporate industrial organization. This approach has achieved an undeniable measure of short-term success.

Conclusion: Some Implications of the Chinese Experience

China's industrial reforms still face a number of difficulties, and it is not certain that the progress of the 1980s can be sustained indefinitely. The labor force in the state sector remains tied almost permanently to its firms and suffers from poor motivation; prices for everything from housing and foodstuffs to steel are heavily regulated and distorted; many large state firms are obsolete and unproductive yet are difficult to close; inflation has been severe at times in the 1980s and has been reined in primarily by cutting credit and slowing economic growth. Some still might be inclined to assert, despite the arguments marshaled in this chapter, that a more thorough privatization of the economy could have created even better growth rates and improvements in productivity.

Furthermore, China's reforms have several political premises and side effects that are likely to be unpalatable in Eastern Europe. First, Communist officials in government and industry remain in charge of their organizations and play an active role in the economy. Second, continued government property rights confer power and privilege on officials at all levels as well as providing them with new opportunities for rent seeking and corruption, a social problem that popularly is perceived to have become serious in the 1980s and was a major political issue in the protests of 1989.[26] In Eastern Europe, where privatization proposals are usually championed as part of a program to dismantle the Communist system and strip former officials of their power and privilege, the Chinese approach is unlikely to have much political appeal.

Politically, the Chinese approach has been to take the path of least resistance. The debate over privatization that has become so lively in the post-Communist states[27] has been suppressed and avoided in China throughout the 1980s. Without a clear overall blueprint for economic reform—or even a clearly articulated conception of what the endpoint of reform shall be—the Chinese Communist Party has sidestepped these politically contentious issues and has proceeded with the business of economic transformation and growth. Whether these transformations will serve in the middle run to further buttress or further undermine Communist Party rule is subject to debate.

The contrast with much of the former Soviet bloc—and especially the former Soviet Union—could not be more striking. While these regimes debate the political and economic consequences of various blueprints for a final economic transition—in some cases while their economies collapse around them—the Chinese have quietly sidestepped such debates for over a decade without a comprehensive plan and have made enviable economic advances. Whatever political changes shall take place in China in the years to come, they are likely to occur in much more favorable economic circumstances than those that prevail in much of Eastern Europe today.

Notes

1. Ellen Comisso, "Property Rights, Liberalism, and the Transition from 'Actually Existing' Socialism," *East European Politics and Societies* 5, 1 (Winter 1991): 162–188.

2. I am indebted to Zhiyuan Cui for pointing out to me the importance of this distinction.

3. David Stark, "Privatization in Hungary: From Plan to Market or from Plan to Clan?" *East European Politics and Societies* 4, 3 (Fall 1990): 351–392; Irena Grosfeld, "Privatization of State Enterprises in Eastern Europe: The Search for a Market Environment," *East European Politics and Societies* 5, 1 (Winter 1991): 142–161.

4. See, for example, Frederick L. Pryor, *Property and Industrial Organization in Communist and Capitalist Nations* (Bloomington: Indiana University Press, 1973); David Granick, *Chinese State Enterprises: A Regional Property Rights Analysis* (Chicago: University of Chicago Press, 1990).

5. Harold Demsetz, "Toward a Theory of Property Rights," *American Economic Review* 57 (May 1967): 347–359.

6. Eirik G. Furubotn and Svetozar Pejovich (eds.), *The Economics of Property Rights* (Cambridge, Mass.: Ballinger, 1974).

7. Demsetz, "Toward a Theory of Property Rights."

8. John L. Campbell and Leon N. Lindberg, "Property Rights and the Organization of Economic Activity by the State," *American Sociological Review* 55, 5 (October 1990): 634–647; John L. Campbell, "Property Rights and Governance Transformations in Eastern Europe and the United States," in Sven-Erik Sjostrand (ed.), *Institutional Development and Change* (New York: Sharpe, 1992).

9. Problems encountered in the enforcement of property rights are central to the economics of contracts, industrial organization, and bureaucracies. While the monitoring and enforcement of property rights is a crucial problem in China's reforms, in this chapter I will limit discussion primarily to the government's reassignment of such rights in the process of reform.

10. In fact, markets in China still are largely restricted to the exchange of finished agricultural and industrial products, precisely because rights regarding the transfer of assets have been widely delegated only with regard to finished commodities. Rights regarding the transfer of assets in all other forms remain highly restricted, and for this reason there are as yet no comparable markets for capital, credit, land, and fixed assets.

11. I say "coincided with" because I am not able to state with any precision how much these specific changes in property rights assignments, and the incentive effects they represent, contributed to the observed economic improvements.

12. Kang Chen, Gary H. Jefferson, and Inderjit Singh, "Lessons from China's Economic Reform," *Journal of Comparative Economics* 16, 2 (June 1992): 201–225.

13. Kang Chen, Jefferson, and Singh, "Lessons from China's Economic Reform"; Dwight H. Perkins, "Reforming China's Economic System," *Journal of Economic Literature* 26 (June 1988): 601–645.

14. Gary H. Jefferson, Thomas G. Rawski, and Yuxin Zheng, "Growth, Efficiency, and Convergence in Chinese Industry: A Comparative Evaluation of the State and Collective Sectors," *Economic Development and Cultural Change* 40, 2 (January 1992): 239–266.

15. Gary H. Jefferson and Wenyi Xu, "The Impact of Reform on Socialist Enterprises in Transition: Structure, Conduct, and Performance in Chinese Industry," *Journal of Comparative Economics* 15, 1 (March 1991): 45–64.

16. Barry Naughton, "Implications of the State Monopoly over Industry and Its Relaxation," *Modern China* 18, 1 (January 1992): 14–41.

17. Naughton, "Implications of the State Monopoly."

18. János Kornai, *The Economics of Shortage* (Amsterdam: North-Holland, 1980); János Kornai, "The Soft Budget Constraint," *Kyklos* 39, 1 (1986): 3–30; János Kornai, "The Hungarian Reform Process: Visions, Hopes, and Reality," *Journal of Economic Literature* 24 (December 1986): 1687–1737; and T. Laky, "Enterprises in Bargaining Position," *Acta Oeconomica* 22, 3–4 (1979): 227–246.

19. Andrew G. Walder, "Factory and Manager in an Era of Reform," *China Quarterly* 118 (June 1989): 242–264; and Andrew G. Walder, "Local Bargaining Relationships and Urban Industrial Finance," in Kenneth G. Lieberthal and David M. Lampton (eds.), *Bureaucracy, Politics, and Decision-Making in Post-Mao China* (Berkeley: University of California Press, 1992), pp. 308–333.

20. Walder, "Local Bargaining Relationships and Urban Industrial Finance."

21. Jean C. Oi, "The Fate of the Collective After the Commune," in Deborah Davis and Ezra F. Vogel (eds.), *Chinese Society on the Eve of Tiananmen: The Impact of Reform,* Harvard Contemporary China Series no. 7 (Cambridge, Mass.: Council on East Asian Studies, 1990); Jean C. Oi, "Economic Management and

Rural Government: Bureaucratic Entrepreneurship in Local Economies," paper presented to the Annual Meetings of the Association for Asian Studies, Chicago, 1990; Jean C. Oi, "Fiscal Reform and the Economic Foundations of Local State Corporatism in China," *World Politics* (October 1992); Christine P. W. Wong, "Between Plan and Market: The Role of the Local Sector in Post-Mao China," *Journal of Comparative Economics* 11, 3 (December 1987): 385–398; and Christine P. W. Wong, "Fiscal Reform and Local Industrialization: The Problematic Sequencing of Reform in Post-Mao China," *Modern China* 18 (April 1992): 197–227.

22. Granick, *Chinese State Enterprises;* Christine P. W. Wong, "Ownership and Control in Chinese Industry: The Maoist Legacy and Prospects for the 1980s," in Joint Economic Committee, Congress of the United States, *China's Economy Looks Toward the Year 2000* (Washington, D.C.: US Government Printing Office, 1986); and Andrew G. Walder, "Property Rights and Stratification in Socialist Redistributive Economies," *American Sociological Review* 57, 4 (August 1992): 524–539.

23. Walder, "Property Rights and Stratification." This claim has yet to be demonstrated with budgetary data, and there are certainly other factors besides amount of budgetary revenue that bear on the incentives and the capacity of government officials to harden budget constraints over their firms. This important question is beyond the scope of this chapter. An alternative argument that is consistent with the same facts is found in Victor Nee, "Organizational Dynamics of Market Transition: Hybrid Forms, Property Rights, and Mixed Economy in China," *Administrative Science Quarterly* 37 (March 1992): 1–27, which attributes differences between urban and rural enterprise to the greater exposure of the latter to market competition.

24. Walder, "Local Bargaining Relationships and Urban Industrial Finance."

25. Oi, "The Fate of the Collective After the Commune"; "Economic Management and Rural Government"; and "Fiscal Reform and the Economic Foundations."

26. It is evident that the extent of such corruption is not so great that it has choked off economic growth. Opportunities for illicit official incomes may even have beneficial incentive effects.

27. Stark, "Privatization in Hungary."

■ 4 ■

Mongolia: Privatization and System Transformation in an Isolated Economy

CEVDET DENIZER AND ALAN GELB

Largely unnoticed by the West, Mongolia began to move away from Soviet domination and a centrally planned economy with the first stirring of glasnost. Though still within the context of central planning, economic decentralization began as early as 1984. By 1990 the country was on the way to implementing a radical transformation program that aimed to create a market economy.[1] Such a program, like those in Eastern Europe after 1990, would need to address the entire spectrum of economic reform, including price and trade liberalization, rapid privatization, and a fundamental change in the economic role of the state. Mongolia's program aimed at all these areas—in particular, privatization, where an innovative voucher plan was initiated earlier than in any country in Eastern Europe. Moreover, the program began under exceptionally difficult conditions because of the withdrawal of Soviet aid and the disruption of trading links within the Council for Mutual Economic Assistance (CMEA).

How could one of the most isolated countries in the world—isolated geographically and also in terms of trade and intellectual interactions outside the Soviet bloc—propose so radical a transformation?[2] What factors encouraged the "big bang" reform strategy, and what hindered it? Was such a strategy successfully implemented, or have the radical steps to the market been slowed down? These are some of the questions discussed in this chapter, which outlines Mongolia's economic transformation program and reports progress to date.

This chapter summarizes the program in four phases: the cautious initial reforms after 1985; the rapid formulation of a radical transformation program from July 1990 to October 1991; an apparent slowdown in implementation and a new, extended timetable for privatization from November 1991 to February 1992; and the subsequent beginning of large-scale privatization and apparent restoration of reform momentum. The final section

67

considers what factors might call for speed versus caution in the reform process and their possible weight in the Mongolian case. An important element of the final section is the assessment, using the simple computable general equilibrium (CGE) model, of the adverse impact of the Soviet aid and trade shock and the interplay between the speed of contraction and movement in a market economy.

Two points should be made before proceeding. First, this chapter does not judge the reform proposals and their execution or predict their future course. Second, policy announcements in Mongolia sometimes have been contradictory, and the data base is limited.[3] There is room for differences of interpretation of the actual as well as the intended evolution both of policies and outcomes.

Mongolia and Its Early Reforms

Mongolia is a large country with a sparse population of only 2.1 million people. High in altitude and landlocked between the former USSR and China, its climate is unusually severe, with temperatures commonly below freezing from October to March. Because of these climatic constraints, animal husbandry traditionally has been important to Mongolian economy and culture. With a national livestock count of 26 million and abundant grazing land, extensive animal husbandry remains the base for its light industry (mostly processing of livestock products) and agricultural exports. Climatic factors limit large-scale crop cultivation. However, Mongolia has significant and largely unutilized natural resources such as minerals and nonferrous metals—including gold and silver, hydrocarbons, and semiprecious stones. It also has ample reserves of coal and copper. Despite large untapped mineral reserves, mining is a major export industry. Mongolia's vast territory, low population density, and inadequate infrastructure result in thin and fragmented markets, making it difficult to realize economies of scale in production.

After its establishment as a nation in 1924, Mongolia became the unofficial "sixteenth" Soviet republic. It remained internationally isolated, and its close relationship with the Soviet Union and ties to other CMEA countries shaped its development framework toward central planning. Gradually, Mongolia became integrated with and dependent on the Soviet and CMEA economies. Starting in the mid-1950s, the Soviet Union and other CMEA countries provided Mongolia with large-scale financial assistance. During the second half of the 1980s, the flow of foreign resources in the form of grants and loans accounted for 30 percent of Mongolia's gross domestic product (GDP) per year. Economic dependence also took the form of increasing trade volume with the CMEA countries until, by the 1980s, about 97 percent of Mongolia's trade took place with these countries. The Soviet Union, which accounted for 95 percent of this total trade volume, supplied all of Mongolia's petroleum, energy, and capital and consumer goods and received in return copper concentrate, wool, leather, and meat.

Some dimensions of Mongolia's structural dependence are shown in Table 4.1. A massive resource deficit of almost 30 percent of the GDP, funded by low-cost Soviet loans, mainly covered the fiscal deficit. Government spending equaled 65 percent of the GDP, with current spending half of the GDP. This spending helped to sustain living standards at an acceptable minimum and supported the country's well-developed social consumption system. Mongolia's exports were concentrated heavily in minerals and raw materials (notably cashmere, leather, and wool), which accounted for 70 percent of the total. Only 5 percent of exports or 1 percent of GDP—almost all raw materials—went to nonsocialist countries, although these countries supplied one-third of imports. Except in the self-sufficient pastoral economy, Mongolia's imports played a critical role in supplying fuels, intermediate and capital goods, spare parts, and consumer goods, including urban foodstuffs.

Before 1921, Mongolia's economy was a simple agrarian one in which the majority of the population lived as nomadic herdsmen. This description still applies to most of the 44 percent of the population living in rural areas. However, after 1960 central planning transformed Mongolia's socioeconomic structure and contributed to the technological dualization of the economy. Buttressed by Soviet aid and mining revenues, industrial investment grew in the 1970s and most of the 1980s, superimposing a modern urban economy onto the traditional one. Spearheaded by industry, the GDP grew at an average annual rate of 5.5 percent between 1970 and 1990, attracting Mongolians to urban areas. By the end of the 1980s, 56 percent of the population was living in the three main cities, most employed either as civil servants (about 212,000 in 1991) or by industry (167,000).

Great achievements were made in the social sectors during this period of economic change. Mongolia achieved a 97 percent literacy rate and a well-developed educational infrastructure. Its health system was effective, with more doctors per capita than the United States and adequate access to medical services. The crude death rate fell from 22 per thousand in 1940 to 8.4 per thousand by 1989. As in Eastern Europe, social welfare was protected by an extensive system of subsidies and transfers. By 1990, some 800,000 persons of Mongolia's population of 2 million received pensions and allowances. This system prevented obvious social dualism by making living standards comparable in town and countryside.

In the second half of the 1980s, Mongolia's economic growth started to experience difficulties. GDP growth slowed from 7 percent during the 1981–1986 period to 4.6 percent between 1987 and 1989, and there were increasing shortages of consumer goods. The slowdown was caused partly by the economic malaise affecting CMEA partners and by the inadequacy

Table 4.1 Mongolia: Structural Indicators

Indicator	1988	1990	1991
		Percent of GDP	
Exports	26	23	
Imports	54	50	
Resource balance	−28	−27	
Fiscal revenues	45	51	
Government exports	65	64	
Current exports	50	52	
Subsidies and transfers	18	20	
Fiscal balance	−20	−13	
Percent foreign financed	100	78	
Total absorption	128	127	
Investment	42	20	
Private consumption	62	75	
Public consumption	24	22	
		Trade Structure	
Percentage of exports			
Minerals	40		
Raw materials	30		
Exports to nonsocialist countries			
Percent of total exports	5		
Share of raw materials	94		
Imports from nonsocialist countries			
Percent of total imports	33		
		Balance of Payments ($ millions)	
Exports	829	468	432
Imports	1,849	1,047	564
Current account	−1,033	−644	−100
		CMEA Dependence: Mongolia and Eastern Europe	
Export share to CMEA (percent)			
Mongolia		95	
Bulgaria		70	
Czechosloviakia		50	
Hungary		40	
Poland		40	
Non-CMEA exports/GDP (percent)			
Mongolia		1	
Bulgaria		15	
Czechoslovakia		15	
Hungary		22	
Poland		12	

(continues)

Table 4.1 (*continued*)

	CMEA Dependence: Mongolia and Eastern Europe
Direct loss from CMEA Shock/GDP (percent)	
Mongolia	30*
Bulgaria	12
Czechoslovakia	7
Hungary	6
Poland	5

Note: *Aid shock only.

of domestic resources to sustain growth. Dissatisfaction with central planning grew and culminated in the removal of Tsedenbahl (Mongolia's leader during much of the period of dependence) in August 1984, an event that marked the beginning of economic and political reform. Influenced by the political changes in the Soviet Union, and with nationalism resurgent (as in the former Soviet republics), Mongolia launched its own program of political openness and economic restructuring. The reforms implemented between 1984 and 1989 included streamlining government agencies, reducing subsidies, decentralizing to reduce expenditures and improve public finance, and giving financial autonomy to public enterprises, resulting in a trend toward self-management.[4]

However, the reforms summarized in Table 4.2 were cautious and aimed to increase the efficiency of the command economy. The government that took office in December 1984 "revised" the eighth five-year plan so that reforms still took place in a planned context. Perhaps because these measures did not alter the central planning structure, they did not improve public finances. While deficits increased throughout the 1980s, public expenditures accounted for more than 60 percent of GDP. About 80 percent of spending was current, and half of current spending consisted of subsidies and transfers. Overall budgetary deficits jumped from 6.9 percent of the GDP in 1985 to 17.7 percent in 1986 and to 19.5 percent in 1988. The USSR financed the deficits entirely and provided the main driving force for growth in 1986–1989.

Mongolia's dependence on the USSR and its susceptibility to external shocks therefore increased. In 1989, Mongolia began to feel the effects of Soviet economic difficulties. The Soviets halved the financial assistance needed to cover the budget deficit in 1988–1990. This was a loss equivalent to 15 percent of Mongolia's GDP, and the CMEA trading system began to crumble. The economy felt contractionary effects of these shocks. Output declined by 2.1 percent in 1990, and there were sharp

Table 4.2 Key Economic and Structural Reforms

1986
  Increase in domestic wholesale prices.
  Limited autonomy granted to public sector enterprises for investment.
  Introduction of long-term bank loans for investment.
1987
  Modification of investment planning system for setting overall targets.
  Expansion of investment autonomy of public sector enterprises.
  Rationalization of number of government ministries.
1988
  Reduction in five-year plan performance indices.
  Further decentralization of budgetary operations to local level.
  Limited liberalization of agricultural pricing and marketing in excess of state
    orders.
  Promotion of private sector cooperatives under new Law on Cooperatives.
  Introduction of more depreciated noncommercial tugrik/US dollar exchange
    rate.
1989
  Liberalization of intrapublic sector enterprise pricing and expansion of operating
    autonomy.
  Modest easing of restrictions on private herd ownership.
  Elimination of monopoly of state trading corporations.
  Increase in selected administered retail prices.
  Easing of foreign exchange surrender requirements.
  Introduction of preferential domestic prices for exported goods.
1990
  Elimination of restrictions on private ownership of herds.
  Freeing of selected retail prices.
  Legalization of two-tiered banking system and establishment of two commercial
    banks.
  Rationalization of government ministries; elimination of State Planning
    Committee.
  Establishment of Customs Affairs Department and Tax Service Department.
  Promulgation of new Foreign Investment Law.
  Devaluation of tugrik versus US dollar for commercial transactions.
  Introduction of foreign exchange auction system.
  Negotiation of most-favored-nation trade agreements with countries in the con-
    vertible currency area.
1991
  Increase in retail prices of most goods.
  Lengthened maturity structure of term deposits and increased interest rates.
  Substantial reduction of budgetary subsidy for imported goods and to loss-
    making enterprises.
  Devaluation of tugrik versus US dollar to Tug 40 = $1.
  Adjustments to wages, pension benefits, and private savings deposits to soften
    impact of price increase.

(continues)

Table 4.2 (*continued*)

1991 (continued)

Privatization Law passed and program for small privatization initiated.

Banking Law passed, and Bank of Mongolia established as the central bank. Separate commercial banks established.

Direct export rights granted to selected manufacturers.

Foreign trading rights issued on nondiscriminatory basis.

Stock market regulation established.

1992

Deregulated all prices (except for public services, utility tariffs, public housing rents, selected medicines, flour, bread, and rationed vodka).

Eliminated mandatory state orders for exports.

Passed Bankruptcy Law.

Issued foreign trading licenses on a nondiscriminatory basis (except for copper scrap, cashmere, timber, and elk horns).

Eliminated budgetary transfers to public enterprises.

Introduced weekly monitoring of budgetary revenues and expenditures.

Established a stock exchange.

Raised central bank lending rate closer to inflation level.

Simplified interbank clearing and payments arrangements.

Assigned responsibility for transportation policy to a single coordinating authority, General Department of Transportation.

Source: The World Bank, 1992.

increases in unemployment and inflation, both entirely new phenomena in Mongolia.

The Formulation of a "Big Bang"

Despite more reforms in January 1990, increasing economic difficulties, shortages of consumer goods, rising prices, and visible unemployment led to popular demonstrations in March 1990. The demonstrations led to a proposal in July by the ruling Communists for a comprehensive program of economic transformation and to the first multiparty election. A coalition government, still dominated by the Mongolian People's Revolutionary Party (MPRP), was formed in September, but some of the most important positions, including that of deputy prime minister with responsibility for privatization, were held by other more reformist parties. A new president also was installed.

Reform measures announced between January 1990 and July 1991 included a doubling of almost all prices, subsidy cuts, devaluation, privatization measures, banking reform—including the creation of a new central bank, tax reforms, the elimination of all restrictions on private ownership of herds, and fundamental legal reforms. Meanwhile, major changes took place in traditional relationships with other CMEA countries, and Mongolia agreed to value trade and settle convertible currencies from the beginning of 1991.

Prices and Markets

Price liberalization was formally extended to cover 60 percent of products,[5] and administered prices were increased by about 100 percent. Nevertheless, the official distribution system dominated trade, and the shrinking pool of foreign exchange was still tightly controlled. Imports were therefore rationed de facto; the result was to squeeze the margin of goods available on parallel markets and slow the emergence of the small-scale private trading sector that was unable to obtain goods. Wages and savings deposits were also doubled to offset price increases. As a result, the ratio of parallel market prices to official prices averaged about two to one, much the same as before the price reform. With the devaluation of the tugrik to 40 to one dollar, domestic prices for many goods and services were still low by world standards. The continued application of trade controls and the dominant public distribution and marketing system kept domestic prices low in an attempt to avoid the adverse social consequences that would result from further sharp price hikes.

Price and market liberalization was incomplete, and there was little movement toward current convertibility. Mongolia's actual reforms fell short of its rhetoric and were less comprehensive than those of Eastern Europe.[6]

Another distinctive feature of Mongolia's reforms was the introduction of consumer rationing in January 1991. Half of the rationed items, including sugar, rice, and flour, involved imports. At 2.7 kilograms for each person a month, meat rations covered about one-third of previous consumption levels.

Private Sector Development

Like Eastern Europe and the former USSR, Mongolia saw some emergence of private activities and spontaneous privatization of state assets during its period of reform.[7] The removal of formal discrimination against private activities in 1988 accelerated private sector development. The number of private cooperatives grew from 180 in 1988 to nearly 3,000 in 1990, and these employed well over 20,000 persons. Other firms also began to appear. By 1990, their number reached 4,200, and they reportedly employed about 32,000 workers. These firms mostly provided services and light manufacturing for the domestic market. Out of a total of about 965,000 workers in Mongolia, some 56,000 persons, including 4,000 who were self-employed, worked in private sector activities by 1990.

The main barrier to greater private activity was the almost total lack of access to goods and foreign exchange because of the continuation of a state distribution system and the shrinking economic resource envelope, which consequently hindered the private accumulation of capital through trading. Private firms sought inclusion in the state distribution system and a quota of 10 percent of trade was reserved for private businesses.[8]

Privatization Program

The most striking development in 1991 was the announcement of the privatization program, which was extremely ambitious both in the number of enterprises and the initial timetable. Three hundred forty-four large enterprises and 1,601 small enterprises were to be privatized by the end of 1992 through free distribution of share vouchers to every citizen born before the approval of the Privatization Law. The program had two distinct components: small or large privatizations, with two types of vouchers. Red vouchers, with a face value of 1,000 tugrik, were for the privatization of the 1,601 small businesses, which included agricultural assets, except land and livestock, and other small assets. The total book value of small assets was 9.4 billion tugrik. Blue vouchers, with a face value of 7,000 tugrik, were for the privatization of the 344 large enterprises, which had a book value of 10.8 billion tugrik. Each citizen was entitled to three red vouchers and one blue. Red vouchers were tradable on secondary markets. Blue vouchers were not tradable but could be assigned twice to nominees.

The face values of the vouchers were only notional, reflecting the estimated historical cost of the assets to be privatized. The actual market value of the assets depended on forward-looking projections. Because they were freely tradable, the market value of red coupons could diverge from their face value even before privatization. Blue vouchers had no secondary market, but they could be used to purchase shares that subsequently became tradable, at prices that reflected their "true" market value.

Assets in the small privatization category were transferred to the private sector at auctions arranged by local authorities, with guidelines set by the Privatization Commission. The commission was responsible for the historical cost valuation and informed the public of these values by listing the assets to be auctioned in newspapers across the country. Only red vouchers could be used to bid; the Privatization Commission would issue the ownership certificate to the winner with the highest bid. However, the employees of the firms being auctioned had the first right to acquire ownership, using red coupons at the value determined by the Privatization Commission.

Blue vouchers were used to auction large enterprises for privatization. These enterprises developed privatization plans and obtained permission to implement them from the Privatization Commission. The commission could value the firms' fixed assets, audit the balance sheets, and issue shares on the basis of net assets. The enterprises then converted to joint stock companies. Ten percent of their shares was granted to the employees, who then were able to participate in the auction on an equal basis with others.[9] The remaining shares were sold sequentially in batches. Bidders could declare a price or price range for shares (in term of blue vouchers) and a time period during which their bids remained valid. Brokers in each *aimak* (province) throughout the country collected declarations and phoned in bids to the stock market. The broker with the highest bid for the batch registered the owners and provided them with ownership certificates. Individuals who were unable to choose a company or did not understand the process could invest in mutual funds operated by the brokerage firms. However, the funds were not allowed to control more than 20 percent of shares of a given company. After full privatization of a sufficient number of enterprises, secondary trading could begin, and foreigners would be able to buy shares.

Like other voucher plans, Mongolia's approach to privatization aims to transfer ownership quickly to a private sector that lacks wealth[10] and is designed to be fair ex ante but not ex post. As noted by Aart Kraay, the voucher system reduces problems associated with "spontaneous privatization" (which damaged the credibility of early privatization efforts in Eastern Europe) by subjecting each enterprise's privatization plans to the approval of the Privatization Commission that also reviews their assets.[11] Although corporate governance may be an issue because the Mongolian privatization program is a "diffuse shareholding" approach, creating suitable core investor groups or intermediaries like the Polish mutual funds would also be a problem in the Mongolian context. Employee preferences and an inclination to invest in local firms probably would result in many employee- or community-owned firms, but there is no reason to assume that alternative core investor groups will not develop once secondary trading begins.

The privatization program assigns the valuation of enterprises for the stock market and minimizes the importance of bureaucratic valuation. The initial valuation of assets by the Privatization Commission was an accounting exercise to determine the number of coupons to be issued. It was not fixed or binding because those values could change in the market according to supply and demand and without reservation prices for assets. However, the announcement of the initial price can have a real impact on the market in a society that has no experience with market prices and has a long tradition of administratively determined prices. With respect to stock market valuation, some researchers argue that these stock markets are not likely to function properly in the transition period.[12] However, the enterprises need to be valued somehow, and, as Kraay pointed out, "if some kind of a stock market is not used to value enterprises for the privatization process, what organization will?"[13]

There is one important caveat. It is not clear that privatization in the Mongolian context implies a swift transfer to private owners of the full set of rights normally assumed to accompany ownership. The creation of effective corporate governance is a three-stage process—issue of vouchers, auctions, and shareholder consolidation through secondary trading. As described below, no company has yet gone through this entire process. Furthermore, until price, market, and foreign exchange liberalization are well advanced, ownership rights will remain circumscribed. There are reports of theoretically privatized enterprises still receiving production instructions from state bodies.[14] In addition, land that the enterprises are built on will still be owned by the state. It is also possible that many enterprises will have negative equity unless the government writes off their debts to commercial banks. In Mongolia's privatization program shareholders have control, at least in theory, but no real ownership.

Slowing the Headlong Rush:
July 1991 to February 1992

The progress of reforms after July 1991 was inevitable, though the program developed more slowly than initially planned. Soviet financial assistance, which had averaged 30 percent of the GDP between 1985 and 1990, totally dried up at the beginning of 1991, causing the economy to deteriorate throughout the year. Following the dissolution of the CMEA, foreign trade declined dramatically. Exports fell from US$795.8 million in 1989 to $444.8 million in 1990 and to $346.5 million in 1991. Likewise, imports fell from $1.53 billion in 1989 to $782.8 million in 1990 and to $391.5 million in 1991. Relative to 1989, exports fell by 56 percent and imports by a whopping 75 percent. Severe shortages of almost all inputs and consumer goods resulted in lower output across all sectors and reduced GDP of 16.5 percent in 1991.

Modern Mongolia had never faced such a crisis. It forced the government to reduce the speed of reforms and increase administrative controls over the economy. In order to guarantee the supply of goods and agricultural produce for the domestic market, state orders were maintained. The government awarded a 25 percent raise in the minimum wage to employees of state enterprises. In addition, the government introduced antimonopoly legislation that set a framework for price controls for a large number of goods, including those in the private sector. The growth of private activities also slowed as continued state orders further constrained the availability of basic inputs to the private sector.

Despite the economic slowdown germane to plans discussed earlier—it was now anticipated that privatization would take at least two years—Mongolia's progress in privatization was rapid compared with development in price and market reform. There was considerable progress, particularly, in small-scale privatization. By the beginning of February 1992, about 80 percent of all small enterprises were in private hands. A secondary market for red vouchers had developed that valued vouchers at about 30 percent of their face value (300 tugrik per voucher, which meant 900 tugrik per holder). Sales of red vouchers by a three-person family would have yielded 2,700 tugrik—about half of a year's average salary.

Another achievement was the preparation of communications and arrangements for large-scale privatization. The Privatization Commission established seven brokerage houses and negotiated special provisions to dedicate Mongolia's limited telephone facilities to the bidding process at specified times.[15] Meanwhile, the commission began to advertise upcoming privatization plans through the press and the radio.

Substantial market liberalization is usually considered a necessary precondition for privatization to be effective.[16] However, some have argued that much private sector activity is a prerequisite for liberalized markets to work in a competitive manner, especially in highly planned economies.[17] These two arguments were reflected in policy debates from July 1991 to February 1992. The political opposition called for rapid price liberalization so that privatization could proceed quickly. The government argued that the private sector and market institutions needed to develop first. This argument reflected the different constraints and incentives that the government and opposition faced as well as greatly diverging points of view within the MPRP. In particular, the differences concerned the social reaction to price increases, which were made more dramatic by the tighter external constraints on Mongolia.

For the first time, the MPRP was facing serious electoral competition and had to gain popular support to stay in power. Partly because of its dealings with international agencies and analysts, the cabinet, including the prime minister and almost all the MPRP ministers who managed the daily running of the country, was more aware than the opposition of the size of the economic crisis and the harshness of the necessary adjustment measures. But party members felt that they had already implemented a credible reform package and that new measures should be put in place gradually. More importantly, they viewed further radical reforms as politically unfeasible in the face of upcoming elections.

Cabinet members who represented other small parties, as well as a sizable number of MPRP deputies in the parliament, argued that the reason for the continued poor economic situation was insufficient reforms and pressed for new measures. Because the main strategy of opposition parties was to advocate reform, they could not have argued otherwise, and their optimal strategy was to blame the government for not pressing ahead with reforms more rapidly. Conversely, a hankering for the old socialist system remained in other sections of the MPRP.

By October 1991, a clear sign of development was that foreign market economies and international organizations were prepared to support reforms through economic assistance. Pledges of foreign aid (including IMF and World Bank loans) of $150 million—equivalent to about 15 percent of the GDP—were made at the Tokyo donors' meeting in May 1991. While a direct comparison is difficult, this might have been equivalent to half of the previous Soviet aid.

Picking Up the Pace: Reforms After February 1992

Pressured by the economic collapse in 1991 and by the opposition, Mongolia's government deepened the reforms in the first quarter of 1992. This move also may have reflected the fact that the flow of external aid and loans was conditional upon further reforms. In the beginning of March, with the exception of a few goods, almost all prices were "liberalized"; however, they remained subject to negotiated price ceilings determined by local price commissions. A new constitution declared that "Mongolia shall have an economy based on different forms of property."

The most important event, however, was the opening of the Mongolian Stock Exchange on February 7, 1992, with the public offering of three large enterprises for vouchers. After the opening, the stock exchange steadily increased its trading volume. By the beginning of June, the exchange had sold 468,400 shares in coupons at a value of more than 100 million tugrik (see Figures 4.1 and 4.2). Between February and June, 34 companies had been listed on the exchange, and their privatization was moving as planned. By June 2, there were 21 fully privatized firms. The list included some prominent establishments, such as the Ulaanbaatar Hotel and Mongol Ceramics.

About 49 percent of the shares of fully privatized companies were acquired by people living in Ulaanbaatar, while 51 percent were sold to people in other areas. Although Ulaanbaatar's share exceeded its 25 percent proportion of Mongolia's population, dispension of ownership was still a notable achievement, considering Mongolia's poor communications and the vastness of the country. The simple process of auctioning off equities in successive blocks seems to have led to a convergence of bidding for the Ulaanbaatar Hotel, but data also suggest that the effect of the announcement of the initial book valuation may have played a role in settling the equilibrium price.

As expected, the use of vouchers also led to diffused share ownership. For example, in the case of the Ulaanbaatar Hotel, 12,000 people obtained shares, and the largest individual owner held only 0.07 percent of the total (see Figure 4.3 and Table 4.3). In June 1992, the new ownership had not yet become effective. As of June 1, a shareholder's meeting had not been held because the board of directors and the management of the hotel were elected by staff and employees prior to privatization.

Figure 4.1 Number of Shares

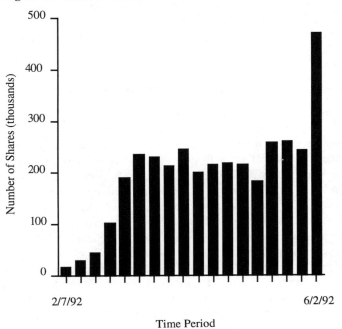

Figure 4.2 Stock Trading Volume

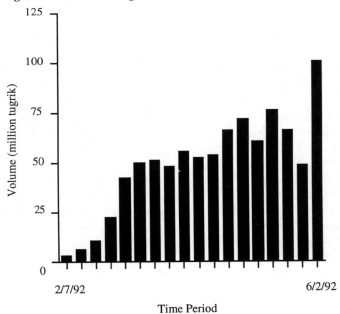

Figure 4.3 Share Price of Ulaanbaatar Hotel

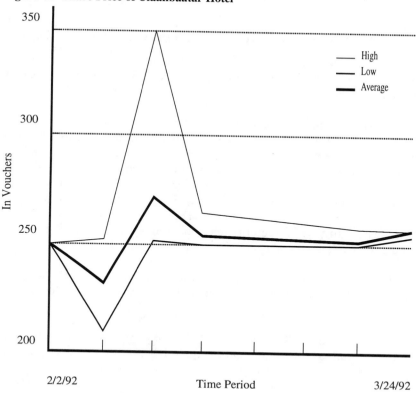

Source: Mongolian Stock Exchange.

Table 4.3 Trading Data on Ulaanbaatar Hotel, Inc., Shares as of June 7, 1992

Trading Day	Number of Shares	Voucher Value	Share Price		
			High	Low	Average
February 2, 1992	9,582	2,395,500	250	250	250
February 11, 1992	22,640	5,345,244	252	210	231
February 18, 1992	12,115	3,150,351	350	251	270
February 25, 1992	40,000	10,200,000	261	250	254
March 3, 1992	45,000	11,490,000	259	250	254
March 10, 1992	75,000	18,970,000	259	250	252
March 17, 1992	65,000	16,400,000	259	250	252
March 24, 1992	45,000	11,445,000	255	252	254
Total	314,157	79,396,095			

Source: Mongolian Stock Exchange.
Notes: Total issued: 335,297 shares; ESOP: 21,140 shares (5.71 percent); total of traded: 314,157 (84.85 percent). Shareholder Data: Total number of shareholders: 12,700; ESOP: 302 people obtained shares through the ESOP plan; Number of shares per shareholder: 26. People with the highest number of shares and the province they reside in: (1) G. Damdin, 269 shares, Dornogobi Aimak; (2) J. Narmandah, 245 shares, Ulaanbaatar; (3) S. Bayraa, 243 shares, Dornogobi Aimak; (4) N. Ouin, 207 shares, Ulaanbaatar; (5) J. Purev, 200 shares, Dornogobi Aimak.

Fast or Slow? Some Considerations and the Case of Mongolia

There are several factors that account for various countries' propensities to adopt radical reform programs or to opt instead for a phased process of incremental reforms.

1. The evolutionary approach to system transformation[18] stresses the need to develop the new from the old. This approach points to the depth and pervasiveness of the changes required in the behavior of institutions and the flow of information in countries long isolated from the global economy. It emphasizes the costs (including social instability and the possible reversal of reform) of attempting to superimpose market structures too rapidly on a centrally planned economy. The institutional capacity and market-related skill base of a reforming country simply may be too low for an abrupt transformation to the market.[19]

On the other hand, the experience of reforming socialist countries suggests factors that encourage the adoption of a radical transformation strategy:

2. A radical transformation program may be favored because the process becomes politicized and delays reforms. The fact that gradual reforms are politicized is an argument for radical measures.

3. A clear model for the transformed society (such as Western Europe) sets standards for reform and accelerates it.

4. Severe macroeconomic imbalances or shocks force swift corrective measures and a choice between liberalizing markets or returning to tighter controls. Shocks can be of domestic or external origin. In many cases, they have been associated with the CMEA trade and payments shock, which is estimated to have been directly responsible for about 10 percent of the decline in Eastern Europe's recorded GDP in 1990–1991.[20] Even though the CMEA shock was self-inflicted by East European countries,[21] when it came, they saw little alternative to economic opening involving comprehensive price and trade liberalization and swift moves toward current convertibility. Non-CMEA trade already accounted for half of total trade in the more open of these countries.

These factors also are relevant to Mongolia, and its experience offers additional insights into how they interact to speed or slow reforms.

1. *Organizational and Institutional Capacity:* Market infrastructure and the institutional capacity for a market economy are inadequate in Mongolia, which is especially relevant to the more open of the East European countries. This factor has constrained the speed of reforms in

many ways. Although the *need* for radical reform was widely appreciated early on, there was not a widespread awareness, even within the government, of what radical reform actually *meant*. This limited the extent to which the actual reforms were supported by a broad consensus and almost surely contributed to inconsistencies between reform plans and their implementation.

2. *Political Factors:* The urge to transform the economy was initially led by a reform-minded group within and outside the MPRP, whose members realized that with the collapse of the Soviet Union, Mongolia would not be able to sustain its economy. As Soviet aid halved in 1990, the Mongolian government began to move away from the official ideology of the MPRP, which continued its official adherence to socialism through 1991. In fact, a law passed in January 1991 banned political parties from operating in government organs and required all government officers, including the president and vice president, to drop their party affiliations.[22] The reformers saw a quick switch to the market economy as the only alternative to communism. After all, was not "Big Brother" (the former Soviet Union) also shifting to the market?

Reform was intertwined also with a resurgence of nationalism and a desire to assert independence from the Soviet Union. The coalition government that formed following the first multiparty elections used much more nationalistic rhetoric than its predecessor, often suggesting that a new economic structure would minimize foreign dependency and reverse past "colonialism." This approach lent credibility to the reform movement and helped to mobilize support. The combination of these factors—reduced Soviet assistance, ideological fragmentation of the MPRP, the insulation of technocrats in the government from political pressures, and some degree of nationalist resurgence—allowed reformers to propose more extensive reform measures. But because general understanding of the nature and implications of reform was very limited, it would be hard to argue that a broad national consensus on the specifics of the reform process existed.

A number of political factors appear to have slowed down the reform process, reactions to the optimistic announcement of more extensive reform measures. As reforms unfolded against the worsening macroeconomic scenario, the size of the needed adjustment and the potential social disruption, particularly in urban areas, became more apparent to reformers within the government. This scenario implied the need to make some difficult choices concerning the pace of reform and the distribution of adjustment costs.[23] At times, the government appeared to be reforming less vigorously than some sections of parliament demanded and more slowly than required by its initial "big bang" approach. But with the upcoming elections in late June 1992, parliament was also delaying the implementation of certain reforms that would have an immediate impact on the welfare of the population. For example, a badly needed sales tax law to increase revenues, long ready in draft, is still waiting in the parliament. A degree of politicization of the reform process—inevitable within a democratic society—has slowed reforms. For instance, representatives of agricultural interests in parliament resisted the abolition of existing industrial support structures in the course of rural privatization—but at the same time, they lobbied against state orders for farm products.

International political considerations also may have played some role in the political calculus. Mongolia needs to retain the good offices of China, on which it is heavily dependent for transport routes and which could become a major trading partner.[24] This consideration may influence the speed of reforms or the estimates of the reformers as to how much social disruption would be tolerable without further political repercussions.

3. *Was There a "Model"?* Unlike Eastern Europe (which looked to Western Europe) or Southern China and Vietnam (which look to the Asian "tigers"), Mongolia's distinctive geographic situation and natural resource structure make it more difficult to identify a clear and plausible model for the transformed economy.

4. *Macroeconomic Constraints and the Shrinking Resource Envelope:* Mongolia's moves toward comprehensive transformation were clearly spurred by the realization that the deteriorating Soviet system would no longer be able to support the Mongolian economy. However, Mongolia's geography and economic orientation made disengagement from the Soviet economy and integration into the global market economy difficult. Comparisons with Bulgaria, the most CMEA-dependent country in Eastern Europe, are illuminating. The terms of trade loss to Bulgaria from the end of the CMEA was estimated at 12 percent of the GDP,[25] while Mongolia's loss of Soviet aid alone was 30 percent of the GDP. Thirty percent of Bulgaria's exports were for convertible currency, and these represented 15 percent of the GDP. Mongolia's convertible currency exports were barely 1 percent of the GDP. However, Bulgaria did not face Mongolia's severe transport difficulties in increasing trade with the market economies.

Between 1988 and 1991, Mongolia's exports fell by nearly half in US dollar value, and the impact was aggravated by a sharp contraction in the financeable current account deficit from over $1 billion to only $100 million. The effect was to cut imports to only 30 percent of their 1988 value, causing pervasive shortages and supply bottlenecks and reducing production levels. Without allowing for terms of trade effects, a total cutoff of external funding would have forced imports back to less than one-quarter of their 1988 level (from 54 percent of the 1988 GDP to only 13 percent). This level is less than fuel imports alone in 1988 and is roughly equivalent to consumer goods imports that year. Sharp output fell in all sectors in 1991, led by construction and industry, and further reduced the GDP, which fell by 16.5 percent. By early 1992, urban unemployment had risen to include about 20 percent of the labor force.

An output decline of 16.5 percent superimposed on an import cut equivalent to 40 percent of the 1988 GDP, and allowing for a halving of commodity exports, would imply a 47.5 percent cut in the absorption of the 1988 GDP. The urban economy, which by 1990 supported 57 percent of the population, would have felt most of this cut. Because Mongolia lacked the transport and distribution systems to rapidly open new mines and reorient exports to world markets (and also lacked familiarity with these markets), its considerable mineral wealth could not be redeployed rapidly. In the short and medium run, pastoral agriculture is the main potential source of foreign exchange—but paradoxically, the traditional sector is the least import-dependent of all.

The impact of trade disruption and cutting off Soviet aid has been simulated[26] by using a computable, general equilibrium model, which seeks to strike a compensating balance between flexible and rigid constraints in the possibilities of adjustment. The model is calibrated to conform roughly to the structural characteristics of Mongolia's economy. It features a rural and an urban sector (heavily dependent on imported intermediaries), revenues from mining and Soviet aid providing external resources, and small rural exports. The results suggest that the rural sector is reasonably well insulated from external shocks but that the urban sector contrasts sharply. This is because both the rural and urban sectors are faced with a combination of supply and demand shocks, but the urban sector is affected more heavily because it is more dependent upon imports than the rural sector. One scenario explored by the model is that of massive reverse migration to rural areas. When Soviet aid was halted and mining exports disrupted, 40 percent of urban residents returned to the rural economy, but even this migration leaves welfare indicators at less than half their preshock levels. The model suggests that preventing a decline in welfare of more than 20 percent would require aid flows of about 15 percent of the GDP, a level not far from the pledges given at the 1991 Tokyo meeting.

If we accept the proposition that macroeconomic shocks tend to accelerate reform, Mongolia's situation raises the question of how far this proposition is likely to apply. As the resource envelope tightens and squeezes away the standard of living margin above subsistence, it will be more difficult to sustain an orderly pattern of reform. In an extreme case, a tightening resource constraint could force a country like Mongolia (or some of the states of the former Soviet Union) to shift from a planned socialist system to a rationed "wartime economy," despite intentions to shift to a market system. It may be significant that even well-established market economies tend to resort to controls rather than market-based adjustment when faced with national emergencies.[27] In addition, severely reduced resources could cause social unrest on a scale that prevented any coherent process of systemic reform.

Such a relationship between resources and transformation is shown in

Figure 4.4. With no external shocks, reasonably good performance along path 1 blunts the impetus to change a socialist system in a radical and perhaps risky way. This path corresponds to China's economy after 1978, for example. Path 2 represents a typical East European country—shocks contribute to a sense that the old system is breaking down and impel rapid reform. Path 3 shows a highly constrained country like Mongolia, facing a far larger shock and with fewer avenues of short-term adjustment through market mechanisms. The difficulty facing such a country is how to implement a rational reform and liberalization process that will enable it to escape from a low-level, crisis-rationed equilibrium without incurring unacceptable social costs. An important role for foreign aid—and one well recognized by Mongolian officials—is to preserve the capacity to implement market reforms and speed the transition to a market economy.

Figure 4.4 Resource Envelope and Reforms

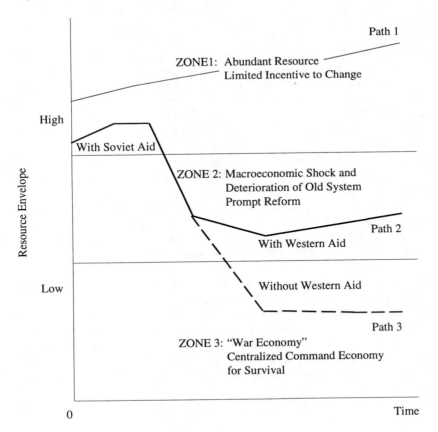

Model of External Shocks in a Mongolialike Economy

The model developed here focuses on three aspects of Mongolia's economy: (1) dualistic economic structure; (2) widespread social protection and a tendency, characteristic of socialist countries, to equalize living standards; and (3) the problem of adjusting to a cutoff of aid and trade disruption with CMEA partners.

Economic Dualism

Since its incorporation into the Soviet sphere of influence in the 1920s, the Mongolian economy has evolved into two broad sectors with very different characteristics. Traditional pastoral farming is largely self-sufficient, but the modern urban economy that now employs the bulk of the population is highly dependent on intermediate imports and capital goods. Imports were funded in the past by a combination of mineral exports (almost all to the USSR) and Soviet aid (which has exceeded 30 percent of the GDP for long periods). Intermediates, in particular fuels, accounted for over half of all imports, with the remainder split equally between capital and consumer products. Aid has supported a high rate of investment, partly in the form of turnkey projects.

Social Protection

At the same time, economic dualism has not translated into intense social dualism. Comprehensive health and education systems and social transfers received by a high proportion of the population have greatly extended the benefits of the modern economy. Although the monetary expenditures of those in the traditional rural sector have been less than those of urban residents, initial estimates of living standards should be comparable in town and countryside. The tendency to equalize rural and urban living standards (even if incompletely) is also notable in other socialist countries.

CMEA Dependence

As a result of aid and exports to the USSR, Mongolia was an open economy as measured by import:GDP ratios; nevertheless, it was almost totally dependent on the Soviet Union. Mongolia's economy was almost totally integrated into the CMEA system and had far fewer trade links outside it than did the economies of Eastern Europe.[28] Transport and logistical barriers make a rapid reorientation of trade exceptionally difficult, at least in the short term. Moreover, the infrastructural requirements for further development of mineral deposits are great, and these barriers limit the speed of such development. The model shows that Mongolia's possible responses to an abrupt cutoff of Soviet aid and to the disruption of barter trading arrangements for its mineral products are limited.

Structure of the Model

The model in Table 4.4 is intended to simulate the consequences of an aid cutoff and trade disruption in a short to medium run of one to three years

Table 4.4   Model Equations and Base Values

Output
Rural	$X_r = \overline{X}_r$
Urban	$X_u = k\,[\alpha L_u(1{-}UN)]^{-2} + (1{-}\alpha)M^{-2}]^{-1/2}$

Labor
Rural	$L_r = \overline{L}_r - MIG$
Urban	$L_u = \overline{L}_u + MIG$

Income
Rural	$Y_r = p_r X_r - YT$
Urban	$Y_u = p_u X_u - p_m M + T + YT$

Demand
Rural	$C_{rr} = \theta Y_r/p_r,\; C_{ru} = (1{-}\theta)Y_r/p_u$
Urban	$C_{ur} = \phi Y_u/p_r,\; C_{uu} = (1{-}\phi)Y_u/p_u$
Balances	$X_r = C_{rr} + C_{ur} + E_r$
	$X_u = C_{ru} + C_{uu}$
	$p_r E_r + T = p_m M$

Exports	$E_r = a.p_r{}^{ee}$
Numeraire	$p_m = 1$

Welfare
Rural	$U_r = (C_{rr}{}^{\theta} C_{ru}{}^{1-\theta})\,/L_r$
Urban	$U_u = (C_{ur}{}^{\phi}\,(C_{uu}{-}I)^{1-\phi})\,/L_u$

Notes: Parameters—Base: $\overline{X}_r = 40$; $k = 2.828$; $d = 3.305 \times 10^{-4}$; MIG = 0; $L_r = 0.475$; $L_u = 1$; YT = 0; T = 50; Soviet aid = 30; mining exports = 20; $\theta = 1/2$; $\phi = 1/7$; a = 5; ee = −100 or −2 or −1; I = 40. Base Values: $p_u = p_r = p_m = 1$; $X_u = 110$; M = 55; nonmining GDP = 95; $Y_r = 40$; $Y_u = 105$; $E_r = 5$; $U_r = U_u = 42.099$.

before radical changes in production capacity are possible. However, the disruption is too long to rely on accumulated stocks or reserves. Rural output, which in reality is the outcome of complex decisions about trading off current sales versus building up herds, is specified exogenously in the model. Labor is the only rural factor of production. Urban output is modeled as a constant elasticity of substitution (CES) function of imported intermediates and domestic value added. The CES is assumed to be 0.33. Urban domestic value added is represented by labor input because simulations typically involve underutilization of domestic capital. The model abstracts from domestic input-output relationships. Urban and rural labor forces are given with the possibility of intersectoral migration allowed in some simulations. A small part of rural output is exported in the base period, but urban output goes to satisfy consumption and investment needs. Rural incomes (assumed to be received by rural households) are set by the value of rural output. Urban incomes are the value of urban gross output less the cost of imported inputs plus a transfer from abroad, which represents the sum of Soviet aid and income from mineral exports that is taken as exogenous. For simplicity, mining is treated as a pure rent and this is separated from rural and urban output. In some simulations a lump-sum tax and transfer may be effected between the rural and urban sectors.

Rural and urban demands are modeled simply as derived from Cobb-Douglas utility functions over rural and urban goods in the two sectors—for simplicity, the model abstracts from final consumer imports. Expressed on a per head basis, these utility functions are used to evaluate the welfare implications of model simulations. Investment demand is treated as a pre-specified quantity of the urban good, which is deducted from total urban demand for the urban good when deriving the utility of urban households.[29] The model is static and does not distinguish between government and private sectors; moreover, it abstracts from all fiscal issues of adjustment.

The model closes or balances through the adjustment of the urban good price (and of the rural good price, if foreign demand is not assumed to be infinitely elastic). Urban consumption is residual after taking investment from urban output. The imported intermediate good is the numeraire, and in the base simulation all prices are defined to be unity. The equations of the model are shown, together with indicators of base structure, which is calibrated to approximate Mongolia before the aid and trade shocks.

This simple specification attempts to strike a compensating balance between flexibility and rigidity in constraining the possibilities of adjustment. On the one hand, experience to date with socialist transformation suggests much capacity to adjust through a variety of structural and productivity gains not easily captured in models of the computable general equilibrium type—for example, through the rapid growth of small businesses and improvements in the distribution and service sectors following the liberalization of markets. On the other hand, the model allows flexible substitution in demand, and possibly in urban production, considering the small size of Mongolia's economy and the interrelationship between key imported inputs (especially fuels) and domestic factors of production.

Another noteworthy feature of the model is its calibration to ensure equal levels of urban and rural welfare in the base period. This reflects the a priori judgment that the costs imposed on the rural sector because of a generally urban-centered Marxist development strategy have been offset by the access to urban-based services. These include health, education, and family allowances that would not otherwise have been available to rural households.

Aid Cutoff and Export Disruption

The first set of simulations explores the impact of drastic cuts in import capacity caused by the end of Soviet assistance (equivalent to 31.5 percent of the nonmining GDP in the base period)[30] and the halving of mining export revenues (21 percent of nonmining GDP in the base) through disruption. Table 4.5 shows the effect both of an aid cut alone and of the cut plus export disruption, using three assumptions about the demand for nonmining exports: very elastic, somewhat elastic, and unit elastic (the elasticity of demand for nonmining exports is respectively 100, 2, and 1). The model assumes an investment level of half that specified in the base period, or 21 percent of the base nonmining GDP. Three model outcomes are shown: rural welfare, urban welfare, and nonmining GDP at base-year prices. These outcomes are relative to their base-year levels. It should be stressed that the GDP measure reported from the model always excludes export mining, which is treated as a pure rent-producing sector.

Table 4.5   Responses to External Shocks

Shock	Base	Shock 1			Shock 2		
Soviet aid/base GDP*(%)[a]	31.5%	0			0		
Mining exports/GDP*(%)	21.0%	21.0%			10.5%		
Nonmining export demand elasticity		−100	−2	−1	−100	−2	−1
Urban unemployment = 0 Response[b]							
Rural welfare	100	99.5	86.7	81.6	99.3	80.7	70.0
Urban welfare	100	70.1	66.5	65.0	41.4	31.4	25.0
GDP*	100	89.5	85.3	83.6	81.1	73.3	69.0
Urban unemployment = 20 percent Response[b]							
Rural welfare	100		85.6			80.4	
Urban welfare	100		61.5			29.6	
GDP*	100		81.9			72.2	

Notes: a. GDP* is GDP excluding mining exports.
b. Investment is halved to 21 percent of base GDP* in response to shocks.

Faced with a major supply shock to the urban sector, the welfare of rural households depends mainly on how easily agricultural exports can be expanded. Nevertheless, the rural sector is well cushioned, with welfare levels remaining at more than 70 percent of their base levels.[31] However, urban households experience a catastrophic fall in welfare as the simulated environment deteriorates. The maximum fall of 30 percent in the nonmining GDP is concentrated in the urban economy.[32] The model also shows the importance of agricultural exports for the urban sector, as increased foreign exchange makes possible more intermediate imports and sustains urban production.

What is the effect of introducing open urban unemployment into the adjustment scenario? The simulations reported in the lower part of Table 4.5 place 20 percent of the urban labor force into that category. This causes output to fall further and urban welfare levels to decline appreciably. As expected, the effect is smaller when urban output is constrained greatly by imports.

Reverse Migration

The emergence of large rural-urban income differentials would be expected to induce reverse migration to rural areas, particularly as Mongolian officials estimate that about half of all urban households retain close ties to the rural economy. Table 4.6 simulates a reverse migration scenario (or a related possibility of income sharing) to reequalize urban and rural welfare, assuming an aid cutoff and mining export disruption and with investment again halved from base levels. Forty percent of the urban population returns to rural areas, raising the population in the traditional sector by 80 percent and reversing decades of urbanization. This social response still leaves overall welfare at below half of base-year levels.

Table 4.6   Reverse Migration and Rural Taxation

Shock	
Soviet aid = 0, mining exports/GDP*[a] = 10.5 percent	
Elasticity of nonmining export demand = −2	
Response	
Migration/urban labor (percent)	40.2
Migration/rural labor (percent)	85.0
Rural = urban welfare (base = 100)	43.1
Rate of rural taxation	
to equalize welfare (percent)	56.0

Note: a. GDP* is GDP excluding mining exports.

Another response to the sharp urban income loss would be to tax the rural sector and equalize welfare in the two sectors. Table 4.6 shows the necessary rural tax rate at over 50 percent. The capacity to collect such a high tax and the real-world consequences of incentives are not considered in the model, where the tax and transfer is simply modeled as costless and lump-sum.

Foreign Aid to Facilitate Transition
Faced with the significant income losses indicated in the tables, a country might be expected to encounter extreme difficulty in implementing a consistent reform program. Table 4.7 shows the use of the model to derive target levels of "Western" aid[33] to sustain an orderly, comprehensive transition to a private market economy. It is assumed (arbitrarily) that declines in living standards of 20 percent are sustainable through the transition without severe social disruption so that the income threshold is 80 percent of the base level. It is also assumed that investment should be sustained at half the preshock level through the transition.

Table 4.7   Cushioning Adjustment Through Aid

Shock			
Soviet aid = 0, mining exports/base GDP*[a] = 10.5 percent			
Nonmining export			
demand elasticity	−100	−2	−1
Outcome[b] (minimum welfare threshold = 80)			
Urban unemployment = 0			
Urban welfare	80.0	80.0	80.0
Rural welfare	99.5	88.3	85.5
Western aid/base GDP* (percent)	13.8	14.3	14.6
Urban unemployment = 10 percent			
Urban welfare		80	
Rural welfare		88.4	
Western aid/base GDP* (percent)		17.4	

Notes: a. GDP* is GDP excluding mining exports.
b. Investment is halved to 21.0 percent of base GDP*

Rural welfare always remains above the 80 percent threshold, declining as the possibilities of exporting are constrained. The range of aid levels suggested by the model is 13.8 percent to 14.6 percent of preshock nonmining GDP. However, this does not include the costs imposed by rigidities in the internal adjustment process. Using a 20 percent urban unemployment rate factor, the aid level rises to around 17 percent of the nonmining GDP. These levels seem to be not too far out of line with the assistance pledges made to Mongolia at the 1991 Tokyo meeting.[34]
The small response of the target aid level to increases in export possibilities for rural products seems counterintuitive, but this is because the simulations in Table 4.7 include no mechanism (such as migration or extended families) for redistributing income between the rural and urban

sectors and also does not include possible gains in export processing. Consequently, a vigorous program of export expansion could permit a progressive decrease in aid levels over time, even considering the initially small export base.

Conclusion

It is still too early to tell whether Mongolia's experience offers lessons to other transitional countries. Certainly the innovative privatization programs provide an example, particularly for the smaller Asian republics of the former Soviet Union, but formally privatizing state property is really an easy part of reform. Making companies profitable and finding new jobs for dismissed workers is the real challenge. Mongolia's privatization has not yet led to restructuring; there have been no bankruptcies and no layoffs. These may come in the future, once share trading concentrates ownership and provides an effective locus for corporate governance. A possible lesson for other countries is that voucher plans are a feasible method of transferring asset ownership rapidly but that they are only a stage in the development of effective ownership. Securities trading, which is needed to concentrate ownership and provide an effective locus of shareholder control, risks manipulations that could damage the credibility of the reform unless there is an adequate regulatory framework for capital markets (which Mongolia does not yet have). Along with other countries in transition, Mongolia has already experienced financial scandals connected with losses from the trading of foreign exchange.

Although Mongolia's small enterprises have been privatized almost completely, they are still under extensive constraints and instructions as to what activities to undertake, and without clear title to their land, investment in such firms will probably be limited.

Another lesson Mongolia may offer for reforming countries is that voters are liable to shy away from radical reformers when faced with growing shortages and a collapsing economy, even if the collapse is caused by factors outside the government's control. In June 1992, the MPRP won an overwhelming victory in the general elections, capturing 72 of 76 parliamentary seats. This apparent socialist rebound does not mean the reversal of reforms. With the changes in the former USSR, a return to the past is impossible. Instead, the recovery of the MPRP probably means slower reforms and greater government attention to preserving as far as possible the social welfare systems and the sense of economic security that characterized the central planning system—for example, by delaying adjustment in the enterprise sector. Like Mongolia, some former Soviet republics face output losses and a drastic tightening of their resource envelopes. This could reduce their ability to liberalize and implement comprehensive reform programs and may strengthen impulses to reimpose direct controls.

Notes

The views expressed in this chapter are not the views of The World Bank or any of its affiliated organizations. They reflect findings, interpretations and conclusions of the authors only.

1. We are indebted to Peter Murrell, professor of economics, University of Maryland, for extensive and extremely useful comments and explanations and to Mete Durdag, senior economist, the World Bank, and Zolzarhgal, chairman of the Mongolian Stock Exchange, for assisting us with information on recent developments in Mongolia's reform. All errors and omissions are the responsibility of the authors alone.

2. Other intellectually isolated socialist countries include Albania and North Korea, neither of which has produced a reform program comparable to Mongolia's. It is difficult to find a comparator for physical isolation.

3. For examples of contradictory policies, see Peter Murrell, Georges Korsun, and Karen T. Dunn, "The Culture of Policy Making in the Transition from Socialism: Price Policy in Mongolia," *IRIS Working Paper Series* no. 32, University of Maryland at College Park (1992).

4. A similar movement toward self-management took place in Eastern Europe and the USSR as enterprises received more autonomy.

5. This figure refers to 60 percent of prices rather than 60 percent of the value of marketed output.

6. For an account of the seemingly contradictory regulation of prices (including phases of apparent reregulation), see Murrell et al., "Price Policy in Mongolia."

7. For an account of spontaneous privatization in the USSR, see Serghei Shatalov, "Privatization in the Soviet Union: The Beginnings of a Transition," Policy, Research, External Affairs Staff Working Paper no. 805, The World Bank, Washington, D.C. (1991). See also Alan Gelb and Cheryl Gray, "The Transformation of Economies in Central and Eastern Europe," Policy and Research Paper no. 17, The World Bank, Washington, D.C. (1991), for a discussion of spontaneous privatization in Eastern Europe.

8. As of April 1992, private firms were still included in the state distribution system. This fact provides another indication of the very limited nature of price and market reform.

9. According to some proposals, employees would also be able to buy shares for vouchers at the price fixed by the commission; see Murrell et al., "Price Policy in Mongolia."

10. Space in this chapter is inadequate to discuss the pros and cons of Mongolia's privatization program relative to other possible methods. Aart Kraay discusses this issue in "A Workable Privatization Program—Lessons from the Mongolian Experience," unpublished paper (1992); see also Branko Milanovic, "Privatization in Post-Communist Societies," *Communist Economies and Economic Transformation* 3, 1 (1991).

11. Kraay, "A Workable Privatization Program."

12. Jean Tirole, "Privatization in Eastern Europe—Incentives and the Economics of Transition," paper delivered at National Bureau of Economics Research Macroeconomics Meeting, March 8–9, 1991.

13. Kraay, "A Workable Privatization Program."

14. Murrell et al., "Price Policy in Mongolia."

15. According to some reports, this arrangement required side payments to employees of the telephone company.

16. Two arguments are usually made: (1) Private activity may not improve

efficiency if guided by the wrong set of relative prices, and (2) privatization requires purchasers of enterprises to appreciate the enterprises' potential in undistorted markets. In the Mongolian context, the latter argument is sometimes countered by the argument that the enterprises have cost the new owners nothing because they were sold through vouchers. This view is contradicted by the trading of vouchers and shares for cash in the period before markets are fully reformed.

17. In this respect, Mongolia's program resembled the Soviet Shatalin's 500-day program, which also stressed privatization over price liberalization. One argument for the sequence in the Shatalin plan was to absorb a money overhang through sales of public assets and to promote the macrostability needed for effective operation of liberalized markets. This argument cannot apply to Mongolia, as assets were sold for vouchers and not for cash. More recently, the same concern about the tension between rapid stabilization and price policies versus reforms and slow supply–side measures have reemerged in connection with Russian reforms. Even though the money surplus has been inflated away.

18. The evolutionary approach is put forward by Peter Murrell, "An Evolutionary Perspective on the Reform of the Eastern European Economies," unpublished manuscript, University of Maryland (1990); see also János Kornai, *The Socialist System: The Political Economy of Communism* (Princeton: Princeton University Press, 1992).

19. To take one example, moving to a market-based financial system risks a serious solvency crisis unless there exists an established accounting and auditing profession and credit appraisal capability. To take another example, without tax administration capacity, relaxing direct government control over enterprise surpluses risks a fiscal crisis.

20. There is no rigorous way of disentangling the effects of the several factors that have contributed to Eastern Europe's economic contraction. This figure is a "best guess" estimate based on the outcome of a July 1992 World Bank–International Monetary Fund conference on the macroeconomic situation in Eastern Europe.

21. Following political changes, East European countries moved as fast as possible to strengthen ties with the West and reduce those with the USSR. This move included a rejection of the CMEA system, despite the high short-run costs.

22. William R. Heaton, "Mongolia in 1991," *Asian Survey* 32, 1 (January 1992).

23. For example, Decree 355 still prohibits the export of raw materials with the objective of protecting the processing industry—even while price liberalization and privatization are in process.

24. August 1991 marked the first visit to Mongolia by China's head of state.

25. Gelb and Gray, "The Transformation of Economies," p. 38.

26. See Cevdet Denizer and Alan Gelb, *Mongolia: Privatization and System Transformation in an Isolated Economy* (Washington, D.C.: The World Bank Country Economics Department, WPS1063, December 1992).

27. In addition to the political factors, there are a number of economic arguments in favor of responding with controls to national emergencies (such as war or natural or other disasters). These crises threaten a dramatic cut in the availability of products for consumption and investment through direct interventions rather than using the price mechanism and indirect controls: (1) Without knowing the shapes of demand and supply curves, it is difficult to set taxes, subsidies, and transfers to achieve a desired reallocation of resources that is different from the original one. (2) The outcome of any market equilibrium reflects a lengthy process of firms and consumers "feeling their way" toward the best allocation of resources. Faced with a

radically new set of incentives, economic agents will need some time to rearrange their responses. Together with (1), this means that any price-guided adjustment to the emergency will be erratic and costly. (3) The particular set of price interventions and income transfers needed to achieve the desired outcome may not be enforceable unless agents are controlled directly or may involve high enforcement costs or confront severe informational problems. Transforming socialist countries face a special version of the problem: It may not be possible to rapidly enforce financial discipline on the economic agents sufficient to rapidly achieve a normal market solution.

For all these reasons, a market-based solution to an emergency may not be credible. This, in turn, will greatly increase the cost of trying to apply such a solution.

For more discussion, see Patrick Bolton and Joseph Farrel, "Decentralization, Duplication, and Delay," *Journal of Political Economy* 98, 4 (August 1990); Martin L. Weitzman, "Prices vs. Quantities," *Review of Economic Studies* 41, 4 (1974); Martin L. Weitzman, "Is the Price System or Rationing More Effective in Getting a Commodity to Those Who Need It Most?" *Bell Journal of Economics* 8, 2 (1978); Gordon Karp and Gary W. Yohe, "The Optional Linear Alternative to Price and Quantity Controls in the Multifirm Case," *Journal of Comparative Economics* 3, 1 (1979); and John Bennett, *The Economic Theory of Central Planning* (New York: Basil Blackwell, 1989). We are indebted to Barry Ickes for drawing our attention to this literature.

28. Mongolia's exports to market economies were about 1 percent of the GDP; in comparison, such exports were 15 percent of the GDP in Bulgaria, a "closed" East European country.

29. For simplicity, investment demand is included in total urban demand as derived from the utility function, but the level of investment goods is deducted from total urban demand to obtain the level of urban consumers' welfare.

30. To avoid the impact of exogenous changes in mineral exports, all ratios are expressed relative to the GDP, excluding mining rent. In the base year of the model, mining rent is equivalent to 21 percent of the nonmining GDP.

31. Because the shocks are on the supply side and are matched by falling urban demand, simulations typically involve only fairly small changes in the relative price of the urban good. Real depreciation is associated with a terms of trade loss to rural exporters who, faced with falling urban demand, try to raise exports with foreign demand possibly inelastic.

32. In reality, the rural sector is also dependent on some urban intermediate inputs and on imports, but the model abstracts from this.

33. For the purposes of this model, Japan and other Eastern market economies are included in the term "Western."

34. The difficulty of converting the GDP measured in domestic currency into foreign currency for socialist countries makes it difficult to express aid flows relative to the GDP. However, assuming a reasonable level for GDP per head of $500, excluding the export mining sector (which is taken as pure rent in the model), the GDP for the country of two million would be about $1 billion, and pledges of $150 million would correspond to an aid level of 15 percent in the model.

In the model (and plausibly in the real world), the marginal value of foreign exchange rises as the supply is cut back, and the marginal value of aid falls as the amount is increased. Some curvature of the utility functions (so that the marginal value of consumption falls with its overall level) would also accentuate this.

■ Part 2 ■
Privatization and Private Sector Reform in Central and Eastern Europe

■ 5 ■

Rethinking Reform: Lessons from Polish Privatization

ANTHONY LEVITAS

In 1989, Polish reformers tried to make up for the historical absence of private property by selling off state assets. They hoped that by auctioning off state enterprises they could both create and allocate property rights, while simultaneously severing socialism's Gordian knot of politics and economics. A year later, after this privatization project had seemed to fail because the market proved too shallow to absorb the offerings, the government tried another approach. In 1991, it announced a plan to give away state property, hoping that a one-time political distribution of property rights would sever economics from politics and allow the market to perform its normal allocative functions. So far, however, only two dozen firms have been sold in public offerings and no firm has been given away. Poland's initial privatization strategies have failed.

However, while these two highly publicized strategies were failing, another little-known and little invested in procedure in privatization was succeeding: The government was reluctantly allowing workers and managers—often with the help of outside investors—to negotiate the value of their enterprises with the state and to lease or buy out all or part of their firms. Surprisingly, these individual negotiations, which are at once political and economic, have not only proceeded faster than market sales and giveaways but also have fused—in practice—the process of privatization with the economic restructuring of firms. In this procedure, the state does not try to divest itself of its assets immediately by auctioning them off or giving them away. Instead, it acts as the monitor of reasonable contracts drawn up by actors who are trying to wean themselves away from the state by simultaneously redefining the ownership structures of their firms, their productive profiles, and the markets in which they expect to function.

The failure of privatization through auctions and giveaways and the comparative success of worker and manager–led buyouts have profound implications for the debate taking place today over the economic transformation of East-Central Europe. This debate is usually framed in a set of mirror-image oppositions: The past was about state property and central planning, the future will be about private property and free markets, and the path from socialism to capitalism is a leap from one set of organizing principles to another. The leap itself is the state's divestment of its assets and their transfer into private hands, a move that once and for all will take the state out of the business of running the economy and allow the market to perform its allocative functions. Within the mainstream debate, the only real question is whether it is better for the state to sell or give away its property.

The mirror-image categories of state and private property, and of central plans and free markets, radically oversimplify both the nature of the Communist past and the much-desired capitalist future. On the one hand, by the time communism collapsed in Poland, forty years of social struggle and the chaos of the transition had left workers and managers acting more as the owners of state property than did the post-Communist state that intended to privatize such property. The state's de facto loss of its ownership rights rendered Polish reformers' understanding of privatization as an act of divestment disingenuous and accounts for the failure of plans to auction off or give away state enterprises.

On the other hand, by the time the Poles began their journey to capitalism, property ownership in the West no longer resembled the individual ownership of *things* that the idea of privatization evoked. Instead, commercial enterprises had become complex social institutions whose boundaries and market relations were constantly being redefined, as much by managers, workers, bankers, and government regulators as by individual property owners looking to maximize returns on a proverbially "free" market.

The comparative success of firm-led privatizations in Poland appears today to be a home-grown attempt to simultaneously redefine not only the ownership structure of enterprises but also their market relations, their relations to the state, and their internal productive structures. This redefinition does not correspond to the nineteenth-century idea of private property as the exclusive ownership of *things*—if that idea were the case, this redefinition might eventually be expected to lead Polish citizens acting through the market to reinvent the complex organizational structures now found in the West. Nor do these firm-led privatizations simply attempt to mimic the complex organizational structures and market relations that have evolved in post-Communist states since the emergence of liberal capitalism.[1] Rather, the process by which workers, managers, state bureaucrats, and outside investors strive to reinvent the identities of Polish enterprises is as historically unique as the processes by which the capitalist nations of the world arrived at their contemporary institutional successes and failures.

Not surprisingly, the attempts of East European countries to redefine property rights, markets, and the boundaries of firms have differed as greatly as the various methods by which Western capitalist countries created their economic structures. In Germany, the state continues to play the dominant role in determining the content of privatization. In Hungary, the government has recently retreated from its attempt to unilaterally control the privatization process. And in former Czechoslovakia, reformers hope to get out of the business of privatization entirely by letting citizens trade government-issued stock vouchers on a newly created market. To understand the real challenge of property reform in Eastern Europe, it is necessary to abandon the mirror-image categories that legitimized the struggle between communism and capitalism. As a result, we might become more sensitive to the global variety of markets and properties that we blithely assume are best understood as free and private.

The State as Auctioneer or Distributor of Its Assets

During the forty years of Communist rule, the Polish state progressively lost control over the enterprises it had created or expropriated. By the early 1980s, waves of social struggle and continual economic reform made state firms legally independent, self-managing, and self-financing. In theory, they were governed by democratically elected employee councils which had the right to hire and fire managers, to control the division of wages and investments, and to veto ministerial decisions over the disposition of firm assets. In practice, power resided somewhere between a managerial elite no longer subject to strict state supervision and no longer effectively defended by the Party and a sullen but well-organized work force that sometimes demanded the recognition of its rights and sometimes simply refused to work.[2]

As the 1980s wore on, rank-and-file pressure increased while the planning apparatus disintegrated. Firms acquired more control over their day-to-day operations, their investment decisions, and their relations with other enterprises. Workers used their powers to demand wage increases, and managers used their relative autonomy to grant them. Over time, wage inflation was compounded by price rises coming from the less heavily regulated new property forms that the Party legitimated in an attempt to jump-start the economy. By the summer of 1989, hyperinflation had set in, while a confusing mix of de jure and de facto property forms existed inside and outside the state sector.[3]

The final collapse of communism, and the post-Communist state's stabilization program, partially clarified the organizational structure of the economy. On the one hand, the evaporation of the Party within firms and attempts by firm managers to appropriate public assets prompted workers to exert their legal powers through the employee councils. On the other hand, the stabilization program required that firms be allowed to set prices and choose their contractual relations if market equilibrium were to be achieved through market means. In short, the historical legacy of the strug-

gle against communism, the more recent battles against managerial appropriation of public assets, and the post-Communist government's stabilization program produced an economic order in which firms legally owned
themselves.[4]

Indeed, Poland's industrial order in 1990 greatly resembled the theoretical model of market socialism. However, many of the economic architects of the post-Communist state, who had earlier fought for the employee
councils and justified their struggles in terms of market socialism, now
rejected suggestions that there might be a "third way" between capitalism
and communism.[5] Instead, reformers declared their intent to create a "normal market economy" with a "normal European property structure" as fast
as possible.[6] To do this, they announced in the fall of 1989 a sequential
program composed of three parts: stabilization, privatization, and industrial
restructuring.

Reformers hoped that stabilization would be achieved by freeing
prices, radically tightening fiscal and monetary policy, and opening the
country to new private ventures and foreign goods. Stabilization, by reducing demand and opening markets, would in turn force state firms to cut
costs, change production profiles, and find new markets. At the same time,
however, reformers believed that stabilization had to be followed rapidly
by privatization because without private owners empowered to choose
investments and profits over wage concessions, the irresponsible spending
of state firms would quickly threaten monetary stability. Rapid privatization was thus considered necessary, not only for the long-term health of the
economy but also for the medium-term success of the stabilization program
itself. By extension, reformers argued that privatization should precede
industrial restructuring lest good money be thrown after bad.

In short, reformers assumed that firms were incapable of adjusting
while owned by the state and that, after divestment, the market would force
new private owners into the most rational pattern of industrial restructuring. But these assumptions and the dependency of the overall transition
strategy on rapid privatization have proved to be the Achilles heel of the
entire reform project.[7]

In January 1990, to anchor the stabilization process and to clear the
slate for the industrial restructuring to come, the government announced an
ambitious privatization program that would run alongside the stabilization
program. First, firms were to be commercialized. Commercialization meant
the elimination of the employee councils and the transformation of state
enterprises into joint stock companies, which at first would still be owned
by the state. The employee councils were to be replaced by boards of directors responsible for management oversight and answerable to the state. In
return for giving up control of their enterprises, employees could purchase
a maximum of 20 percent of stocks at preferential prices, as long as the

sum total of preferences did not amount to more than a year's average wages.

Once commercialized, the firms were to be sold on the open market. By offering the stocks of good firms at low prices, the government hoped to generate a cycle of self-sustaining investor confidence that would make possible the rapid sell-off of state assets. As a side benefit, the sales would also take "hot" money off the market and cool inflation.[8] Moreover, the Ministry of Finance argued that the power to commercialize firms at will would give the state an insurance policy against the presumably perverse behavior of employee council–run firms, particularly with respect to managerial selection. In fact, the state would assume all ownership rights, and commercialization was renationalization by another name.

The reformers' faith in rapidly privatizing the state sector through public offerings expressed a naive neoclassical orthodoxy: Neoclassical economics assumes that if private property and free markets exist, then the allocation of assets and resources should approach optimality. Polish reformers, recognizing that (at least) half of the neoclassical economic structure was missing, sought to create private property by defining the state as the auctioneer of its own assets and letting the market determine the optimal distribution of ownership rights. Cash sales would tie investment to ownership and risk to possible gain. The assumption of risk would make the process politically legitimate because only those willing to face losses stood the chance of making gains. Indeed, the whole operation had an air of normalcy about it that was much desired by a country that felt as if it had just awakened from a bad dream. To make matters worse, commercialization was vigorously encouraged by the international consultants and accountants who flocked to Poland to take part in the great transformation.

In early 1990, the Ministry of Finance's Agency of Ownership Change selected twenty "good" firms whose employee councils had agreed to commercialization and public sale. The agency quickly discovered, however, that even when employees fully cooperated in evaluating the worth of a firm, it was hard to set reasonable opening stock prices. After all, the firm's profitability would be contingent on radical adjustments made in a volatile environment. At the same time, the sharp reduction of inflation, real wages, and savings that came with stabilization made it painfully clear that even if the agency could prepare many firms for auction, multiple offerings would rapidly push stock prices toward zero. Trivial stock prices in turn vitiated the political and economic logic of public offerings by inviting wild speculation. Despite considerable effort and expense, the agency only managed to privatize five firms through public offerings in 1990 and another six in 1991.[9]

Throughout the spring of 1990, the draft legislation on privatization was hotly debated in parliament. Not surprisingly, employee council activists opposed the state's plans to commercialize firms at will. More importantly, they were joined by others who, while not fond of the councils, realized that the ministry's plans for widespread commercialization would meet with political resistance inside and outside the firms. Worse, mass commercialization was potentially an economic disaster, they argued; given the necessarily slow progress of auction sales on shallow markets, such an approach would entail the recentralization of economic control by a state that barely controlled its office space. As Tomasz Stankiewicz, the director of commercialized firms at the Ministry of Ownership Change, noted, mass commercialization would "have made me a second Hillary Minc" (the economic tsar of Polish Stalinism).[10]

While the debate over privatization dragged on and the difficulties of public offerings became more clear, the idea of giving away state assets became more attractive. Giveaways seemed to avoid the problems caused by shallow markets and hard-to-establish values. At the same time, it seemed that the ownership question could be manipulated to involve citizens by removing it from an arena in which only firms and ministries had something at stake: Stocks would be given to citizens through intermediary institutions such as mutual funds and without reference to workplaces.[11]

While public offerings were justified by reformers' neoclassical faith in the market's ability to optimally allocate resources (including property rights), the justification for giveaways grew out of more recent attempts to save neoclassical economics from its own failure to specify exactly what is meant by private property. Here, property rights theorists argue that the meaning of private property cannot simply be assumed when so much of economic life is concerned with defining its boundaries and content. They argue that many of the phenomena that neoclassical economists understand as market "failures" result from poorly defined property rights that make it impossible for actors to use the market. Market "failures" are therefore the product of prior political lacunae and cannot be admitted as evidence of the market's inability to perform its allocative functions.[12]

From this perspective, the slow pace of public offerings looked more like a problem of poorly specified property rights than a problem of market failure. The neoclassical view of privatization was inverted: With market sales, the Polish state attempted to make up for the historical absence of private property by relying solely on the market; later, giveaways aimed to bring the market to life by rapidly creating property rights. In short, each strategy was one-legged. Public offerings attempted to avoid the political problem of redefining property rights by relying only on the market, while free stock distribution sought to avoid the economic problems of restructuring markets by once and for all redefining property rights.

Like public offerings, however, mass privatization required the government to determine privatization procedures unilaterally. Legally, there was no difference between the state as the auctioneer and the state as the distributor of its assets. Both approaches required that firms give up their current rights, and once again the question for parliament was whether firms should have the right to refuse to participate in the government's privatization programs.

In the end, the privatization legislation passed by the Polish parliament in July 1990 was a curious document. The Agency of Ownership Change was transformed into a separate ministry and given wide powers to sell commercialized firms. The employee councils, however, were ceded the right to veto commercialization.[13] The legislation recognized mass stock distribution as a possible instrument in the privatization process but did not specify how it should be used. Almost as an afterthought, a paragraph was added that enabled the employee councils, after approval by the ministry, to legally dissolve their firms and rent, lease, or sell the assets to a new corporation created for that purpose. Significantly, the new corporation could be owned solely or partially by its employees. The paragraph essentially provided a loophole for employee ownership.

In December 1990, one of the principal advocates of stock distribution became minister of ownership change, and the focus of the state's privatization program officially shifted from public offerings to mass privatization. A large, primarily foreign-funded operation was set up within the ministry to select firms, create the mutual funds to control the stocks, and plan the distribution of shares to the population. Initially, the ministry hoped to include 500 large and medium-sized firms in the first round of the program. But, as with public offerings, the ministry soon faced a daunting array of problems concerning the selection of firms, the design of the funds, the procedures for choosing and regulating fund managers, and the means of distributing fund shares to the population. It also had to convince firms to participate.

As reformers began to ponder the economic implications of various giveaway schemes, and to explain their logic to firms, the idea that a one-time political resolution of property rights would enable the market to operate normally became less tenable. The very design of the mass privatization program turned out to involve making complicated judgments about the kinds of markets and firms that were desirable. Worse, once state planners began to make decisions about what kinds of firms and markets were desirable, it became far from clear that mass privatization offered a reasonable way to create them.[14] Sensing this, firms either withdrew their agreement to participate or refused to sign on. By spring 1992, the ministry's target population of firms had shrunk to 200, and the overall program still was being reconsidered and modified. While it is unlikely that mass privatization will be abandoned entirely, the program will never fulfill the expectations reformers had for it.

Despite the humble results of the state's attempt to sell firms on the market and to privatize them through giveaways, the Ministry of

Ownership Change continues to attribute the failure of privatization efforts to the government's inability to win the political right to renationalize firms from parliament.[15] According to officials of the ministry and others at the World Bank and the IMF, the chief obstacle to both industrial adjustment and privatization is the employee councils that refuse to participate in government programs, block sales, and sit by passively while their firms disintegrate.[16]

While these accusations no doubt contain some truth and much desperation, it is worth considering the fate of the 250 firms that the state convinced to become commercialized properties of the treasury.[17] In some of these firms, managers and workers agreed to commercialization because they expected that afterward they would receive financial support or tax relief from the state, or that the state would find them creditors or foreign buyers. Ironically, these firms wanted to be privatized in order to regain the state's patronage. By late 1991, the government feared that the ministry would be swamped by a wave of bad firms eager for renationalization and that the state would become responsible for large numbers of loss-makers.[18]

In other firms, managers and employee councils decided on commercialization because they were already negotiating or planning to negotiate with potential buyers. Indeed, for them commercialization was a necessary first step toward privatization. Once these firms were commercialized, however, ownership rights reverted fully to the state, and firms lost control over the choice of buyers and the terms of the sale. Suspicious of sweetheart deals, afraid of sanctioning corruption, and seeking to maximize revenues from sales, the ministry almost inevitably tried to involve buyers in the bidding for the newly commercialized enterprises other than those already engaged in negotiations. Earlier negotiations frequently stalled or collapsed entirely. The state sometimes chose buyers against the will of the firms and, in a few cases, clearly made ill-advised and suspect choices.

Irrespective of the reasons for commercialization or the time when privatization was actually to take place, the state hoped that eliminating the employee councils and strengthening management would improve firm performance. This result has yet to be achieved. Indeed, the ability of firms to adjust has, contrary to expectation, frequently deteriorated after commercialization. Managers remain as reluctant to introduce radical changes as before, despite their relative autonomy versus the work force. Instead of claiming that they will be fired by the employee councils if they undertake reforms, managers now argue that radical changes will produce unrest that will scare away potential buyers or creditors, or that change is pointless until the desires of a new owner are clear. Meanwhile, the newly created boards of directors have neither the authority nor the information to force managers to change policy. Worse, board members often are hastily trained newcomers who are more interested in their salaries than in restructuring the firms they have been appointed to supervise.

Moreover, labor relations frequently deteriorate in commercialized firms. Eliminating the employee councils severs a major line of communication between management and labor. It also removes an institutional counterbalance to the wage and employment demands of the unions because the employee councils more frequently adopt the view of firm survival than do the unions. In many firms where adjustment efforts had begun, reform ceased as the state tarried and labor and management awaited ownership decisions over which they had little control. It seems that renationalization does little to improve the performance of firms. Instead, it may impede the efforts of the dominant existing asset holders, workers, and managers to find new owners and to restructure their economic operations.[19]

The State as the Monitor of Reasonable Contracts

Ironically, the least organized of the government's efforts to privatize state firms has proved the most successful—enterprise-led liquidation. These procedures, not to be confused with bankruptcy, were made possible by a clause inserted in the privatization legislation at the very end of the negotiations. They allow for the legal dissolution of the enterprise and its lease or sale to a new corporation created primarily by the existing work force.

So far, 415 firms have been privatized using these procedures.[20] Though most have been small or medium-sized firms, the numbers are nonetheless impressive when compared to the 26 firms that have been sold in public offerings and trade sales and the complete failure of mass privatization.[21] They are all the more striking when one considers how little has been done politically or organizationally to facilitate insider-led privatizations and how much initiative they require from firms themselves.

To begin liquidation, an enterprise must employ a consulting firm recognized by the ministry to estimate the value of its assets according to three different procedures. A general meeting of the work force is then called to determine whether employees are willing to buy at least 20 percent of the newly evaluated assets. If so, the firm enters into negotiations with the Ministry of Ownership Change to arrange which valuation of the assets will be used to set the price of the enterprise or whether another price will be chosen.

Firms may also solicit stock commitments from interested outside buyers. Depending on the negotiated price, the willingness of employees to buy shares, and the level of outside commitments, the assets of the enterprise can be purchased outright, rented, or—as happens most often—leased. As with the price of the assets, the terms of the lease are the product of intense negotiations with the ministry. In most cases, the newly created corporation becomes the sole owner of the old state firm's assets after ten years. In the interim, the stocks of the new corporation are freely tradable. On average, these procedures take nine months to a year to complete.

At any time, the ministry can refuse to allow the liquidation to go forward, and it can raise the capital requirements of the venture high enough to force firms to find outside buyers. However, the state's control functions are different from the powers that come with renationalization. Enterprise-led liquidation succeeds because the impetus for reform comes from the people who know most about the firm's situation. The firm looks for outside buyers, decides which of these buyers to let into the process, and determines roughly how it will turn a profit.

Because the success of these transformations depends on the actions of insiders, many see them as sophisticated forms of theft by either the industrial nomenklatura or coalitions of workers and managers. However, the employee councils have prevented egregious managerial theft by forcing managers to be accountable to a democratically elected local body, and the potential for undervaluation of assets by coalitions of workers and managers has been tempered by the state's ability to reject liquidation proposals, demand higher capital outlays, and set lease terms. Moreover, the risk of undervaluation, or at least its overall social costs, could be reduced further by including a windfall profits tax agreement in the lease or buyout arrangement. The state would then be able to exact higher than normal taxes if it turned out that assets had been grossly undervalued. So far, however, such agreements have not been tried.

Although these enterprise-led privatizations require the dissolution of the employee councils and their replacement by corporate boards, the councils have not only gone along with change but have frequently led it. Here, at least, they have come to see survival as being linked to privatization. In all the cases examined, whether the initiative to liquidate a firm came from management or labor, the employee councils played a major role in explaining the process to the work force, dealing with consulting firms and provincial authorities, and sometimes in ministerial negotiations. Unlike privatization through commercialization, there is a clear connection between efforts to change the structure and functioning of firms before and after the actual legal transformation of the enterprise itself. Layoffs and radical structural reforms often precede the actual legal transformation of the firm as workers, managers, and outside investors anticipate their future market strategy.

Blue-collar workers purchase significant numbers of shares (between 20 and 60 percent) in most firms privatized through liquidation procedures. Nonetheless, what is striking about the capital structure of these new corporations is the plurality of major shareholders. Sometimes this share structure is fostered by ministerial requirements for outside capital; sometimes it is the product of the firm's prior internal and external negotiations. Typically, the largest group of shareholders is white-collar workers, and the managing director is frequently the dominant player. Yet insiders frequently find outsiders to buy into the new enterprise. No matter where the initiative to find these outsiders comes from, they are usually drawn from the network of the firm's suppliers and buyers. Sometimes they acquire a controlling interest. Most frequently, they are significant but not dominant shareholders. Stocks are often more or less evenly divided between managers, blue-collar workers, and outside investors.

Thus, most privatizations to date have been nursed into the world by the employee councils, the institution that the state has regarded as being most opposed to property reform. Moreover, privatization proceeds faster when firms are allowed to take the initiative and the state's role is reduced to preventing theft and monitoring the reasonableness of contracts. Finally, and most importantly, firm-led privatizations, unlike all others, tie property reform to the reconstruction of the economic identity of firms, in terms both of their internal structures and of their external relationships with suppliers and buyers. This link exists partly because some insiders acquire a direct interest in making their firms profitable and partly because even those who are not interested in profit are more interested in the firm's survival than the state's. In either case, reform takes place because local actors know more about their firm's economic possibilities than the ministries.

Conclusion

Throughout East-Central Europe and the former Soviet Union, reformers are trying to transform the confused property regimes left by communism's collapse. In most of these countries, reformers have been tempted to reassert state control over enterprises and then to divest the state of the enterprises as quickly as possible. In Germany, the legitimacy and largess of the Bundesrepublik has made it possible for its property agency, the Treuhandanstalt (Treuhand), to renationalize the firms of the former German Democratic Republic (GDR). This example is the exception that proves the rule, and elsewhere in the region post-Communist reformers can only dream of Germany's capacities and resources. Moreover, the apparent success of the Treuhand in selling off firms is being interpreted elsewhere as a vindication of both renationalization and unilateral divestment through market sales.

Nonetheless, the practice of the Treuhand, if not its rhetoric, vitiates part of this interpretation: Instead of simply auctioning off firms, the Treuhand is deeply involved in restructuring the property rights and the markets of the enterprises it sells and in negotiating the boundaries of both elements with inside and outside parties. Moreover, it may be left holding large numbers of firms that, while waiting for new owners that never arrived, squandered their resources and hence their own capacities for adaptation.[22]

In Hungary, as in Poland, the decomposition of central planning left in its wake legally self-managed enterprises. However, the employee councils have been dominated by managers, and the organization of workers is weak. In 1989 and 1990, the appropriation of state assets by managers led the post-Communist government to renationalize state firms and recentralize decision-making about the privatization process. With the recentralization of power, privatization slowed dramatically. Recently there have been renewed attempts to decentralize the process and to limit the state's role in privatization to monitoring plans drawn up by firms.[23]

In Czechoslovakia, where the legal system of industrial regulation changed relatively little under the Communists, the post-Communist state has succeeded in preserving at least de jure title to state assets. On the basis of these de jure rights, the government plans to divest the state of its assets by distributing stock vouchers directly to the citizenry at large. Nonetheless, firms retained the right to submit their own privatization plans to the state prior to the creation of a stock market, and the relation of these individual plans to the state's attempt to distribute ownership claims remains unclear. At the same time, there are indications that managers are using their inside positions to gain control over the secondary market in shares, and that they think (perhaps correctly) that stock ownership will be so diffuse that their positions will remain unchanged. Consequently, privatization might mean the preservation of existing state monopolies, or it might mean that insiders are redefining the political and economic boundaries of their firms for themselves. But these problems do not suggest that the rationalization of firm structures follows only after divestment and only when outside owners begin to look for profits. Most importantly, it is too early to say whether the Czech experiment will work at all.[24]

In Poland, reformers initially tried to auction off state assets, believing that only the market could rationally allocate resources and property rights. When the market "failed," they turned to giveaways, arguing that if property rights could be specified, then the market would spring to life. The failure of these two projects indicates that markets cannot be used to unilaterally determine property rights and that the property rights of complex assets cannot be given away to create viable markets.

Meanwhile, privatization has been most successful when the existing asset holders have been allowed to negotiate among themselves and with outsiders—but under the supervision of the state—a property settlement that they believe permits them to survive in the markets they will face. In policy terms, the success of these cases suggests that the state's role in privatization is best conceived as the monitor of reasonable contracts, which are drawn up by the actors closest to the assets. Theoretically, the success of this program suggests that property rights, the productive profiles of enterprises, and markets are mutually dependent and historically created social institutions, whose boundaries must be (re)defined together.

The unexpectedly confused nature of property rights left in communism's wake, the inability of divestment-type privatization strategies to reorder these rights, and the comparative success of enterprise-led property reform suggest that the bipolar categories of plans and markets and state and private property do more to obscure the challenges at hand than help resolve them. Ironically, communism's collapse should not be read as the unilateral victory of free markets and private property over central planning and state property. It should be understood as a call to rethink the mirror-image economic categories bequeathed to us by Marx and Smith and reinforced by the Cold War. Perhaps if we begin to rethink these categories, we will have a better chance of understanding the relationship between economic performance and the configurations of properties and markets that exist today.

Notes

1. There is a burgeoning literature on the interdependent and indeterminate nature of market structures and economic organizations and on their larger historical contingency. For an introduction to these issues, see Mark Granovetter, "Economic Action and Social Structure: The Problem of Embeddedness," *American Journal of Sociology* 91 (1985): 481–510; Oliver Williamson, *Markets and Hierarchies: Analysis and Antitrust Implications* (New York: The Free Press, 1957); Michael Piore and Charles Sable, *The Second Industrial Divide: Possibilities for Prosperity* (New York: Basic Books, 1984); Frank Pyke and Werner Sengenberger (eds.), *Industrial Districts and Local Economic Regeneration* (Geneva: International Labor Organization, 1992); and Sharon Zukin and Paul DiMaggio (eds.), *Structures of Capital: The Social Organization of the Economy* (Cambridge: Cambridge University Press, 1990).

2. On the history of employee councils in Poland, see Michal Federowicz and Anthony Levitas, "Works Councils in Poland: 1944–1991," in Joel Rogers and Wolfgang Streek (eds.), *Contemporary Works Councils* (Chicago: The University of Chicago Press, forthcoming); and Kazimierz Kloc, *Historia Samorzadu Robotniczego w PRL, 1944–1989* (The history of worker's self-management in the PRL, 1944–1989), Monograph 351 (Warsaw: Szkola Glowna Handlowa, 1992).

3. On the structure of the Polish economy in the 1980s, see Adam Lipowski, *Mechanism rynkowy w gospodarce polskiej* (The market mechanism in the Polish economy) (Warsaw: Panstwowe Wydawnictwo Naukowe, 1988); and Janusz Beksiak, Stefan Kawalec, and Danuta Mlczewska, *Zarzadzanie Przedsiebiorstwami. tom. 4: Zachowania Uczestnikow Zycia Gospodarczego* (Enterprise management, vol. 4: The behavior of economic actors) (Warsaw: Panstwowe Wydawnictwo Naukowe, 1990). On the private sector, see Jacek Rostowski, "The Decay of Socialism and the Growth of Private Enterprise in Poland," *Soviet Studies* 2 (April 1989): 194–214.

4. For three different views on the worker-run system of firm management, see Janusz Dabrowski, Michal Federowicz, and Anthony Levitas, "Polish State

Enterprises and the Properties of Performance," *Politics and Society* 19, 4 (1991): 403–437; Mark Schaffer, "Poland," in David Dyker (ed.), *The European Economy* (London: Longman, 1993); and Manuel Hinds, *Issues in the Introduction of Market Forces in Eastern European Economies* (Washington, D.C.: The World Bank, IDP-0057, April 1990), pp. 1–150. On the appropriation of state assets by managers, see *Prokurator General: Sprawozdania no. dkI RK 728/89* (Report of the prosecutor general, no. dkl RK 728/89) (Warsaw, January 1990), pp. 1–85.

5. It is worth mentioning the names of some of the prominent figures in the Polish council movement who later came to occupy key positions in either the Ministry of Finance or the Ministry of Ownership Change: Leszek Balcerowicz, Stefan Kawalec, Tomasz Stankiewicz, Jurek Strzelecki, Janusz Lewandowski, and Tomasz Gruszecki. For a more substantive treatment of the journey council advocates made to neoliberalism, see Federowicz and Levitas, "Works Councils," and Kloc, *Historia.*

6. See *Program Gospodarczy: Glowne zalozenia i kierunki* (The economic program: Main assumptions and directions) (Warsaw, October 1990). The plan broadly paralleled, and was clearly influenced by, the ideas of Jeffrey Sachs. See Jeffrey Sachs, "My Plan for Poland," *The International Economy* 3, 6 (December 1989). Jeffrey Sachs and David Lipton, "Creating a Market Economy in Eastern Europe: The Case of Poland," *Brookings Papers on Economic Activity* (April 1990).

7. For a larger critique of the overall strategy, see Dabrowski et al., "Polish State Enterprises," especially pp. 425–430. While different policies might have facilitated faster privatization in Poland, the hopes that the government placed in rapid privatization were greatly exaggerated. We, however, also overestimated the possible speed of privatization and succumbed to the temptation to want to resolve it once and for all through stock distributions in early 1990. See Janusz Dabrowski, Michal Federowicz, and Anthony Levitas, "State Enterprises After Five Months of Fiscal Discipline," Center for European Studies, Working Papers on East-Central Europe no. 7, Harvard University (November 1990).

8. See "Kierunki Prywatyzacji w roku 1990" (Directions of privatization in 1990) (Warsaw: Ministry of Finance 4389/90, October 1990); and Stefan Kawalec, "Zarys Programu Prywatyzacji Polskiej Gospodarki" (Outline of a privatization program for the Polish economy), in *Propozycje Przeksztalcen Polskiej Gospodarki* (Warsaw: Polish Economics Association, 1989), pp. 29–33.

9. See Andrew Berg, "The Logistics of Privatization in Poland," paper presented at the Conference on Transition in Eastern Europe, The National Bureau of Economic Research, Cambridge, Mass., February 26–29, 1991; and Tomasz Gruszecki, "Privatization in Poland During 1990," *Working Papers of the Stefan Batory Institute* (Warsaw: Stefan Batory Institute, 1990), pp. 1–103. The economic performance of these privatized firms, with a few exceptions, has been disappointing. In most, stock values have fallen.

10. Conversation with Tomasz Stankiewicz, November 30, 1990.

11. In 1988, Janusz Lewandowski and Jan Szomburg proposed using a voucher scheme to privatize state assets in Poland. See "Uwlaszczenie jako fundament reformy spoleczno-gospodarczej" (Propertization as a fundamental aspect of socioeconomic reform), in *Propozyce Przeksztalcen Polskiej Gospodarki* (Warsaw: Polish Economics Association, 1989), pp. 63–81. For more recent formulations see Janusz Lewandowski and Jan Szomburg, "A Transformation Model for the Polish Economy" and "The Strategy for Privatization" in the series *Economic Transformations,* nos. 1 and 7 (Gdansk: The Gdansk Institute of Market Economics, January 1990), pp. 1–25.

12. The seminal essay here is Ronald Coase's "The Problem of Social Cost," *The Journal of Law and Economics* 3 (October 1960): 1–44. See also the work of Armen Alchian, Yoram Barzel, Steven S. Cheung, and Harold Demsetz.

13. Their veto powers could be overturned by a majority vote of the Council of Ministers if the vote was approved by the prime minister. These powers have yet to be used.

14. Typical of proposed solutions to these problems was the announcement that mass privatization was to be joined by a new program of sectoral privatization. This program was supposed to take into account the fact that the problems of some firms could not be resolved by privatization alone and that privatization had to be accompanied by reform at the branch level. The program was later abandoned.

15. For this kind of criticism of privatization efforts, see Jan Szomburg, "The Structure of the Decision-Making Process in Polish Privatization," in John Earle (ed.), *Privatization in Eastern Europe* (Stanford: Stanford University Press, 1993).

16. See, for example, Fabrizio Coricelli and R. de Rezende Rocha, "Stabilization Programs in Eastern Europe: A Comparative Analysis of the Polish and Yugoslav Programs of 1990," and Ryszard Frydman and Stanislaw Wellisz, "The Ownership Control Structure and the Behavior of Polish Firms in 1991: Macro-economic Measures and Micro-economic Responses," in Vittorio Corbo, Fabrizio Coricelli, and Jan Bosak (eds.), *Reforming Central and Eastern Europe Economies: Initial Results and Challenges,* mimeo (Washington, D.C.: The World Bank, 1991). See also Hinds, *Issues in the Introduction of Market Forces.* For less pessimistic assessments, and their significance for the overall reform strategy, see Dabrowski et al., "Polish State Enterprises."

17. The empirical material on privatizing enterprises is drawn from a report on 20 privatized state enterprises by Janusz Dabrowski, Michal Federowicz, Anthony Levitas, and Jan Szomburg, "The Course of the Privatization Process in the Polish Economy: A Report to the Ministry of Ownership Change," in the series *Economic Transformations,* no. 23 (Gdansk: The Gdansk Institute of Market Economics, January 1992), pp. 1–46. See also Dariusz Chelminski and Andrzej Czynczyk, "Spoleczne Bariery Prywatyzacji: Prawomocnosc ladu instytucjonalnego w przedsiebiorstwach skomercjalizowanych" (The social barriers to privatization: The authority structure of the institutional order of commercialized enterprises) (Warsaw: Warsaw University Department of Management, August 1991), pp. 1–28.

18. See Szomburg, "The Structure of the Decision-Making Process."

19. At the firm level people are rarely opposed to privatization (foreign or otherwise) if they have some assurance that the purchase of their enterprise will allow at least some employees of the firm to survive. This is true for the local unions as well, though the national organizations are more suspicious. See Janusz Dabrowski, Michal Federowicz, and Anthony Levitas, "State Enterprises in 1990: Research Results," in the series *Economic Transformations,* no. 11 (Gdansk: The Gdansk Institute of Market Economics, January 1991), pp. 1–59, especially pp. 48–52.

20. Again, this material is based on Dabrowski et al., "The Course of the Privatization Process."

21. Another 534 firms, generally small ones, have been bankrupted. Some of their assets have been sold off by receivers.

22. See Horst Kern and Charles F. Sable, "Between Pillar and Post: Reflections on the Treuhand's Uncertainty About What to Say Next," paper presented at the Workshop on the Treuhandanstalt, Center for European Studies, Harvard University, November 16, 1991.

23. See Gyorgy Hollo, "Privatization in Hungary," Center for European

Studies, Working Papers on East-Central Europe, Harvard University (March 1992). It also should be noted that while the recentralization of state control over privatization clearly slows down the process, it is not at all clear that state control actually makes the process more just or less corrupt: One ministerial official may be more easy to bribe than a handful of democratically elected members of the work force.

24. See Gerald McDermott, "The Political and Social Reconstruction of Property Rights and the Firm in East-Central Europe: The Case of Czechoslovakia," mimeo (Cambridge, Mass.: Massachusetts Institute of Technology, May 1992).

■ 6 ■

Path Dependence and Privatization Strategies in East-Central Europe

DAVID STARK

Capitalism by Design?

Across the ruins of communism, a clear breeze blows from the West. Like the "fresh winds" from the East across the ruins of war more than four decades ago, this breeze promises prosperity through sacrifice. Like the old socialist vision with its road maps to the promised land, this new vision comes with packaged formulas for applying economic science to institutional reconstruction. In 1991 no less than in 1948, devastation is seen as mandating bold action but also as presenting opportunity: The collapse of the old order demands ambitious experiments and offers the occasion to build anew, this time by creating capitalism by design.

As the juxtaposition of post–World War II Bolshevism and post–Cold War designer capitalism suggests, this chapter takes a highly skeptical view of the concept that the economic transition in East-Central Europe should be approached as a problem to be solved by the rationalist design of economic institutions. Three sets of reasons inform this skepticism.

First, proposals for institutional change according to comprehensive blueprints suffer from an inadequate comparison of socialist and capitalist economic systems.[1] Misled by the superior economic performance of capitalist institutions, such proposals mistakenly conclude that these institutions can easily be replicated. The deeper lesson is that the causes of the failure of socialism were rooted in the attempt to organize all economic processes under a grand design. The notion that institutions can be implemented by conscious design duplicates socialism's rationalist fallacy—for example, the Leninist notion that property relations could be changed overnight by decree. Moreover, the premise that efficient institutions can be drafted as a system ignores, as Peter Murrell observes, the operation of existing capitalist structures.[2] Capitalism in the West did not originate by

115

blueprint, its development has not been directed by conscious design, and its processes for selecting technologies and organizational forms are governed more by routine than by rational choice.[3]

The second reason to be skeptical about cookbook capitalism is that systems designers who fly into the region with little knowledge of its history approach the problem of transition through the lenses of their own models. To such a gaze, differences among the countries in the region are merely differences in degree (the timing and rapidity of collapse, the strength of elite commitment to reform, the speed of introducing new policies, and the like). Consequently, these designers' analyses are simple measurements of the degree to which a particular strategy conforms to or departs from a given therapist's prescriptions. Instead, we should regard East-Central Europe as undergoing many transitions, both across the region and within any given country. We also find many transitions in different domains—political, economic, and social—and the timing of these processes is often asynchronous, their articulation seldom harmonious.[4] Most important, because these models of economies are abstracted from the social institutions in which societies (and hence economies) are reproduced, analyses that begin with blueprints ignore the constraints placed on policymakers by the citizens of the new democracies of East-Central Europe. Capitalism cannot be introduced by design in a region where 40 years of experimentation have made citizens cautious about big experiments. A new social order cannot be created by dictation—at least not when citizens want a voice in determining the new institutions. These voices will be loudest where economic transformations are painful and difficult. Attempts to reduce production costs and lower transaction costs can be successful only when a society is willing to bear the transition costs.[5]

Because the actions of policymakers will be shaped by their perceptions of society's tolerance of economic burdens, we should analyze policymakers' resources for securing support instead of focusing on their recipes for change. Such resources are not likely to be evenly distributed across the countries in the region. Even more important, resources for garnering support are not simply material, financial, or economic but are above all political. These resources involve patterns of mediation between state and society that differ from country to country. In such a view, social change is not directed from above or initiated from below but is a result of interactions in which the designs of transformation are themselves transformed, shaped, and modified in response to, and even in anticipation of, the actions of social groups.[6] By attending to these interactions, our examination shifts from the idea of "one best way" to manage transition to a comparison of the diverse institutional configurations among the countries.

The third reason for skepticism about analyses that begin with blueprints is that the analyses often take the collapse of communism to indicate an institutional void. But the devastation wrought by communism and the quick demise of its party-states has not left an institutional vacuum. My concern is not with lingering traces of socialist ideology or the new look of the old nomenklatura but with the institutional legacies of the transitions themselves. To extend the metaphor of collapse, these societies will find the materials with which to build a new order in the ruins of the old. Therefore, differences in how the pieces fell apart will affect the ways in which political and economic institutions can be reconstructed.[7] In short, it is the differing paths of extrication from state socialism that shape the possibilities of transformation in the subsequent stage.

My analysis thus takes as its point of departure a proposition that is implausible only on first acquaintance: The economic transformations in East-Central Europe will be marked by path dependence. Why should we expect continuity when departures are imperative? The strength of the concept of path dependence is precisely that it helps to explain outcomes where strategic actors are searching for departures from routines and attempting to restructure the rules of the game.[8] Actors who seek to move in new directions find that their choices are constrained by existing institutional resources. Institutions limit the field of action, preclude some directions, and constrain certain courses. But institutions also favor the perception and selection of some strategies over others.[9] Actors who try to introduce change need resources to overcome obstacles to change. This use of existing institutionalized resources is a principal part of the seeming paradox that even (and especially) instances of transformation are marked by path dependence.

This view does not preclude the possibilities of dramatic change, but it differs emphatically from approaches that argue for a rapid, radical, extensive replacement of the current institutions, habits, and routines of the former economies by an entirely new set of institutions and mentalities. The idea of path-dependent change rejects such whole-scale replacement not because of some nostalgia for socialism but from an appreciation of the evolutionary character of capitalism. The massive social engineering that would be required to create radical change is not only undesirable but unlikely.[10] I argue that the structural innovations that will bring about dynamic transformations are more likely to entail reconfiguration of institutional elements than their immediate replacement.

From this perspective, we become more circumspect about such notions as "the transition to capitalism" or "the transition to a market economy"—alert to the possibility that behind such seemingly descriptive terms are teleological constructs in which concepts are driven by hypothesized end-states. Presentist history finds its counterpart here in futurist transitology. In place of transition (with the emphasis on destination), I analyze transformations (with the emphasis on processes) in which the introduction of new elements takes place in combination with adaptations, rearrangements, permutations, and reconfigurations of already existing institutional forms.

This chapter examines these transformative processes by comparing strategies of privatization in the four East-Central European economies: the former Czechoslovakia, Hungary, Poland, and the former East German territories. The purpose of such a four-way comparison is not to construct some essentialist model of privatization, in which the respective cases differ only in degree, but to produce a comparative framework in which the specificity of each case will be revealed through its simultaneous contrast with the other cases.[11] The study of East European capitalism is best begun not by comparing a general model of capitalism or even many models of existing capitalist systems (in which East European cases are approximations of various West European counterparts) but by an analysis in which the specific content of the analytic categories is developed through a relational comparison of the East European cases themselves.[12] The privatization programs of the region lend themselves to such a methodological strategy. Despite the similarities in the systemic problems encountered, there are significant differences in the privatization programs, which typify transformative processes in the four national cases. In the concluding section, these differences in the first phases of transformation are traced to differences in the earlier stage of extrication. We shall see that these privatization programs are not derived from master blueprints but are shaped by the specific institutional resources that are the legacies of the path of exit from state socialism. Seen from this vantage point, transformative processes taking place in contemporary East-Central Europe resemble not architectural design but bricolage, or construction with whatever comes to hand.

Specifying the Dimensions of the East European Variant(s)

"Privatization" in this chapter refers to the process of transferring ownership rights of productive assets held by the state. Although in the contemporary East European context such transfer is usually seen as the principal means of creating a private sector in an economy dominated by a public sector, the two processes—privatization and creation of a private sector—should not be confused or conflated. First, transferring ownership from state to private hands is unlikely to be sufficient to create a dynamic private market economy.[13] Second, a private sector might be produced more effectively by measures to stimulate the start-up of new ventures and expansion of existing units in the nascent private sector (formerly, the second economy) than by transforming state assets into private assets.[14] Nonetheless, each new government in the region looks to privatization, that is, ownership transfer, as the fundamental step toward the creation of a market economy. This chapter brackets the question of that causal relationship and focuses on the variation in privatization strategies across the four cases. How do these new governments differ in their policies for transferring ownership of the assets of state enterprises? While acknowledging similarities among the cases, the chapter identifies the distinctive privatization programs that characterize each new government's strategy during its initial period in office.

For a typology to portray these differences, I propose three central questions to define three dimensions that must be addressed by any program of privatization: (1) How are the state's assets evaluated? (2) Who can acquire these assets? and (3) With what resources are ownership rights acquired? In the following section I specify the categories of these dimensions for the East-Central European variant(s) of privatization strategies.[15] I then analyze the country cases and identify programs that are examples of the combinations of methods of asset evaluation, identities of participants, and resources for participation in privatization.

Valuation of Assets
The polarities of this first dimension are straightforward. At one pole, assets of the large public enterprises are evaluated by administrative means. In an extreme case, we would find a single state agency responsible for every aspect of the privatization process. That bureaucratic agency would assess the economic viability of firms, select some for foreclosure and others for privatization, and seek buyers for those to be privatized. Although bureaucrats might solicit economic assessments of market performance for these evaluations, decisions would be made on the basis of administrative measures rather than spontaneous market mechanisms. The opposite pole is already anticipated in our presentation of the first: Valuation would take place directly through market mechanisms. In this case, policymakers see markets not only as an outcome of privatization but also as a means of privatization. In an extreme case, we would find spot market transactions in the form of public auctions where auctioneers could announce a figure at which bidding might begin, but the final selling price would be determined by competitive bidding.

The two poles do not entirely capture the complexity of this dimension. Between them are some mechanisms of price formation and valuation that are either combinations of bureaucratic measures and market mechanisms or alternatives to them. Examples of such hybrid mechanisms are relational contracting (in which state agencies contract the task of privatization to consulting firms based on their international reputation or in anticipation of long-term associations in which agency and firm would share information) or bargaining (in which price setting is strongly influenced by network connections that differ from purely market transactions or by political considerations that differ from purely administrative criteria).[16]

Actors Targeted to Acquire Assets
In constructing a strategy of privatization, the governments of emergent democracies can present privatization as a process that will increase the wealth of the nation. They can argue that firms will be more accountable, more likely to economize on costs, and more efficient when property rights are exercised by private owners instead of by state bureaucrats. But if privatization will increase the national income, it will also increase private wealth. Regardless of how they choose to portray private gain as contributing to the public good, governments that undertake privatization on a scale so potentially vast as that in East-Central Europe (where over 85 percent of productive assets are state property) must address questions of distributive justice.[17]

One question is whether these new governments will attempt to forge an explicit link between the economic objectives of privatization and the new civic principles of the emergent democracies. Specifically, is citizenship, with its attendant concept of the abstract equality of the citizen, invoked as a principle for distributing property rights? At issue is not whether individuals are favored over groups but whether individuals are targeted as citizens to receive property rights in the privatization of large public enterprises' assets.

Some governments will use civic principles to target citizens as recipients of the state's former assets, and others will use purely economic principles to target corporations. In this latter case, although private persons might participate in some programs of privatization (in agriculture, retail shops and restaurants, etc.), the fundamental strategy for the privatization of the large state enterprises will be to distribute property rights to corporations. In short, privatization strategies will differ according to whether the state specifically seeks to involve civic persons (citizens) as participants or, alternatively, designs large-scale privatization around legal-economic persons (corporations).

Resources Used to Acquire Ownership Rights
Privatization strategies can also vary according to the kinds of resources that are used or converted to acquire ownership rights. Monetary or financial resources are the obvious first consideration in this dimension. But, besides the differences in their financial holdings, actors in the transitional societies of East-Central Europe also differ according to the powers and capacities associated with their social, professional, or political positions. In fact, the prohibition of private property in productive assets meant that the stratification systems of state socialist societies were organized more around differences in position than differences in wealth. Thus, at the very moment when these economies embark on privatization, they must deal with a continuing legacy of the social stratification system of state socialism, where advantages accrue according to position.

Thus, the third dimension contrasts privatization schemes and strategies that are organized primarily around the use of monetary resources with those in which the participating agents capitalize on their positions. The concepts of position and "positional property" carry connotations of office holding.[18] I start from that Weberian concept but find it useful to extend the concept from office holding to a broader set of organizational posts and positions. This attention to positions should not be interpreted as a narrow preoccupation with the fate of those who held political positions in the old order and whether and how they are converting their political capital to economic capital.[19] My concern is more with economic job holding than with political office holding. Some privatization strategies will be structured so that the occupants of certain positions will have an advantage in acquiring property rights. Managers, for example, might be able to use their positions to gain ownership rights. Similarly, privatization strategies that place importance on employee ownership plans are instances of inclusion or exclusion strategies in which ownership rights are acquired through position.

The three dimensions are cross-classified in Figure 6.1 to yield a preliminary typology of privatization strategies in East-Central Europe. The

Figure 6.1 A Typology of Privatization Strategies in East-Central Europe

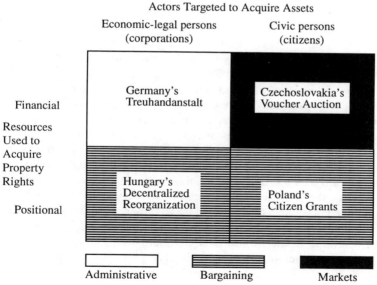

dimensions referring to actors targeted to acquire assets and resources used to acquire ownership rights form a two-by-two table. The remaining dimension, referring to the method of evaluating assets, is represented through shading ("administrative" lightest and "markets" darkest, with "bargaining" in between). Also located on Figure 6.1 are the strategies for privatizing large public enterprises that most closely illustrate four possible combinations of the categories along the three dimensions.

To avoid possible misunderstandings in interpreting this typology, it is worthwhile to state the limitations of its object of study. First, the typology addresses the privatization of large public enterprises and does not include schemes for privatizing retail trade, catering establishments, and agricultural cooperatives.[20] Second, the selection of country cases was done to illustrate particular intersections of the typology's dimensions. My task here is to identify distinctive traits rather than to produce an exhaustive description of the full range of privatization programs in each country. Location of a particular country case in a given cell is not meant to capture all aspects of its privatization.[21] Third, my typology focuses on the strategies of policymakers in approximately the first year of the newly elected governments. How these strategies will be reshaped during later interactions with the relevant social actors must be the subject of a later investigation.

Distinctive Features of the Country Cases

Germany's Treuhandanstalt
Our discussion of privatization strategies in Figure 6.1 begins with administrative evaluations of assets that favor corporations using monetized resources. No privatization strategy better illustrates this particular combination of elements than Germany's Treuhandanstalt. Charged with the task of performing triage on the wounded enterprises of the former East German economy, the Treuhandanstalt—or trust—has singlehandedly carried out functions that are performed in other countries in the region by government units scattered across the Ministries of Industry, Planning, Finance, Labor, and Privatization. Following the monetary union of the two Germanys in July 1990 and their unification on October 3, 1990, the Treuhandanstalt became the world's largest industrial holding, with a staff of 2,500 to privatize and monitor the operations of the former East German state enterprises, which employed more than three million wage earners.[22] By May 1991, the Treuhandanstalt had privatized 1,670 firms of the approximately 7,000 that had been operating in the former East German lands, making its largest strides in the branches of energy, foodstuffs, construction, trade, and tourism. Ninety percent of these properties were sold to West Germans (primarily corporations), 5 percent were purchased by foreign (that is, non-German) capital, and 5 percent are now held by their former managers. In

preparation for further privatizations, the Treuhand also split up 316 Kombinat (megaconglomerates in the old socialist economy) into 8,500 smaller firms involving some 45,000 plants.[23]

This aggressive posture of attacking a problem by using a strong bureaucratic agency with an almost unquestioned mandate to impose radical and rapid restructuring is the defining feature of the German privatization strategy. But although the German state has moved with greater speed and determination than other East-Central European governments in the first stage of privatization, there are some indications that its greatest difficulties lie ahead. Recent developments indicate that these obstacles will not be met with an even quicker pace and stronger administrative measures but that the difficulties facing the Treuhand will retard its speed and lead to some modification of its methods.

The irony of the East German case is that the very strength of the West German economy, which was expected to lead to a smooth transition, has proven initially to be a source of problems. In particular, the dramatic surge of demand for consumer goods in the newly incorporated lands was met at first by expansion of output by West German firms. Although it might be the case that the "wealthy brother" will save the situation in the long run by buying firms, in the short run he began by selling goods to his poorer sibling. Uncompetitive on the world market, unable to sell goods on the West German market, and now uncompetitive on their own territory, the former East German enterprises saw their markets evaporate within weeks. With no orders and no work, millions of employees in these failing enterprises have been receiving a scarcely disguised unemployment compensation in the form of "short-time work" in which they remain on the payroll with little or nothing to do.[24]

For some intellectuals who attempt to shape German public opinion, the most attractive solution to this problem is massive westward migration. "Everyone who is willing to work hard can find a job here in our prosperity," they say. But even if such migration could absorb a significant proportion of people seeking work, the consequences might prove catastrophic to the national social fabric and devastating to the local economies the emigrants leave behind. Massive migration, even on a scale far lower than some policymakers have in mind, could lead to a massive devaluation of the human capital of the economy of the former East German lands. Such devaluation would be triggered not simply by the aggregate loss of highly skilled individuals but also by the destruction of the work teams in which those skills had previously been used. As an unintended consequence of macroeconomic mismanagement by state socialism, the organization of work in the microsphere of the redistributive enterprise evolved into a forced autonomy and distorted flexibility.[25] At the level of the shop floor, work teams were forced to develop ways to adjust quickly and flexibly to supply shortages and other irrationalities of central mismanagement. Such adaptations should not be idealized—they were constrained and distorted—but these teams evolved into work units in which the human capital of a team was more than the sum of its parts. In such a case, the departure of two or three from a team of a dozen can shatter a small but potentially significant resource that might otherwise be a basis for reconstructing a failed economy. In short, migration stimulated by the close proximity to prosperity on the same national territory might alleviate unemployment, but it might also erode organizational capacities and retard the development of a dynamic economy in the former East German lands.

Unemployment and severe economic crisis will have important consequences for the further work of the Treuhandanstalt. As the situation of the eastern enterprises deteriorates, it will prove more difficult to find buyers for them. Meanwhile, as unemployment explodes, pressures will mount to slow the pace of liquidation. Firms (which will number in the thousands) that can be neither sold nor shut down will remain under the bureaucratic authority of the Treuhand, and the Treuhand will be forced to intervene directly in reorganizing these properties, using subsidies to keep them afloat in the meantime.[26] But we can expect relentless pressures on the Treuhand to demonstrate that it remains committed to privatization. After all, its mandate was for sweeping and rapid privatization—politicians and government officials will not look favorably on an agency that resorts to subsidizing instead of privatizing, and bureaucratic superiors will frown at subordinates in the agency whose quarterly record of completed privatizations falls below the norm. Therefore, we can expect that the Treuhandanstalt will increasingly look to current managers as a pool of potential new owners for the failed but salvageable smaller units that have been or will be broken off from the large state enterprises. In this scenario, the evaluation of assets is increasingly likely to take place through bargaining between the agency and enterprises, with the result that managers will exercise expanded property rights. A recent study indicates that this process has already begun, and restructuring has become the critical task of the Treuhand. To organize the market for potential buyers, firms first must be reorganized.[27] The Kombinat are too big to sell all of a piece, and the parts that can be broken off and sold by themselves are too small to make a difference. Restructuring thus often entails the dismantling of several large enterprises and the strategic recombination of these newly available parts (from across different enterprises) to create new ventures.

Czechoslovakia's Voucher-Auction Program

In strong contrast to the decidedly statist orientation of the German privatization strategy, the Czechoslovak strategy evaluates assets directly by the market, involves participation on the basis of citizenship, and uses monetary resources. In fact, this combination of categories along our three dimensions is represented by a single institutional innovation in the

Czechoslovak strategy—public auctions of citizen vouchers for shares of the large state enterprises.[28]

The program that the Czechoslovak economic authorities are launching involves the distribution of over 50 percent of the equity of more than 1,000 large public enterprises through a citizenship voucher scheme. Each Czechoslovak citizen over 18 years of age receives vouchers equal to 1,000 "investment points." These investment points can be exchanged for shares in the enterprises designated for privatization through the voucher program. But although every citizen receives these vouchers as a matter of right, only those who pay a registration fee of 1,000 korunas will be able to use the vouchers in the public auctions.[29] To indicate that the equity shares obtained through the voucher program are not a free gift from the state, to signal that there will be risk involved, and to filter out citizens with no serious interest in share ownership, Czechoslovak officials have designed a voucher scheme that combines citizenship participation and monetary resources.

The actual process of exchanging vouchers for shares is fairly complex, and Czechoslovak authorities undertook a major program to educate the public about its basic principles and logistic intricacies. The first stage of the voucher-auction program began May 18, 1992. For each wave of privatizations, the Ministries of Privatization designate the enterprises whose equity will be distributed by auction.[30] For each enterprise, the ministries post an initial asking price for the shares of that particular firm. To understand the principles of the auction, it is important to note that this price is expressed not in monetary units but in terms of investment points. That is, the state announces the number of investment points at which it is willing to exchange a share of a given enterprise. A single share of a blue-chip company, for example, might begin at an initial level of 200 investment points; a share of a firm with a less prominent record or less promising future prospects might be posted at only 10 investment points. In the first round of the auction, then, one citizen might decide to place all 1,000 of his investment points on five shares of the blue-chip company, another could indicate his willingness to exchange all 1,000 of his points for 100 shares in the less promising venture, and a third could diversify his "portfolio" of investment points across firms with differing initial asking prices.

Equally important in understanding the principle of asset evaluation in the voucher-auction program is the fact that the auction is conceived as an iterative process occurring in multiple rounds. That is, although economists in the Czech and Slovak Ministries of Privatization must conduct a rough-and-ready evaluation of the performance of firms to set the initial price of shares in the first round of bidding, the final price in investment points in the simulated market of the voucher-auction (and, more important, the later price of shares bought and sold on an actual market) will be determined by the supply and demand for these shares. What Vaclav Klaus and his team in the Ministry of Finance seem to have in mind is a kind of Walrasian auctioneer.[31] The auctioneer (actually a computerized network) accepts offers to buy shares of a given enterprise at a certain asking price in investment points. Unlike a commodities exchange (or the typical estate sale or auction of objects of art we might know), the citizen-bidders are not, strictly speaking, bidding up the price in a given round. At the end of the first round, the auctioneer identifies shares for which demand exceeded supply as well as those in which the reverse was the case. As the seller, the state can either accept offers from that round or adjust prices upward or downward for the next round, to be held two weeks later. The auction proceeds for three or four rounds, with the state accepting offers or revising prices. One concept currently in circulation among the designers of the voucher-auction program is that the state should accept offers when the demand for shares of a particular enterprise is lower than their supply (the number of shares for each firm in the auction is fixed) and revise prices upward for shares for which demand exceeds supply.

This is not the place to elaborate all the technical and political complexities of the voucher-auction. For example, what percentage of assets will the state retain, even for the auctioned firms, and how will this factor influence the bidding process? What are the likely consequences of different decisions about when the state should accept offers or when it should revise prices upward or downward? What if the overall participation rate is so low that virtually all shares are undersubscribed?[32] Our attention is addressed instead to the major principles that underscore the voucher-auction as an important feature of the Czechoslovak strategy of privatization.

First, and most importantly, the Czechoslovak leadership appears committed to using a simulated market to rapidly achieve a functioning equity market in the shares of a significant proportion of former state enterprises.[33] The question of whether investment points reflect the real value, even a true relative value, of shares is beside the point because the purpose of the voucher-auction is to get shares into private hands, where they can actually be bought and sold.[34] According to the designers of the voucher-auction, it is in such a market (where speculators are to be not disparaged but encouraged) that the real evaluation of assets will take place.[35] For this reason, rather than because of the registration fee, we locate the Czechoslovak privatization strategy in Figure 6.1 in the cell representing the intersection of market evaluation and monetary assets.[36]

Second, with a capital market organized around the stock exchange stimulated by the voucher-auction program, the Czechoslovak economy appears to be heading in the direction of raising investment funds through markets typical of the Anglo-American system rather than through the Japanese-German system, in which banks play a more central role in monitoring and directing the performance of their creditor firms (for a contrast, see the Polish case discussed next in this chapter).

Third, the Czechoslovak leadership appears to be prepared to accept relatively dispersed ownership in the initial stage of its privatization program in the hope that later transactions in the actual capital market will yield relatively rapid concentration of ownership in midlevel enterprises. Several design features currently being discussed (for example, the combination of offering the shares of some firms at initially low asking prices and accepting offers even when the supply of shares exceeds demand) suggest that Czechoslovak officials hope that some enterprising individuals will quickly buy up the relatively cheap shares and gain controlling interest in these firms. Such a scenario would likely be accompanied by continuing dispersal of ownership in the most highly prized enterprises because the economic leaders have more confidence in the enterprises' managerial talent and are therefore more willing to tolerate the managerial control that comes with highly diffused shareholding.[37]

These same features also suggest that the Czech leadership is aware of the likelihood of resistance to the voucher-auction by managers of the enterprises designated for auction and is designing some features to help neutralize or mitigate this resistance. At the bottom end, firms whose shares find no buyers might be more easily liquidated after a strong vote of "no confidence" by the citizen-investors. At the top, economic officials can point to the likelihood of diffused shareholding in the blue-chip companies to persuade the enterprises' managers (precisely the ones with the most bargaining power) that the auction is not against their interests and should not be resisted.[38] For the broad range of enterprises in between, the Czech ministers can probably count on resistance from managers, but they seem to hope that relatively quick concentration of ownership through share sales will bring these firms under the control of the new owners.

Poland's Universal Citizen Grants and Employee Shareholdings
The story of Poland's privatization strategy begins in Gdansk, the birthplace of the first and, for a time, the largest independent trade union in Eastern Europe. But Solidarity and Lech Walesa, the most famous offspring of the Lenin Shipyards and now the president of the Polish Republic, are only half the story. Not without historical irony, yet not entirely by coincidence, Gdansk was also the birthplace of Polish neoliberalism. During the mid-1980s, while the intellectuals of Warsaw and Budapest debated in urban coffeehouses, a group of young private businessmen and young provincial intellectuals in Gdansk formed a Liberal Club and at its meetings began reading and discussing major theoretical statements on property rights. From the practical experiences of these entrepreneurs and the circle of intellectuals close to them arose the Liberal Congress, a small but extraordinarily influential party that has produced Jan Krzysztof Bielecki, the former prime minister, and a disproportionate share of cabinet ministers in the government formed after the election of President Walesa.

Privatization in Poland, of course, began not under the leadership of Walesa's Polish liberals but under Wojciech Jaruzelski's Polish Communists. During the power vacuum of 1989, an untold number of apparatchiks landed comfortably ("not perestroikists but parachutists," went the expression) as the new owners of promising units carved out of former state enterprises. The liberals thus came to office (first with Finance Minister Leszek Balcerowicz and later with Prime Minister Bielecki and his larger retinue) in a period in which the scandals of such "nomenklatura capitalism" could be widely heard in public circles. Property reform was clearly on the agenda, and the Tadeusz Mazowiecki government announced a program of clean privatization, using the British model as its centerpiece with the promise of foreign investors and large public offerings. But foreign investors were slow and few (they were looking more to Hungary and the former East Germany), and the public offerings made little dent in the state-owned assets of the large socialist enterprises. In fact, the major achievement of the first year of the Ministry of Property Transformation, a few unrepresentative foreign buyouts aside, was privatization through liquidation. This was a dubious achievement, given the stated aims of the ministry, because the assets of 159 of these 160 so-called privatizations were leased to the managers and employees of the liquidated firms.[39]

After the election campaign in which he promised "acceleration" of privatization, President Walesa turned to Janusz Lewandowski, the new minister of property transformation from Gdansk, and asked him to elaborate and specify the sweeping program for "mass privatization" that Lewandowski and his Gdansk compatriot, Jan Szomburg (currently director of the Research Center for Marketization and Property Reform), had proposed years earlier.[40] The young transformers confronted two obstacles. First, from another side of the Gdansk story, they faced the Workers' Councils, reactivated after 1989, which viewed property transformation as their opportunity to solidify employee ownership.[41] Second, they faced the enormous problem of the fact that domestic savings could cover only a fraction of the assets of the large state enterprises. On this subject Lewandowski had said that "privatization is when someone who doesn't know who the real owner is and doesn't know what it's really worth sells something to someone who doesn't have any money."[42]

The program of mass privatization formally announced in June 1991 calls for the property transformation of some 400 Polish enterprises in the first stage of its operation. Contained within the program is a major peace offering to the Workers' Councils: Employees in the privatized firms will receive a free 10 percent of the shares of their companies. That is, lacking savings and credit, employees will be able to use their positional resources as jobholders to gain an ownership stake in their enterprises.[43]

At the center of the mass privatization program, however, stands a universal citizens' grant in the form of share vouchers issued to every Polish citizen. In marked contrast to the Czechoslovak program, no registration fee is required to participate. By this signal, and through all its rhetoric, the Polish government seems eager to send the message that these vouchers are emphatically a free gift from the state.

In another variation from the Czechoslovak schemes, Polish citizens will not exchange their vouchers directly for shares in a privatized enterprise. Instead, the vouchers will be exchanged for shares assigned to an "asset manager" who will, in turn, exchange the vouchers for shares in transformed enterprises that the manager chooses (or is assigned). Current proposals call for this manager role to be played by experienced foreign companies, perhaps as few as ten. These asset managers should not be confused with the managers of pension funds or mutual funds, to whom they bear only a superficial resemblance. According to the intentions of the program's designers, these asset managers will not influence firms indirectly by buying and selling shares on the market. Instead, they will exercise authority through active and aggressive property management and be directly involved in formulating the policies and business strategies of the firms under their control.[44] Thus, in place of the Czechoslovaks' imitation of Anglo-American practices, the Poles seem to be looking now to models in Germany and Japan.[45]

Several other features of the Polish program of mass privatization complete the contrast with the Czech voucher schemes. According to Polish experts, the situation is not likely to be developed enough in the immediate future to establish an "open-ended" program in which citizens are free to withdraw shares and change asset managers. Presumably to avoid inflation, citizens will be limited at first to collecting dividends from the results of the voucher–asset manager program. That is, for an undetermined period (which certainly will last at least several years) citizens cannot capitalize their shares by turning them in for their nominal value. The system is further "closed-ended" because it prohibits citizens from changing asset managers. Because executives of the limited number of asset managing companies will not be exposed to the discipline inherent in the possibility of disappointed shareholders who seek higher dividends elsewhere, the mass privatization program includes a complex incentive program for these managers. Meanwhile, the reformers hope that the managers of the former state enterprises will now be under the firm discipline of the foreign asset managers. Obviously more concerned than the Czechs about the consequences of dispersed shareholding, the Poles are hoping to target citizens as "owners" while using the universal citizens' grant as a vehicle to achieve extraordinarily concentrated corporate control.

With its unrestricted access to shares, the Polish voucher program is more inclusive than the Czechoslovak schemes. Yet its citizens' participation is almost entirely passive. What can the Polish citizen do with his share? He cannot capitalize it, nor can he withdraw that share from his current asset manager and deposit it with another. In exchange for his passivity he gets only a dividend.

Why then have a voucher program at all? The answer lies in the Polish program's goal to yield aggressive property management to foreign companies within the constraints of a politicized citizenry. No Polish politician or official could propose an outright giveaway of Polish firms to foreign asset managers, and, strictly speaking, this is not what they will do. In a legal and political sense, they will have given the ownership to the Polish citizenry, and the stewardship of the citizen-owned assets will rest in the hands of presumably competent managers. The Polish voucher program will not be "popular capitalism" in the sense of millions of small active investors with an interest in the ups and downs of the market. Instead, its designers hope to increase the chances that a capitalism with quite concentrated effective ownership can be made popular with the Polish citizenry.[46]

Hungary's Institutional Cross-Ownership

Hungary exemplifies the fourth cell in our typology—characterized by the combination of bargained evaluation of assets, corporate owners, and positional resources. Although Hungary's centralized State Property Agency (SPA) has a strong legislative mandate (and a firmly established bureaucratic office) to supervise and control all aspects of the privatization process, asset evaluation in Hungary is not conducted through administrative means, as in Germany. And although shares of Hungarian firms can be sold on an embryonic stock exchange, the evaluation of assets, unlike Czechoslovakia's auction program, is not primarily performed by market mechanisms. Because Hungary is between the polarities of administrative and market evaluation, it is represented in Figure 6.1 as "bargaining," yet this residual definition fails to convey the more precise institutional character of asset evaluation as performed by the Hungarian authorities. In the spontaneous but controlled transformation of property rights that is occurring through decentralized processes initiated by the large public enterprises, bargaining is indeed the prevalent form. But within the SPA itself, the mechanism of asset evaluation would be more accurately characterized as relational contracting—especially for the largest firms designated by the agency to be sold to foreign investors for hard currency to reduce the state deficit.

Within months after taking office in the spring of 1990, Hungary's coalition government under Prime Minister Jozsef Antall of the leading party, the Hungarian Democratic Forum, responded to the criticisms of the opposition parties by adopting the opposition's call for the "privatization of privatization." The central feature of this measure was a dramatic increase in the role of international investment banks and consulting firms in the privatization of the large state enterprises. When the SPA nominated a list of 20 enterprises to be sold in the first round of privatization, the agency also announced an open invitation to investment banks and consulting firms to place proposals with the agency indicating, in general terms, how they would evaluate assets, arrange credit, and find a buyer for a given enterprise. That is, the agency put up for tender the rights to manage the restructuring of a particular company. The investment and consulting firms that won this competition would be compensated with a percentage of the final selling price. In an important sense, the SPA was not directly selling enterprises but instead was selling the rights to lead and manage their privatization.

Dozens of consulting firms and investment banks responded to this offers, and whole rooms in the State Property Agency offices held stacks of proposals from floor to shoulder height. Several of the most internationally prominent firms (Solomon Brothers, Goldman Sachs, Barclays, Price Waterhouse, Coopers and Lybrand, and others) submitted prospectuses for eight or even more of the tendered enterprises. Each firm thought that, if selected on its merits, it would be leading several of the reorganizations. But when the SPA announced its decisions only three weeks later, it became obvious that its assignment of the enterprises was based less on careful reading of the proposals than on the aim of increasing the number of cooperating partners in the first round: The 20 enterprises slated for privatization were distributed among 20 leading banks and consulting firms.

In more recent months it is becoming clear that these organizations are forming the core of a relatively stable set of participants in an ongoing relationship with the SPA. In assigning state firms (and even in selecting enterprises to be restructured) in later rounds of privatization, the SPA is working closely with the international partners with whom it had positive experiences in the first round. Invitations are not entirely open; in some cases the agency approaches only a few international firms to sound them out about plans for this or that enterprise. And, although we have no documentary evidence, we should not rule out the possibility that decisions are being made before the announcement of competitive bidding for the rights to manage a particular restructuring. When making contracts in these cases, both sides are calculating not simply in terms of the immediate contract but in terms of past performance and in anticipation of future exchanges.

Our purpose here is not to denounce a too-cozy relationship between the SPA and the communities of international banking and consulting. On the contrary, these practices have an economic rationale: Relational contracting provides a mechanism by which both parties can gain more information than through more restricted market transactions. On the side of the SPA, such relational contracting lowers transaction costs (for example, the administrative costs of handling an overabundance of bids or the costs of time and resources in working with too many partners) and can yield more extensive and better information (about capital markets, about international investors, about the marketing and production strategies of foreign companies, and the like) than might be obtained when contracts are made through open competition on a strictly case-by-case basis.[47]

We would seriously fail to understand the process of privatization in Hungary, however, if we focused our attention too narrowly on the State Property Agency—for, although the SPA has the legal authority to supervise privatization, the predominant process of restructuring the ownership rights to the large public enterprises is not taking place at the agency's initiative. Instead, the prevalent form of transformation in Hungary is the decentralized reorganization of property. Simplifying from a more complicated web of transactions and a wider network of connections, the basic course of such reorganization can be outlined as follows: Under the pressure of enormous debt, declining sales, and threats of bankruptcy; to forestall takeovers (in the cases of more prosperous enterprises); or to attempt to increase independence from state ministries, directors of many large public enterprises are taking advantage of legislation that allows state enterprises to establish joint stock companies (RTs) and limited liability companies (KFTs). In the typical cases of such reorganizations, the state enterprise is not itself transformed into a joint stock enterprise; rather, the managers of the enterprise break up the organization (along divisional, factory, departmental, or even workshop lines) into numerous corporations.[48] As newly incorporated entities with legal identities, these new units are nominally independent and are registered separately, with their own boards of directors and separate balance sheets. The more interesting question, of course, is: Who owns the shares of these new units? An examination of the computerized records of the Budapest Court of Registry indicates that the controlling shares (in overwhelming proportions) of the corporate satellites launched around the large public enterprises are held by the state enterprises themselves.[49] For this reason, I prefer to use the term VKFT (in Hungarian vállalati-KFT, or enterprise limited liability company) to denote these new units' semiautonomous organizational status and to indicate their continuity with an organizational innovation of internal subcontracting (the VGMK, or enterprise economic work partnership) that had appeared in the earlier stage of transition.[50]

Property shares in these satellite organizations are not limited, however, to the founding enterprise. The typical cases involve patterns of more mixed ownership. Top and midlevel managers, professional and other staff, and (more rarely) highly skilled workers can be found on the lists of founding partners. But their shares are not large and should not be taken as evidence of "managerial buyouts." More important is the participation in share ownership by other RTs and KFTs—sometimes by other VKFTs in orbit around the same enterprise, more frequently by RTs or VKFTs organized around some other enterprise with lines of purchase or supply to the corporate unit.[51] Most important among the outside owners are banks. In many cases, the establishment of VKFTs and other corporate forms was triggered by enterprise debt, and in the reorganization the creditors, whether commercial banks (whose shares as joint stock companies are still predominantly state owned) or other credit institutions (also state owned), exchange debt payments for equity.

What then is the fastest-growing new ownership form in the Hungarian economy?[52] The terminology is cumbersome, but it reflects the complex, institutionally intertwined character of property transformation in Hungary: a limited liability company owned by other limited liability companies owned by joint stock companies, banks, and large public enterprises owned by the state.

Has the decentralized reorganization of property rights taken place beyond the control and outside the purview of the governmental agents responsible for privatization? Consistent with its campaign rhetoric in the parliamentary elections, the new Hungarian government, when it took office in May 1990, adopted a deliberate strategy to slow down privatization and provide for its centralized management.[53] But within months, the SPA seems to have realized that it has neither the capacity nor the ability to oversee directly the privatization of thousands of state enterprises. Toleration of decentralized reorganization appears to be the agency's current posture. This statement does not mean that the SPA is unaware of the character of these reorganizations. If a corporate spin-off of the kind described above involves assets valued above 30 million forints (approximately $400,000), or a series of such spin-offs represents in the aggregate more than 50 percent of the assets of the state enterprise, the reorganization must be approved by the agency. Although approval is not automatic, the approval rate for such proposals is extraordinarily high.[54] This high rate suggests that negotiations with the agency may precede the submission of an actual proposal for reorganization. Moreover, case studies and summary reports of corporate reorganizations indicate that the dominant form of asset evaluation in these cases is unquestionably bargaining.[55] Whether at the level between the state enterprise and its affiliated corporations or between the enterprise and the state agency, actors exploit every available means of bargaining power.

In what direction will corporate reorganization evolve? Any answer would be premature, but three alternatives can be stated clearly. In the first scenario, the current ambiguities in the distribution of property rights will be clarified in favor of the managers of these enterprises. That is, decentralized reorganization will lead to a further concentration of managerial control.[56] In the second scenario, decentralized reorganization will set the stage for a later round of genuine privatization. That is, although senior management may have broken up enterprises to buffer the firm from inevitable bankruptcies or increase its autonomy from state authorities, the establishment of even semi-independent corporate forms might create inviting opportunities for takeovers by foreign firms or by indigenous private entrepreneurs, whose means to acquire properties were more limited when they were dealing with the large state enterprises.[57]

In the third scenario, decentralized reorganization is but the first phase of a reconsolidation of state ownership.[58] This outcome might only seem to be paradoxical. State elites may be willing to tolerate corporate reorganization (even on a wide scale and together with some genuine privatization of the smaller units[59]) provided that the controlling shares remain with institutions over which the state can continue to exercise control.[60]

Whatever the outcome, we can observe in the meantime that the predominant form of the transformation of property relations in Hungary is the outcome of bargaining about asset evaluation and takes the form of institutional cross-ownership in which enterprise managers use their resources as officeholders to extend their exercise of property rights. For these reasons, Hungary exemplifies that cell in our typology representing the intersection of bargaining, corporate owners, and positional resources.

Paths of Extrication and Patterns of Transformation

The typology of privatization strategies and the discussion of the country cases provides a preliminary analytic framework that might stimulate more systematic comparisons of these cases. The eventual outcomes of these strategies will be shaped by the continued tug and pull of politics and the interaction of the state and various groups in these four societies. But whatever the outcomes, it is not too early to observe that privatization strategies in East-Central Europe are beginning from four quite distinctive starting points.

How can we explain these differences? In my view, an explanation of the variations in these strategies of privatization must begin by taking into account their distinctive paths of extrication from state socialism; that is, reunification in Germany, capitulation in Czechoslovakia, compromise in Poland, and electoral competition in Hungary.[61] These diverse paths of extrication, and the differences in social structure and political organization that brought them about, have led to significantly different current political institutions and forms of interest mediation between state and society across our four cases.

The collapse of communism in East Germany resulted in the colonization of its new political institutions during incorporation into the powerful state of the German Federal Republic. The capitulation of Communist authorities in Czechoslovakia after decades of suppressing almost all institutions of civil society resulted in the rapid restructuring of its political institutions with few remnants from the earlier period.[62] Communism did not collapse in Hungary and Poland; its demise was negotiated in both countries. Faced with a powerful, indeed mono-organizational, opposition with deep roots in Polish society, Poland's Communist leaders attempted a compromise. The legacies of this path of extrication, with its institutional guarantees for Jaruzelski and company, remain today in the compromised parliament, strong presidency, and nationwide (though weakening) workers' movement.

Hungary's reform Communists, by contrast, attempted to salvage some of their power by entering into direct electoral competition with a seemingly weak political opposition. That political opposition, of course, is now in the government and parliament, but the legacy of Hungary's peculiar path remains. In the nearly two years since its roundtable negotiations, Hungary has seen its political parties flourishing without roots in society; its weak labor movement becoming further fragmented; and its enterprise managers (as the best-organized social group during the previous decade) becoming the most powerful actors in the society.

Thus, the relationship between different types of democracy and different types of capitalism, rather than the abstractions of democracy and capitalism, holds the clue to explaining differences in contemporary Eastern Europe.[63] The diverse paths of extrication from state socialism yield distinctive patterns across a triangle formed by the state, the market, and the society. It is in terms of these patterns that I conclude the discussion of privatization strategies in East-Central Europe.

With their political incorporation into the German Federal Republic, the citizens of the former East German territories found their futures charted by a political leadership with a strong commitment to thorough marketization. Together with an abiding confidence in the market, this political leadership has profound confidence in the state. However, this trust is accompanied by a deep and almost indiscriminate distrust of East German society. Forty years of communism, according to the German leadership, have produced a terrible human tragedy—the personality structures, habits, dispositions, expectations, and mentalities imposed by Communist rule on the citizens of the newly democratized lands have made them incapable of managing their affairs. It is not their fault, but they are no longer trustworthy. They must be remolded and reeducated, not simply with industrial skills but with new mentalities. Those too old or too thoroughly spoiled by old habits and inclinations must be prevented from obstructing the new course; in the yet undamaged youth of the eastern lands lies future good fortune.[64] It follows that the German leadership will use the state to transform the economy and reconstruct the society.

The Czechoslovak leaders also have profound confidence in the market. Unlike the Germans, they lack a strong state; yet unlike the Poles, they are not faced with deeply rooted institutions in civil society that might negate their leadership. Therefore, it follows that the Czechoslovak political leaders are trying to use the market to transform the economy. So deep is their confidence in the market that they will use it to privatize the economy. Citizen vouchers in Czechoslovakia are not an ideological means to win support through some extra-economic means; instead, they are the institutional vehicle to achieve direct economic goals that will provide the basis for short-term and longer-term social support. It would be entirely misleading, therefore, to interpret the Czechoslovak leadership's use of a civic principle as an indication of its deep and abiding commitment to equality. In fact, if these leaders do indeed auction the assets of the large public enterprises at the pace and scope proposed, that scheme is likely to give rise to a relatively rapid differentiation of wealth—because some individuals (not without certain risk, of course) will be able to acquire properties at truly bargain-basement prices.

Hungary is in many ways the opposite of the Czechoslovak case. There we find a state elite that is profoundly ambivalent about the market and even distrusts the market. But at the same time, this state elite is highly uncertain about society's trust in its leadership. The current government was popularly elected. It enjoys legitimacy, but that legitimacy does not mean that the burdens that will necessarily accompany marketization will be accepted by the population. Nor could a likely replacement government, formed from parties of the same political elite, anticipate greater public confidence. Lacking intermediary institutions (such as strong and cohesive trade unions) with whom it could publicly negotiate, the elite has very few means to know what the limits of the society's tolerance might be. Thus, political leaders avoid taking decisive steps because of their fear of society's reaction. All the while, the government engages in a cyclical process of here tightening, there loosening the reins on the galloping enterprise managers.

While the German government trusts the state to remake the society, the Czechoslovaks trust the market to remake the economy, and the current Hungarian leadership distrusts the market while being distrusted by the society, in Poland the state must win society's faith in the market to keep the society's trust. Like the Czechoslovak voucher program, Polish citizens' vouchers are intended to perform an economic function of promoting privatization where domestic savings are too little to cover the value of the assets. But unlike the Czechoslovak program, the Polish strategy of appealing to the civic principle is not simply auxiliary to, or instrumental for, an economic logic. In Czechoslovakia the voucher system is a means of achieving a market that is seen as self-legitimating, while in Poland the citizen voucher system is a means of legitimating the market.

Conclusion: A Market Economy or Modern Capitalism?

These privatization programs will inevitably be modified as the work of the transformers is transformed by the societies of East-Central Europe. The resulting process will resemble bricolage, innovative adaptations that combine seemingly discrepant elements, more than architectural design. We should not be surprised, however, if the blueprints of foreign experts continue to figure in the transformative process. Although the grand designs of cookbook capitalism will not be used faithfully as guidelines for action, they will, nonetheless, be useful resources. This hypothesis stems from a perception that contemporary East-Central European policymakers are balanced between populations that must bear the transition costs and international agencies and foreign governments that may provide capital, aid, and access to Western markets.

A master blueprint is not a substitute for stabilization measures, but which East European finance minister would dare enter into negotiations with international lending institutions (the World Bank, the IMF, the European Bank for Reconstruction and Development, and the like) without one? With the diffusion of grand models from one economy to the next, we should expect, however, that formulas for external legitimation will be "decoupled" from actual practices.[65] At the same time, we should note the possibility that politicians may present their own policy preferences as if mandated by international agencies. ("The IMF made me do it.") The question of who is legitimating what and by what means is much more complicated than a matter of powerful international agencies dictating to East European politicians who have no choice but compliance.

Will this bricolage result in market economies? A definite prognosis is, of course, premature. But functioning markets are more likely to come from trials and errors that can be corrected, and new opportunities are more likely to be perceived and exploited when transformative processes are decentralized than when grand experiments are centrally imposed on society.

The more important question is whether far-reaching marketization of all aspects of economic life should be the policy goal in contemporary East-Central Europe. Advocates of such a goal suffer from two analytic shortcomings: (1) They mistake one possible means as the end itself, and (2) they operate in a theoretical universe in which the dichotomies of state or market exhaust the range of coordinating mechanisms in modern economies. Surely the goal of marketization has been, among other ends, to modernize production processes and improve the international competitiveness of these damaged economies. Yet, as various currents of thinking in political economy indicate, there are sectors in which the most competitive forms of economic coordination are neither market nor statist but new forms whose operations we are only beginning to understand and identify (with such preliminary labels as "networks," "alliances," "interfirm agreements," and the like).[66] An exclusive policy of all-encompassing marketization across all sectors would therefore pose a new obstacle and not a means to international competitiveness.

Such obstructionism is likely so long as the policy debate in transitions from state socialism is dominated by those who mistake the triumph of capitalism as the triumph of the market and look only to the "market revolutions" of Reagan and Thatcher, although the real victories were won by industrial reorganizations in Germany and Japan that were neither market oriented nor hierarchical. Modern capitalist economies should not be reduced to only one of their constitutive parts: Markets are but one of many coexisting coordinating mechanisms in modern capitalism.[67] Transformative schemes that rely on a single coordinating mechanism do not emulate existing capitalism as much as they echo the implementation of state socialism, and, like socialist structures, these schemes court the danger of sacrificing the dynamic efficiency and flexibility that depend on diverse organizational forms.[68]

Notes

An earlier version of this chapter appeared in *East European Politics and Societies* 6, 1 (Winter 1992): 17–54. Research for this paper was supported by a grant from the National Council for Soviet and East European Research. My thanks to László Bruszt, Valerie Bunce, Janusz Dabrowski, István Gábor, Péter Gedeon, Peter Katzenstein, János Lukács, Gerald McDermott, Peter Murrell, Victor Nee, László Neumann, Andrzej Rychard, Jan Szomburg, Marton Tardos, Éva Voszka, and especially Monique Djokic Stark for helpful criticisms and suggestions at various stages of researching and writing this paper.

1. See, for example, Merton J. Peck and Thomas J. Richardson (eds.), *What Is to Be Done? Proposals for the Soviet Transition to the Market* (New Haven: Yale University Press, 1991).

2. Peter Murrell, "Conservative Political Philosophy and the Strategy of Economic Transition," *East European Politics and Societies* 6, 1 (Winter 1992): 3–16.

3. See especially Michael T. Hannan and John H. Freeman, *Organizational Ecology* (Cambridge, Mass.: Harvard University Press, 1989); Richard Nelson and Sidney Winter, *An Evolutionary Theory of Economic Change* (Cambridge, Mass.: Harvard University Press, 1982); Paul David, "Understanding the Economics of QWERTY: The Necessity of History," in W. Parker (ed.), *Economic History and the Modern Historian,* (Oxford: Basil Blackwell, 1986), pp. 30–49; and Brian W. Arthur, "Competing Technologies and Lock-in by Historical Events: The Dynamics of Allocation Under Increasing Returns," *Economic Journal* 99 (1989): 116–131.

4. Sensitivity to these differences is obscured by the very events that brought so much attention to the region. "Nineteen eighty-nine" was a double conjuncture—both in the near simultaneity of events across the countries of the region and in the rapid acceleration and reciprocal effects of changes across political, economic, and social domains. But "1989" will stand in the way of understanding developments in the region if we take it as a universal beginning or culmination. That is, we must begin to disaggregate the idea of "the transition," perhaps even dispense with it as a concept, and try to understand how changes in the different countries and in the different domains have very different time frames. Changes in social institutions, for example, are not simply slower but might have been taking place much earlier than more visible political developments. If pace and timing differ across domains, we also should not assume that changes within different societies necessarily move in the same directions.

5. See László Bruszt, "Transformative Politics: Social Cost and Social Peace in East Central Europe," *East European Politics and Societies* 6, 1 (Winter 1992): 55–72.

6. Unlike the designers' schemes, in which the actions and preferences of subordinate social groups are a hindrance to the speedy enactment of the prescribed formulas (or at most take only a reactive role at the voting booth by approving or removing programs and parties), in the perspective adopted here the institutionalized interactions between state and society play a formative role in shaping actual strategies.

7. I take this to be the key analytic insight of Theda Skocpol's *States and Social Revolutions* (Cambridge: Cambridge University Press, 1979). See also László Bruszt and David Stark, "Remaking the Political Field in Hungary: From the Politics of Confrontation to the Politics of Completion," in Ivo Banac (ed.), *Eastern Europe in Revolution* (Ithaca, N.Y.: Cornell University Press, 1992), pp. 13–55.

8. By "path dependence" I am not referring to processes whereby the societies of Eastern Europe are seen to return to the natural "historical trajectories" of the interwar period from which they had temporarily deviated. See, for example, the argument of Ivan Szelenyi in *Socialist Entrepreneurs* (Madison: University of Wisconsin Press, 1988). Unlike these notions of already existing roads or the concept of trajectories, the concept of path dependence is not that of a vector.

9. My conception of institutions as embodied routines and my emphasis on practices instead of preferences and on predispositions instead of rational calculations draw on the work of Pierre Bourdieu, especially *The Logic of Practice* (Stanford: Stanford University Press, 1990). For a similar conception of institutions as not simply constraining but enabling, see Paul DiMaggio and Walter Powell's introductory essay to *The New Institutionalism in Organizational Analysis* (Chicago: University of Chicago Press, 1991), pp. 1–38.

10. The pertinent lesson of state socialism is that large-scale social engineering might so badly tear the social fabric that its damage will take decades to repair and preclude the longer-term calculations so central to the efficient functioning of economic institutions. That is, the greater the scope of an experiment, the greater the risk of catastrophe. See Murrell, "Conservative Political Philosophy." My intention here is not to denigrate institutional design. Institutional designs do matter and can bring about improvements, especially if they are delimited in scope to solve particular problems of governance and coordination for specific sectors or localities (rather than as global solutions to the problems of an entire economy). In place of grand experiments, we should hope for more, not fewer, "designs"—partial solutions to limited problems in which transformation becomes a process undertaken by many dispersed agents at many institutional sites.

11. For the use of a similar comparative methodology, see David Stark, "Rethinking Internal Labor Markets: New Insights from a Comparative Perspective," *American Sociological Review* 51, 4 (August 1986): 492–504; and David Stark, "Bending the Bars of the Iron Cage: Bureaucratization and Informalization Under Capitalism and Socialism," *Sociological Forum* 4, 4 (1990): 637–664.

12. This lack of comparison of the East European cases is the major limitation of Ellen Comisso's interesting argument in "Political Coalitions, Economic Choices," *Journal of International Affairs* 45, 1 (Summer 1991): 1–29. For Comisso, the "options" available to the economies of Eastern Europe are given by the array of existing West European national economies, for example, the "French model," the "Swedish model," "modified Thatcherism," and so on.

13. David Stark, "Privatization in Hungary: From Plan to Market or from Plan to Clan?" *East European Politics and Societies* 4, 3 (Fall 1990): 351–392.

14. János Kornai, *The Road to a Free Economy* (New York: Norton, 1990); and Stark, "Privatization in Hungary."

15. The analytic categories are given content in terms of the specific historical and social setting that is contemporary East-Central Europe. The Weberian notion of historically grounded concepts should be familiar to most sociologists. My method here is antithetical to the hollow antinomies of "deduction versus induction" or "theory versus historicism" resuscitated in the recent rational choice literature, for example, Edgar Kiser and Michael Hechter, "The Role of General Theory in Comparative-Historical Sociology," *American Journal of Sociology* 97, 1 (July 1991): 1–30.

16. On relational contracting and other forms of coordination between firms that lie between (or outside) the dichotomy of markets and hierarchies, see Oliver Williamson, *The Economic Institutions of Capitalism: Firms, Markets, and Relational Contracting* (New York: Free Press, 1985); and Rogers Hollingsworth and Wolfgang Streeck, "Countries and Sectors: Concluding Remarks on Performance, Convergence, and Competitiveness," in Roger Hollingsworth, Philippe Schmitter, and Wolfgang Streeck (eds.), *Comparing Capitalist Economies: Variations in the Governance of Industrial Sectors* (New York: Oxford University Press, 1992).

17. Strategies of justification lie at the core of strategies of privatization. Although I raise these issues explicitly in this subsection, processes of justification are an important aspect of each of our three dimensions. My intention here is to see how the specific work of justification can vary from case to case as shaped by the broader transformative politics. On strategies of justification in the transitional period on the shop floor, see David Stark, "La valeur de travail et sa retribution en Hongrie," *Actes de la recherche en sciences sociales* 85 (November 1990): 3–19 (available in English as "Work, Worth, and Justice in the Hungarian Mixed Economy," Center for European Studies, Working Papers on East-Central Europe no. 7, Harvard University (1990). For an ambitious theory of justifications, see Luc Boltanski and Laurent Thevenot, *De la justification: Les économies de la grandeur* (Paris: Gallimard, 1991).

18. Obviously, we think here of the work of Pierre Bourdieu on different forms of "capital" in modern societies. See, for example, his "Forms of Capital" in John G. Richardson (ed.), *Handbook of Theory and Research for the Sociology of Education* (Westport, Conn.: Greenwood Press, 1986), pp. 241–258.

19. The old political capital suffered a massive devaluation, and, in the current period, the publication of memoirs is one of the few remaining avenues of such direct conversion. In fact, there are good reasons to expect that in the current period monetary rather than positional resources will be important as an avenue of ownership for former apparatchiks whose earlier assets were exclusively political.

20. A more comprehensive examination would also have to address the disposition of real estate and the question of the reprivatization of property. Restitution or compensation of former owners is an important question, with significant implications for the timing, pace, and methods of privatizing large public enterprises. In particular, uncertainties about reprivatization can pose serious obstacles that inhibit potential buyers and delay privatization in the state sector.

21. For example, our location of "Hungary's decentralized reorganization" in the lower lefthand cell indicates that policymakers there have, to date, designed ownership restructuring around corporate owners through bargaining processes and favoring positional resources. This structure does not imply, for example, that financial or monetary resources are not mobilizable in Hungary or that positional resources are not mobilizable in Germany. Similarly, the use of citizen vouchers in

Poland and Czechoslovakia does not exclude corporations from participating in privatization in those economies—although it is interesting to note that the governments of Germany and Hungary have, thus far, excluded the principle of citizens' grants from their strategies for privatization.

22. *The World Bank/CECSE* 2, 5 (May 1991): 3.

23. For an excellent description of the work of the Treuhand in its first months of operation and a balanced analysis of the difficult problems facing it in the near future, see Roland Schönfeld, "Privatization in East Germany: Strategies and Experience," paper presented at the Conference on Transforming Economic Systems in East-Central Europe, Munich, June 1991.

24. Such short-time work was originally scheduled to expire on June 30, 1991, prompting some estimates that there would be 3.5 to 4 million unemployed (as high as 45 percent of the previously active earners in 1989) by the end of the summer of 1991. See Schönfeld, "Privatization in East Germany." These nightmares were not realized, partly because short-time work was extended beyond the deadline. By late 1991, high-level Treuhand officials acknowledged an effective unemployment rate of about 30 percent. See Horst Kern and Charles F. Sabel, "Between Pillar and Post: Reflections on the Treuhand's Uncertainty About What to Say Next," paper presented at the Workshop on the Treuhandanstalt, Center for European Studies, Harvard University, November 16, 1991; see also comments by Treuhand officials at that conference.

25. Stark, "Rethinking Internal Labor Markets"; and János Lukács, "Organizational Flexibility, Internal Labor Markets, and Internal Subcontracting, Hungarian Style," in Rudolf Andorka and Lázló Bertalan (eds.), *Economy and Society in Hungary* (Budapest: University of Economics, 1986), pp. 15–34.

26. Schönfeld, "Privatization in East Germany"; and Kern and Sabel, "Between Pillar and Post."

27. Kern and Sabel, "Between Pillar and Post."

28. The designation "Czechoslovakia" is used here because the voucher-auction program was developed before the split of Slovakia and the Czech Republic. Moreover, the first wave of voucher privatization took place in both countries. Slovakia is unlikely to continue privatization through vouchers.

29. Presumably to increase participation rates, the registration fee was reduced from initial proposals for 2,000 korunas (equivalent to about half the average monthly earnings of industrial employees).

30. By late 1991, the ministries had received proposals for 3,588 privatization projects from some 900 enterprises. Some 2,800 of these projects were in conformity with the requirements of the voucher scheme. I am grateful to Gerald McDermott for providing these figures.

31. We might also observe that the auction that Klaus is proposing has some resemblance to the schemes of Oscar Lange for setting prices through a simulated market within a socialist economy.

32. According to public opinion polls at the beginning of 1991, interest in participating in the voucher-auction program was very low. See Franz-Lothar Altmann, "Privatization in Czechoslovakia," paper presented at the Conference on Transforming Economic Systems in East-Central Europe, Munich, June 1991. For an excellent account of the economic landscape in which the Czechoslovak privatization programs are occurring, see Gerald A. McDermott and Michal Mejtrik, "The Role of Small Firms in the Industrial Development and Transformation of Czechoslovakia," *Small Business Economics* 4 (1992): 51–72.

33. The Czechoslovak leadership appears prepared to accept relatively high transaction costs (the voucher-auction will be costly) in the distribution of shares in

its privatization strategy in anticipation that these one-time transition costs will quickly reduce overall transaction costs in the newly privatized economy.

34. For the problem that the citizenry might not have information about the market, the Czech strategists seem to have a market solution in mind: Investors who take risks will want better information, and the demand for information will stimulate the business of gathering and selling information. The simulated market, they believe, will help to set in motion the secondary institutions (brokerage houses, market analysis, etc.) required for smoothly functioning capital markets.

35. Prominent among the Czechoslovak citizens who will have money to speculate on the stock exchange will be former Communist officials and black-marketeers. The cynicism of the architects of the Czech privatization strategy is undisguised: "It's sure there is dirty money here," said Tomas Jezek, Czech Minister of Privatization. "But the best method for cleaning the money is to let them invest it." *New York Times,* January 27, 1991, p. 10.

36. The architects of the Czechoslovak voucher-auction program hope that a simulated market will stimulate a real market. An element of learning by doing is built into the program. By playing the voucher market (and this is really playing a game), at least some groups of citizens get accustomed to "buying and selling" and might be drawn into playing the real market. (For a very different conception, see the Polish case, which highlights the distinctiveness of the Czech case.) Whether the institutions of a stock exchange can be created in such a manner, of course, remains to be tested.

37. For enterprises at the very bottom of the list (where citizens were not willing to exchange points for shares), the state will, of course, face the difficult decision of whether to close them or continue operating them under state management.

38. Anticipation of managerial resistance would lead us to expect that there should be active bargaining between ministries and enterprises in the initial asset evaluation determining the initial asking price in the first round of the auction. Such an observation does not threaten our typology because that initial asset evaluation is only a preliminary one to set in motion the auction (and the later market for shares) in which the effective and determinate asset evaluation will take place.

39. See Jan Szomburg, "Poland's Privatization Strategy," paper presented at the Conference on Transforming Economic Systems in East-Central Europe, Munich, June 1991. For an overview of the ambitious goals but limited achievements of early privatization efforts in Poland, see Tomasz Gruszecki, "Privatization in Poland in 1990," *Communist Economies and Economic Transformation* 3, 2 (1991): 141–154.

40. Lewandowski and Szomburg had proposed a stock distribution plan as early as 1988. See their "Uwlaszczenie jako fundament reformy spoleczno-gospodarczej" (Property change as a fundamental aspect of socioeconomic reform) in *Porpozyce Przeksztalcen Polskiej Gospodarki* (Warsaw: Polish Economics Association, 1989), pp. 63–81. A similar program of mass privatization was later elaborated by David Lipton and Jeffrey Sachs, "Privatization in Eastern Europe: The Case of Poland," *Brookings Papers on Economic Activity* (1990): 293–341.

41. Ownership claims coming from the Workers' Councils arise in some places from strong bargaining positions and in others from weakness. For an excellent analysis of reorganization at the level of enterprises, which cautions against any global statements about the activities of "workers," "trade unions," or "management," see Janusz Dabrowski, Michal Federowicz, and Anthony Levitas, "Stabilization and State Enterprise Adjustment: The Political Economy of State Firms After Five Months of Fiscal Discipline," Center for European Studies, Working Papers on East-Central Europe, Harvard University (1990).

42. Szomburg, "Poland's Privatization Strategy."

43. Debated but not yet resolved is the question of whether Workers' Councils will be disbanded in all transformed enterprises. If so, workers would be asked, in effect, to exchange a set of implicit organizational rights inherited from the transition period for a set of explicit ownership rights in the new period of transformation. The question will not be answered without much bargaining.

44. See, for example, Janusz Lewandowski and Jan Szomburg, "The Strategy of Privatization," paper presented at the Research Centre for Marketization and Property Reform, Gdansk, October 1990.

45. The distinction between "credit based" and "capital market based" (roughly, banks versus a stock exchange) is presented in John Zysman, *Government, Markets, and Growth* (Ithaca, N.Y.: Cornell University Press, 1983).

46. By late 1991, Poland's program of mass privatization showed signs of unraveling. The 400 firms scheduled for the voucher program had been reduced to 230, and the program was under attack from all quarters. See Ben Slay, "Privatization and De-Monopolization in Poland," unpublished manuscript, Research Institute, Radio Free Europe/Radio Liberty (November 1991). If citizen vouchers recede in importance, we should expect that the locus of privatization and reorganization will shift even more to the level of firms and localities and especially to the Workers' Councils—one of the most important economic institutional legacies of Poland's extrication from state socialism. For an excellent analysis of decentralized reorganization in Poland, see Janusz M. Dabrowski, Michal Federowicz, and Anthony Levitas, "Polish State Enterprises and the Properties of Performance: Stabilization, Marketization, Privatization," *Politics and Society* 19, 4 (1991): 403–437.

47. To the legitimate objection that such an arrangement should be designated as a "market" because it bears strong resemblance to the organization of some capital markets in developed economies, we have three replies. First, see the discussion later in this chapter on the continuing nature of these contracts. Second, this observation might lead some researchers to further explore features of "relational contracting" in capital markets in Western economies. (Such research is already ongoing. See for example, the extraordinary analysis of networks in investment banking by Joel Podolny, Ph.D. dissertation, Department of Sociology, Harvard University, 1991.) Third, for the purposes of our typology, this institutional arrangement (so prevalent in the Hungarian case) deserves some distinctive terminology to set it apart from the use of spot markets (auctions) in the Czech case.

48. Such a restructuring would require preparation of a comprehensive transformation program under the guidelines of the 1989 Law on Transformation, with the direct involvement of the State Property Agency.

49. I am grateful to László Neumann and Éva Voszka for providing me with these data.

50. The term VKFT is not my invention but comes from workers I interviewed (in collaboration with János Lukács) in January 1990 during field work in several Hungarian factories. These workers were using the acronym to allude to an earlier hybrid organizational form, the VGMK (enterprise economic work partnership), involved in a primarily internal system of subcontracting. Although participants were free to make contracts and had significant autonomy in organizing production and allocating their "entrepreneurial fees," in the VGMK form the ownership of fixed assets remained in the hands of the parent enterprise. With the term VKFT, the workers were denoting the semiautonomous character of the new limited liability companies spinning around the enterprise. On the VGMK as a hybrid organizational form and precursor of new mixed property forms, see David Stark,

"Coexisting Organizational Forms in Hungary's Emerging Mixed Economy," in Victor Nee and David Stark (eds.), *Remaking the Economic Institutions of Socialism: China and Eastern Europe* (Stanford: Stanford University Press, 1989), pp. 137–168.

51. See especially the important study by Éva Voszka, *Tulajdon—reform* (Property—reform) (Budapest: Közgazdaság és Jog Könyvkiadó, 1991), and also her "From Twilight to Twilight," paper presented at the Congress of Hungarian Sociology, Budapest, June 1991. For excellent case studies of such reorganization, see Éva Voszka, "Rope Walking: Ganz Danubius Ship and Crane Factory Transformed into a Company," *Acta Oeconomica* 43, 1–2 (1990): 285–302; see also Mária Móro, "Az állami vállalatok (ál)privatizációja (Pseudo privatization of state enterprises), *Közgazdasági Szemle* 38, 6 (1990): 565–584.

52. In the past eighteen months the creation of new economic units has increased by two-and-one-half times, but the number of corporations has grown by seventeen times (Voszka, "Rope Walking"). If we preferred to measure by capitalization instead of counting units, the new semiautonomous corporate forms would be even more preponderant.

53. In this phase, as Éva Voszka succinctly describes, on issues of privatization the government was much more preoccupied with the question of who should be the seller than who should be the new owner. Voszka, "Rope Walking."

54. After consulting with the leading Hungarian experts in this field, our best estimates are that only about 10 percent of such proposals are rejected by the SPA. According to the best available data, the official rate of approval of corporate reorganization is 70 percent. But most practitioners in the field acknowledge that many rejected proposals are approved after minor technical changes (or, on occasion, with no revision).

55. Voszka, "Rope Walking"; Móro, "Pseudo privatization"; and László Neumann, "Labour Conflicts of Privatization in Hungary" (Budapest: Institute for Labour Studies, 1991).

56. This first scenario envisages a further extension of patterns of institutional cross-ownership and suggests a research agenda to investigate patterns of interlocking directorates in the Hungarian economy.

57. In this scenario, the debt for equity exchange so prevalent in the first round of reorganization could play an important part in the second. The overwhelming problem of enterprise debt (some owed to banks, some in the disguised form of interenterprise debt as firms increasingly delay paying their suppliers in the state sector) is leading to solvency problems in the banking sector. There are recent indications that some banks are beginning to act like owners—demanding dividends from the KFTs and RTs affiliated with state enterprises. Where profits are low to nonexistent, some state enterprises may be forced to sell some of their affiliated units to pay such dividends. But the prospects for privatizing these units to domestic entrepreneurs are far from encouraging. Where will entrepreneurs find the capital to make such investments? The same financial crisis that triggers the sales places restrictions on credit.

58. In such a scenario, the relationship between enterprises and the state would take the form of bargaining and would reflect the continuity of ambiguous property relations in Hungarian state enterprises from the 1968 reforms to the present. But there would be discontinuities as well: In place of the earlier "plan bargaining" and the later "regulatory bargaining," under decentralized reorganization and reconsolidation of state ownership the new relationship would be characterized as dividend bargaining. For a discussion of the continuities and discontinuities in these bargaining relations, see Erzsébet Szalai, "A hatalom metamorfózia?" (Metamorphosis of power?), *Valóság* 6 (1991): 1–26.

59. Encouraging but limiting, such privatization would be consistent with a policy choice that sought to rationalize the state's ownership role (trimming down the size of its assets) while consolidating its ability to intervene in the economy as an (indirect) owner.

60. In this case, as in all the scenarios, the question of who controls the banks is of fundamental importance. The dismissal in June 1991 of three bank presidents following a sharp dispute over the banks' dividend policies indicates that the state is attempting to use its authority in appointing senior banking officials to control the shares in state enterprises held by the banks. It remains to be seen how the state's influence over banks will be changed by the new banking law that took effect on December 1, 1991. Under that legislation, only banks or other financial institutions may hold more than 25 percent of the shares of a bank. The state has until 1995 to reduce its direct ownership of shares in commercial banks.

61. For an elaboration of these concepts, see László Bruszt and David Stark, "Remaking the Political Field in Hungary: From the Politics of Confrontation to the Politics of Competition," in Ivo Banac (ed.), *Eastern Europe in Revolution* (Ithaca, N.Y.: Cornell University Press, 1992), pp. 13–55.

62. Czechoslovakia's current trade unions, for example, bear relatively little resemblance to the pre-1989 unions—in contrast to Hungary, where the old official union remains the largest (if tired) trade union federation, and to Poland, where both Solidarity and the Ogólnopolska Porozumienie Zweigzków Zawodowych (OPZZ) are the continued legacy of the 1980s. See Bruszt, "Transformative Politics."

63. On the concepts of different types of capitalism and different types of democracy, see the insightful work of Philippe Schmitter, "Modes of Sectoral Governance: A Typology," unpublished manuscript, Stanford University (1991); and Terry Karl and Philippe Schmitter, "Modes of Transition in Latin America, Southern and Eastern Europe," *International Social Science Journal* 128 (March 1991): 269–284.

64. The reader who suspects exaggeration here would benefit from reading, for example, Werner Gumpel's "The Mentality Problem in the Transition Process from Centrally Planned Economy to Market Economy," paper presented at the Conference on Transforming Economic Systems in East-Central Europe, Munich, June 1991. I have paraphrased Professor Gumpel in the passage above. To quote him directly: "These people must be made to unlearn most of what they were brought up with."

65. The rapidity with which some packages of innovation have become institutionalized (that is, come to be taken for granted) has been extraordinary. No one was shocked, for example, when Yeltsin announced shock therapy for the Russian economy. On diffusion across national boundaries, see David Strang and John W. Meyer, "Institutional Conditions for Diffusion," paper presented at the Workshop on New Institutional Theory, Department of Sociology, Cornell University, November 1991. On the decoupling of formal structures celebrating institutionalized myths from actual organizational practices, see especially John W. Meyer and Brian Rowan, "Institutionalized Organizations: Formal Structure as Myth and Ceremony," in Walter W. Powell and Paul J. DiMaggio (eds.), *The New Institutionalism in Organizational Analysis* (Chicago: University of Chicago Press, 1991), pp. 41–62.

66. See especially the research presented in Roger Hollingsworth, Philippe Schmitter, and Wolfgang Streeck (eds.), *Comparing Capitalist Economies: Variations in the Governance of Industrial Sectors* (New York: Oxford University Press, 1992); Schmitter, "Modes of Sectoral Governance"; Robert Boyer, "The Transformations of Modern Capitalism in Light of the Regulation Approach and

Other Theories of Political Economy," paper presented at the Conference on Comparative Governance of Economic Sectors, Bellagio, June 1989; and Walter Powell, "Neither Market nor Hierarchy: Network Forms of Organization," in B. Staw and L. L. Cummings (eds.), *Research in Organizational Behavior* (Greenwich, Conn.: JAI Press, 1990), pp. 295–336. The key analytic move in this new literature is to shift from the preoccupation with micro- or macrophenomena to a mesolevel focus on sectors. These studies suggest an exciting agenda for similar mesoanalysis of sectors and localities in contemporary Eastern Europe.

67. On the multiple meanings of the term "market," see the excellent paper by Robert Boyer, "Markets Within Alternative Coordinating Mechanisms: History, Theory, and Policy in the Light of the Nineties," presented at the Conference on the Comparative Governance of Sectors, Bigorio, Switzerland, April 1991.

68. Michael T. Hannan and John Freeman, *Organization Ecology* (Cambridge, Mass.: Harvard University Press, 1989), especially p. 3; and David Stark, "Coexisting Organizational Forms," especially p. 168.

■ 7 ■

Strategy, Structure, and Spontaneous Privatization in Russia and Ukraine

SIMON JOHNSON, HEIDI KROLL & SANTIAGO EDER

Since 1987, new laws have enabled managers and workers in the former Soviet Union to acquire significant property rights in their enterprises on their own initiative. This process, known as "spontaneous privatization," remains extremely controversial. There are accusations that it is simply theft[1] and that it primarily benefits the old Communist nomenklatura. At the same time, there have been suggestions that it offers the only feasible way forward for state enterprises.[2] What is the evidence for the arguments about spontaneous privatization, and how should we interpret it?

We first require a clear definition of spontaneous privatization. Using the approach of Grossman and Hart,[3] we define a firm as a set of assets and consider ownership to consist of residual control rights over those assets. Residual control rights constitute the de facto ability to determine how a firm's assets are used in all circumstances other than those specified in implicit or explicit contracts.[4] Contracts are ex ante agreements, the terms of which are established before all contingencies are known, and residual control rights confer the right to make decisions as contingencies occur.

Using this basic definition, the owner of a firm is that person or persons who has the right to decide how assets are used, given that the firm fulfills its contractual obligations.[5] In the old Soviet system, most of these residual control rights rested with supervisory bureaucrats rather than with managers of state enterprises. Consequently, we define spontaneous privatization as occurring when managers acquire, on their own initiative, residual rights of control over their firms.[6] (Note that we use the term *state enterprise* to refer to a particular legal form and *firm* to refer to a set of assets.) If property rights are considered in this light, it is evident that a change in the legal form of a state enterprise—de jure privatization—is neither necessary nor sufficient for spontaneous privatization.[7]

What causes this reallocation of property rights? In particular, how is the managerial acquisition of residual control rights linked to other changes in such matters as internal organization and product mix, which are evident

147

in state firms? To answer these questions properly we need to define two further concepts.[8]

Both of these definitions are drawn from the conceptual framework used by Chandler. First, we adopt the definition of managerial strategy as "the determination of the basic long-term goals and objectives of an enterprise, and the adoption of courses of action and allocation of resources necessary for carrying out these goals."[9] *Strategy* will be used here to mean both what managers want to do and how they go about doing it.[10]

Chandler also defined structure as "the design of organization through which the enterprise is administered."[11] However, in order to be appropriate for the former Soviet Union, our second definition will be an extension of Chandler—*structure* in this chapter includes both the internal organization of the firm and the way in which the firm is related to other entities, such as government bodies and other firms. Chandler was concerned with the response of large US companies to changes in their operating environment and how they responded with new internal organizations. Our line of inquiry for the former Soviet Union is similar, but we will look primarily at organizational changes external to the firm.[12]

These definitions facilitate our analysis of how the existing structure of a firm conditions the strategy pursued by managers and what managerial strategy implies for a firm's structure.[13] De facto residual rights of control, contractual arrangements, and legal property forms are all essential parts of a firm's structure; thus changes in residual control rights should not be evaluated independently of the overall change in a firm's structure. Using these definitions, spontaneous privatization can be understood as a series of phenomena that are much more complex than the simple theft of property.

The legal reforms of perestroika initiated changes in the external control structure of state enterprises. In effect, the supervising bureaucracy was forced to give up some of its control rights, but these rights were not clearly transferred to anyone else—there was ambiguity about precisely who had residual control rights over firms. At the same time, the allocation of inputs and outputs by the bureaucracy was disrupted, and managers of many state enterprises found that their firms could not survive by operating as before. Managers found they needed to develop new strategies in order to sustain their enterprises, and these new strategies required further changes in structure.

The new structures went far beyond the original intentions of government reform by allowing managers to obtain more residual control rights; the acquisition of these rights by managers further weakened the remaining mechanisms of central control. Managers did not initiate perestroika, but they responded to the new problems and opportunities by restructuring their firms in ways that suited themselves and their purposes—this is spontaneous privatization.

Spontaneous privatization is clearly important, but how can one obtain further information about it? Published official statistics do not deal with spontaneous privatization except by recording some of the de jure transformations of property forms. Newspaper accounts are sporadic and often do not include vital details. Fortunately, our research has shown that it is now possible to collect information directly by interviewing managers.

We initially decided that to select a sample of firms from across the whole former Soviet Union would involve too many unmeasurable selection biases. Instead, we began this research by conducting a survey of all the industrial state enterprises with more than 250 employees in one city— Kiev, capital of newly independent Ukraine.[14] Table 7.1 provides details on sectoral and size distributions of the 198 nonmilitary enterprises in Kiev and the distribution by sector of the 68 interviews that we have conducted so far in Kiev.[15]

Table 7.1 Distribution of Firms in Kiev by Sector and Number of Employees

	Number of Employees				
Sector	250–1000	1000–5000	5000+	Total Firms	Interviewed So Far
Energy	3	1	—	4	0
Nonferrous metallurgy	2	—	—	2	0
Chemical and petrochemical	9	3	1	13	0
Machine building and metalworking	37	17	5	59	18
Glass and porcelain	2	1	—	3	1
Construction materials	23	4	—	27	11
Wood, woodworking, and paper	9	1	—	10	3
Light industry	17	12	—	29	11
Food processing	16	3	—	19	3
Pharmaceuticals	—	3	—	3	0
Flour, groats, and animal feed	2	—	—	2	0
Microbiology	1	—	—	1	0
Printing	2	2	—	4	3
Other	15	6	—	21	0
Total	138	53	6	197	50

Source: Kiev City Statistics Department, September 1, 1991, private communication.

Our ultimate goal is to use the Kiev survey as a benchmark against which data from other cities and from follow-up work in Kiev can be compared. However, to date we have conducted only a small number of systematic interviews with non-Kiev managers, and we are unable to generalize—in the sense of estimating how widespread spontaneous privatization is in Ukraine or in the former Soviet Union.[16] Instead, this chapter provides a qualitative assessment of our interview results through the summer of 1992. Hopefully, an analysis of the strategies followed by managers of state enterprises in Kiev sheds light on the wider process.

These strategies appear to be strongly affected by the previous structure of the firm and particularly by who had jurisdiction over the enterprise up to mid-1991. Enterprises in Ukraine previously existed under one of three supervising bureaucracies: all-Union ministries, republican ministries, and local government. The all-Union ministries usually controlled larger enterprises in heavy industry, defense, and machine building, while the Ukrainian ministries supervised light industry and producers of consumer goods. Local government was in charge of construction, some food processing, and services.

Most of the new managerial strategies involve spontaneous privatization, but the role played by changes in residual control rights and contract structures varies greatly between different strategies. Specifically, we can identify three roles for spontaneous privatization: to help reconstruct former hierarchies, to build new hierarchies, or to make the firm more independent.[17] Reallocations of residual control rights and, more generally, the creation of new structures, are an integral part of managerial strategies. These changes in structure—often radical—are usually accomplished without any alteration in the legal form of the original state enterprise.

This way of analyzing changes in property rights draws heavily on the markets-versus-hierarchies approach first proposed by Coase[18] and elaborated more fully by Williamson[19] and others. However, our emphasis is somewhat different. Most studies of these issues in Western economies seek to understand how firms grow and what limits the extent of vertical and horizontal integration. In contrast, we are trying to understand why the collapse of one hierarchical system sometimes leads firms to become more independent—so that their relations with other firms are primarily market based—and sometimes leads to the creation of new hierarchies. We also are concerned particularly with the meaning of changes in residual control rights when the legal form of a state enterprise remains unaltered.

Elsewhere, we have described in detail how legal changes under perestroika enabled managers and workers to take control of their enterprises.[20] The next section of this chapter reviews the main legal and organizational aspects of spontaneous privatization, and the subsequent section outlines government privatization plans in Russia and Ukraine as they existed in the summer of 1992. A following section provides pertinent evidence from our interviews with managers. We conclude with an assessment of the likely conflicts between managerial strategies and government actions.

The Organizational Basis of Spontaneous Privatization

A major catalyst for the process of spontaneous privatization in the former Soviet Union was the emergence after 1987 of a variety of new property and business forms alongside traditional state enterprises. A partial list includes cooperatives, leasing businesses, small enterprises, joint ventures, joint stock companies, concerns (interbranch state associations), associations, state corporations, and holding companies. The diversity of forms is misleading, however, because in practice there is no discernible difference between some of the forms, which often are used interchangeably. The new organizational forms have served as the basis for several basic types of spontaneous privatization.[21]

The earliest form of spontaneous privatization was the establishment of cooperatives, small enterprises, and other types of subsidiary firms under and around existing state enterprises, usually as a means of circumventing the production plans (state orders), wage and price controls, tax obligations, and other restrictions applied to state enterprises. Mikhail Gorbachev's initial enterprise reforms fueled this movement by keeping state enterprises under a tighter regulatory leash than the cooperatives while at the same time authorizing the establishment of cooperatives attached to state enterprises. Over 80 percent of the 260,000 cooperatives operating at the end of 1990 were attached to state enterprises. The boom in cooperatives was facilitated by laws enabling groups of workers to lease equipment and premises from the sponsoring enterprise for a fixed term.

The small enterprise (*maloe predpriyatie,* or MP) emerged in 1989 as an alternative to state-sponsored cooperatives that were tainted by speculation and price gouging. Instead of establishing cooperatives, state enterprises were allowed to hive off shops, subdivisions, and other structural units as substantially independent, albeit nominally state-owned, enterprises. Legislation passed in 1990 permitted private ownership of MPs, fixed ceilings on the number of their employees, and bestowed them with a host of special tax concessions to promote their development. The number of MPs mushroomed in 1991 as many existing cooperatives and subunits of state enterprises took advantage of the opportunity to reduce their tax liabilities by converting themselves into small enterprises. Notwithstanding the de facto legalization of hired labor within permitted limits, formal ownership of the vast majority of MPs remained vested in the state.[22]

The next stage of spontaneous privatization was the establishment of shareholding corporations as a vehicle for management-employee buyouts of enterprises. Such takeovers usually have been accomplished by converting state enterprises into joint stock companies (*aktsionernye obshchestva,* or AOs) of the closed type, in which shares are not tradable outside the firm, by freeing enterprises from the direct administrative control of ministries without establishing a system of corporate governance by shareholders. This arrangement results in the complete entrenchment of managers.

Above the enterprise level, there also has been a widespread transformation of the ministries and intermediate-level main directorates (*glavki*) into a variety of commercial forms.[23] The "corporatization" of the ministries began when groups of enterprises separated themselves from their ministries on their own initiative and organized "from below" three interbranch state associations (*mezhotraslevye gosudarstvennye ob"edineniya*, or MGOs), which were also sometimes called concerns (*kontserny*). In the wake of a major cutback in the ministerial apparatus in 1989, corporatization was appropriated as a survival strategy by ministries that were targeted for liquidation. Liquidated ministries were reincarnated as state concerns and associations (*assotsiatsii*). This process accelerated after the failed coup of August 1991. One by one, former all-Union ministries were abolished and replaced by state concerns, associations, corporations, and holding companies.

The progressive disintegration of the centralized distribution of supply also led to spontaneous changes in the way enterprises acquire inputs. The wave of corporatization and mergers described above played an important role in this process. Enterprises protected their supply channels by joining concerns and associations and by distributing shares to their suppliers. There also has been an increased reliance on barter. Most striking was the rapid development of a network of commodity exchanges (*birzhi*) that mushroomed to over 200 exchanges by the summer of 1991. Most exchanges were founded by large industrial enterprises and by the commercial centers and territorial administrations of Gossnab, the former state supply organization. Thus, as in the case of other new business forms, the rapid growth of exchanges largely reflects the transformation of existing state structures rather than the initiative of independent entrepreneurs.

From Spontaneous to Managed Privatization?

In 1991, a leading study of the transition problems in the Soviet economy adamantly opposed spontaneous privatization on the grounds both of equity and efficiency.[24] The study suggested that by transferring ownership of firms to managers and workers, spontaneous privatization would create arbitrary inequalities in the distribution of income and wealth, encourage firms to allocate income to wages and salaries at the expense of investment, and fuel a political backlash. The opposition to management and workers becoming dominant owners, combined with a recommendation favoring the sale of shares over free distribution, supported by implication a strategy of privatizing to sell firms to outsiders through public offerings of shares and sales to foreign investors.

This view of spontaneous privatization recently has been challenged by a growing number of economists and practitioners who espouse a more benign view.[25] The "revisionist" view emphasizes that spontaneous privatization, once in progress, cannot be halted or reversed easily and that it has positive properties that can be harnessed usefully in the service of rapid formal privatization. This view draws a lesson from the Hungarian and Polish experience with strategies that initially favored "outsider" privatizations. The pace of privatization under these strategies proved much slower than expected or desired, in part because of resistance by insiders to proposed sales but also because of the scarcity of acceptable buyers. In contrast, spontaneous privatization proceeds rapidly because it is initiated by the managers themselves.

The revisionist prescription is not to prohibit spontaneous privatization but rather to regularize it by establishing a clear legal framework designed to place the process under supervision by competent authorities and to make it fairer, more efficient, and politically acceptable. For some proponents, this means that the privatization strategy should recognize the ownership claims of managers and workers by granting them concessions that are structured both to clarify the ownership rights of insiders and to persuade them (and possibly other claimants) to cooperate with and actively support formal privatization. Proposals to grant workers a substantial block of shares in their firms at the moment of their conversion into joint stock companies (corporatization or commercialization) are an example of this type of policy.[26]

The basic legal framework of privatization in Russia has been elaborated in stages, beginning in July 1991 with a law on the privatization of state enterprises,[27] continuing in December 1991 with the "Basic Provisions of the Privatization Program"[28] and supplementary guidelines on various elements of the program,[29] and concluding in June 1992 with the approval by the Russian Supreme Soviet of a set of amendments to the 1991 privatization law[30] and a comprehensive state program for privatization.[31] The stated intent of the original privatization program was to stop the process of "nomenklatura privatization" by putting into place uniform and transparent procedures designed to ensure that state enterprises are sold only through competitive processes, such as auctions.[32] The program has been attacked by advocates of employee ownership for slighting the interests of workers.[33] Nevertheless, the program tacitly acknowledges the process of spontaneous privatization by building in significant concessions for managers and workers. Subsequent amendments to the program have reinforced this policy.

For small enterprises such as shops, the program ensures that management-employee buyouts will be an important method of privatization by establishing procedures that favor insiders. Small enterprises are to be auctioned off or sold through competitive tenders, in which nonprice criteria are considered.[34] If workers win ownership, they are entitled to a 30 percent discount on the sale price and a one-year deferment of payment. In addition, enterprises are permitted to set up privatization funds out of net profits and incentive funds to buy enterprises.[35] As a result of such concessions, 42 percent of the shops sold at a pilot auction held in Nizhny Novgorod in April 1992 were purchased by those who work in them.[36] Further, whereas the original provisions of the program banned competitions and auctions with fewer than two participants, the amended rules allow enterprises to be sold to their workers if they are the only bidder.[37]

For large enterprises to be privatized through corporatization, the program seeks to prevent the complete entrenchment of managers by requiring that the enterprises be converted only into open joint stock companies with tradable shares and boards of directors.[38] Under a planned mass privatization program, each citizen of the Russian Federation will receive a voucher entitling him or her to purchase shares in state enterprises either directly or through an intermediary investment fund.[39] There are, however, generous concessions to the claims of insiders. To begin with, workers receive 10 percent of the proceeds from the sale of shares in their enterprises, with the exception of shares sold to members of the workers' collective themselves. Beyond the right to share in the proceeds from privatization, each enterprise is required to choose one of three options for granting privileges to members of the enterprise work force.[40]

Under the first option, workers receive, free of charge, 25 percent of the shares, up to a limit of 20 times the minimum monthly wage per worker. While the shares are immediately tradable, they are preferred, or initially nonvoting. In addition, workers have the right to purchase another 10 percent of voting shares for vouchers and cash at a 30 percent discount of their face value and with payment deferred for up to three years. Managers can purchase 5 percent of the shares at face value using vouchers or cash.[41] The idea is to give workers and managers incentives to cooperate with and support the privatization process.

The remaining 60 percent of the shares will be sold to outside shareholders for a combination of cash and vouchers. Ideally, a controlling stake of up to 50 percent of the shares will be sold in a single block to a "strategic investor," which may be a foreign company, mainly through auctions or tenders. The final 10 percent of the shares will be offered to the public exclusively for vouchers. By transferring an appreciable stake in the enterprise to a key investor, Russian privatization officials hope to ensure that owners will have sufficient incentives and power to exercise effective oversight of enterprise management. In addition, state officials can counter the effects of the voucher system by dispersing ownership among a large number of shareholders. To this end, voucher holders can exchange their vouchers for shares in private mutual funds, which in turn can use the vouchers to bid for a controlling block of shares in firms.

The original "Basic Provisions of the Privatization Program" provided only for this first option, which was designed to prevent workers from gaining control of their enterprises before they are privatized. A second option, giving employees the right to buy control of their enterprises, was added in response to pressure from managers and workers. If a two-thirds majority of the work force votes in favor of this second option, workers can purchase 51 percent of the enterprise's capital through closed subscription. The price per share is determined according to a methodology developed by the Russian State Property Committee. Under this plan, workers can pay for up to 50 percent of their shares with vouchers, but they forfeit their rights to the free distribution of shares and the purchase of shares on preferential terms that are provided under the first option. The remaining balance of shares will be sold to outside shareholders, including a 10 percent tranche auctioned to small investors exclusively for vouchers.

Under the third option, a group of employees assumes responsibility for executing the enterprise privatization plan and for preventing the enterprise from going bankrupt by obtaining the consent of the workers' collective to conclude a corresponding contract for a term not to exceed one year. Upon successful fulfillment of the contract, the group members are given the right (an option) to purchase 20 percent of the shares of the enterprise at face value. If the group fails to fulfill the contract, this right is forfeited. While the contract is in effect, the group has the right to vote 20 percent of the shares belonging to the property fund. Under this option, all the enterprise workers, including the group members, can purchase simple shares composing 20 percent of the charter capital, up to a limit of 20 times the minimum monthly wage per worker, at a 30 percent discount of the face value and with a deferred payment of three years. The balance of shares is again to be sold to outside shareholders.

Privatization in Russia is further complicated by conflicts among different levels of government (city, oblast, and central) over control of state enterprises and by the existence of ethnic republics that have asserted ownership claims to enterprises located in their territories. The privatization program assigns to local governments the right to privatize small enterprises,[42] but the governments could use their ownership rights to derail privatization.[43] A full discussion of this issue is beyond the scope of this chapter.[44] It is worth noting, however, that the Russian program attempts to induce the various levels of government to carry out privatization by buying them out with a large share of the privatization proceeds.[45]

The legal framework of privatization in Ukraine comprises a package of privatization laws passed by the Ukrainian parliament in March 1992[46] and the State Privatization Program approved by the parliament the follow-

ing July.[47] As in the case of Russia, the extent to which managers and
workers should be allowed to become the owners of the enterprises in
which they work has aroused considerable controversy in Ukraine. The
laws on the privatization of state enterprises reflect the bias against worker
ownership held by the officials who drafted them and are much less generous in providing benefits to workers and managers than even the original
Russian privatization program. But as a result of an amendment introduced
into the State Privatization Program by the Ukrainian parliament, the privatization process may prove to be more favorable to managers and workers
than the drafters of the privatization laws intended.[48]

Under the privatization laws, small enterprises are to be sold on a competitive basis through auctions and tenders. Unlike their Russian counterparts, however, Ukrainian workers do not get a discount on the sale price in
purchasing their enterprises at auctions or tenders. The primary concession
to employees of small enterprises is the right to make payments under an
installment plan over a period of up to three years. Employees have a preferential right to purchase the enterprise over other bidders, but only under
the condition that all other terms are equal.

Employees of large enterprises have the preferential right to purchase
at face value an amount of shares equal to the value of the privatization
voucher to be issued to each employee and up to one-half the value of the
voucher, using their own funds. Any additional shares will have to be purchased on the same terms available to outsiders. Since it is unlikely that
workers will choose to invest all their vouchers, together with a substantial
portion of their savings, in their own enterprises, the possibility that large
enterprises will be privatized with sizable employee share ownership seems
remote. Even if they were to pool together all their vouchers, Ukrainian
workers probably would not be able to afford to buy the 25 percent block of
shares in their enterprises that Russian workers receive free of charge.

While these provisions of the privatization laws remain in effect, an
amendment introduced into the State Privatization Program by the
Ukrainian parliament has confused the situation by removing previous
restrictions on the power of workers' collectives to lease their enterprises.
In conjunction with a law on leasing passed by the Ukrainian parliament in
April 1992, this amendment could make it extremely difficult for the
Ukrainian government to prevent workers' collectives from bypassing the
privatization laws and leasing out their enterprises directly.[49] Since the law
on leasing contains a buyout option that must be exercised within three
years of signing the lease, it is conceivable that this amendment would
enable Ukrainian workers to circumvent the obstacles to buying control of
their enterprises that are built into the privatization laws. There is also a
danger that the confusion created by the apparent contradictions between
the privatization laws and the State Privatization Program could delay and
ultimately derail the privatization process.

Structure and Strategy

The most interesting result of our interviews concerns the differences between managerial strategies and the meaning of spontaneous privatization at three types of state firms: former all-Union enterprises, republican enterprises, and local government enterprises. The most important distinction between enterprises appears to be their initial structure in the sense of the bureaucratic jurisdiction under which they operated before the dissolution of the Soviet Union.

The primary reasons for this systematic variation appear to be differences in endowments and in the way state control disintegrated. Former all-Union enterprises are larger, with more labor and capital, and often have a more diversified production line. Furthermore, direct bureaucratic control over their operations began to weaken in 1989 and had almost completely disappeared by the end of 1991. By now the strongest firms have become effectively independent.

In contrast, republican enterprises are still subject to bureaucratic control. These firms are medium-sized, have more specialized production, and more of them have remained within reorganized hierarchies. Finally, local government enterprises tend to be small and subject to a great deal of detailed bureaucratic supervision. Most of these firms have retained the same hierarchies as before.

Former All-Union Enterprises

Before perestroika, most all-Union enterprises were subordinate to three tiers of hierarchical control: ministry, main directorate (*glavk*), and *ob"edinenie*. The ministry controlled all enterprises in its general area, the *glavk* was responsible for a group of related enterprises under the ministry, and an *ob"edinenie* consisted of a main enterprise and several subsidiaries. All enterprises in an *ob"edinenie* were usually involved in the same production process.

Most all-Union managers report that between 1989 and 1991 their ministries had either been abolished or fused with other ministries. By the spring of 1991, these enterprises were under the control not of a ministry but of an all-Union concern, association, or *ob"edinenie*. These all-Union organizations were, as a rule, composed of all the enterprises that once belonged to a particular *glavk,* although some were composed of enterprises from different *glavki* and even from different ministries. Managers report that while in principle they were supposed to join these concerns "voluntarily," they were not really given a choice—the responsible authorities in Moscow simply declared that a particular concern was in control.

According to our interviewees, these interrepublican organizations operated only up to November 1991, when, on the orders of the Ukrainian government, all hierarchical links between enterprises in Ukraine and controlling organizations in Moscow were broken.

Former all-Union enterprises have had to reregister with an appropriate committee (the new name for a ministry) of the Ukrainian government, and although it is evident that the new Ukrainian committees would like to be influential, they are still very inexperienced, understaffed, and ineffective. In particular, these Ukrainian bureaucrats are not capable of supplying firms with resources such as intermediate goods, machinery, and hard currency at the level previously provided through Moscow. As a result, they have little effective control over former all-Union enterprises, and managers of these firms have both enormous freedom and complete responsibility for their enterprises.

Given this dramatic, politically induced change in structure, how have managers responded? We find one of two distinct managerial goals in former all-Union firms: reintegrate the firm in some form of hierarchy, or achieve full independence for the firm.[50] Each goal involves a different set of actions, and each can be described accurately as a separate strategy. Furthermore, within each of the two strategies there are a number of variants and each of these implies a different role for spontaneous privatization.

Hierarchy. Some managers have reacted to the collapse of all-Union ministries by attempting to rebuild hierarchical structures from below, involving either vertical or horizontal integration of production. According to the managers' precise goals for this new structure, an appropriate form of spontaneous privatization—a new contract and control rights structure—is selected.

Several companies we interviewed are trying to vertically integrate within one firm—both upstream and downstream—the entire chain of production for a good. Such integration usually is not attempted for the whole range of an enterprise's products but rather for a particularly profitable product or subgroup of products. For example, a firm that manufactures agricultural machinery has entered into an association with several producers and consumers of potato harvesting equipment. The director stated that this move is intended to ensure a steady flow of inputs and outputs. Likewise, a factory that manufactures machine tools has joined with its suppliers and customers to develop a laminating technology that was previously manufactured only in enterprises outside Ukraine. This new organization is explicitly intended to deal with the effects of trade disruption between Ukraine and other former republics.

These organizations are based on new—and often implicit—contracts between firms. The organizations are usually new property forms that have unclear de jure rights. However, there is always a related reallocation of residual control rights over relevant parts of participating enterprises. Someone has to decide how to deal with unforeseen contingencies, and there is no way these decisions can be made by the same person as before, because the old control structures no longer exist. This is spontaneous privatization.

The second type of hierarchical strategy involves the creation of new organizations that horizontally integrate firms producing the same goods or related goods. These new horizontal organizations come in three main forms.[51] The first unites enterprises that produce complementary goods and enables them to increase their combined product range. For example, a large military enterprise in Kiev that produces voltage-measuring equipment has already pursued an aggressive policy of diversification into kitchen appliances. The management now wants to expand into production of an entire range of domestic appliances, including goods for which it simply does not have the technological know-how or production capacity. At the beginning of 1992, it was negotiating with other firms that already produce electric appliances in order to form an alliance that would sell newly produced equipment under one brand name.

An example of a different type of horizontal reorganization is provided by the electronics sector in Ukraine, in which 145 enterprises have agreed to form a holding company with the aim of duplicating some of the tasks previously handled by the ministry. As a manager in one participating firm said, "We are uniting to survive." The holding company will attempt to coordinate the distribution of supplies that are hard to obtain, organize some parts of the production chain, and lobby the Ukrainian government.[52] Residual control rights have been reassigned again—in this case, ending up partly with the holding company.

A third type of new horizontal organization unites enterprises producing the same type of goods to form a cartel. These cartels usually involve a small number of firms that together account for most of a particular good's production in Ukraine. In Ukraine, for example, most of the larger enterprises that produce printing presses and book-binding machinery have formed such an organization. Their aim is to have a small staff that will coordinate their production, handle negotiations with suppliers, and represent their interests to the government. A similar organization has been formed by enterprises that produce electrical cable in Ukraine. This organization was formed when the Ukrainian factories were forced to disengage from a similar all-Union association headquartered in Moscow. The aim—as stated to us in interviews—is to coordinate production and to present a united front to the government when asking for resources.[53]

Independence. The strategy of independence is completely different from any version of the hierarchical strategy. Managers who want independence seek to retain all residual control rights at the level of their firm. Their interaction with the outside world will be through arm's-length contracts and market transactions rather than participating in an organization that has any kind of hierarchical structure.

As a rule, three conditions must exist for an enterprise's management to choose an independent strategy. The first is that top managers (directors) must want to free themselves from bureaucratic interference. If enterprise directors are afraid of operating by themselves, they will instead choose some form of hierarchical strategy. Second, workers and lower-level managers (i.e., the whole "work collective") must agree with the strategy. The legal arrangements through which a firm can gain independence are actually agreements between some branch of the state and the work collective. Interestingly, we have not yet encountered a single case in which managers were unable to convince workers to support their strategy. The third condition for an independent strategy is that the enterprise produce a good that is in high demand and for which the supplies are secure. It is really no surprise that firms that begin with a stronger market position are more likely to pursue the strategy of independence.

Former all-Union enterprises seeking independence can be grouped in three different categories, according to their progress towards this goal. The first and smallest group includes enterprises that have been privatized de jure because they already have complete independence. These enterprises usually started an active dismantling of their ties to the state in 1989 or 1990. They have all found ways to avoid, or receive an exemption from, the November 1990 decree that imposed a moratorium on Ukrainian state enterprises changing their property form. A leading example in Kiev is a factory that produces agricultural machinery. The enterprise was leased "with the right to buy" from its all-Union ministry by the workers' collective in September 1990. According to our interviewee, the firm was the first enterprise within this ministry to be leased, a step that was made easier by the fact that officials in Moscow felt the enterprise was "far away" in the provinces.[54] Within three months of signing the lease agreement, the managers had maneuvered to buy the firm from the ministry.[55]

The managers of this firm wanted to become independent primarily because there is a strong demand for their output both from state firms and new private farmers. High demand has put the firm in a position of strength vis-à-vis its customers. In 1992, this position enabled the firm to demand payment through barter rather than in money because the accelerating inflation in Ukraine made monetary payments relatively unattractive. In addition, this firm has an established export market, which enables it to purchase inputs and technology, using hard currency, from suppliers both inside and outside the former Soviet Union. Relations with its traditional suppliers—most of whom are located in Russia—have become more difficult, but the firm plans to diversify away from Soviet suppliers. For example, it is planning two joint ventures that will assemble foreign-designed excavators and use primarily foreign-made components. The firm simply does not need to cooperate on a hierarchical basis with other Russian or Ukrainian firms.

The second group of firms seeking independence consists of enterprises that are already leased from the state by the workers' collectives. Many enterprises with this status signed a lease agreement that actually gave them the right to buy the enterprise. However, the 1990 Ukrainian moratorium on property change has prevented most outright purchases, so the majority of leased enterprises are still formally owned by the state.

Even though immediate purchase is not possible, these lease agreements allow gradual transfer of ownership to the workers' collective. According to the provisions of the all-Union law on leased enterprises, after the lease agreement is signed any new assets belong to the workers' collective—even if they are financed from retained earnings. Therefore, in most leased enterprises a significant percentage of the assets is already the property of the workers, and in some cases the workers' collective now owns as much as 50 percent.

Furthermore, we have interviewed managers in several leased enterprises who claim they have been able to have their rent payments included as part of their taxes—while paying the same level of taxes as equivalent firms that are still state property. In effect, these enterprises make no additional payment for the lease because they are able to be more independent than before. These managers believe it will be easier eventually to become fully private if the firm is already on a lease.

The third group of independence-oriented enterprises includes firms that have neither privatized nor gone on lease but have simply found themselves under very weak control from above and have not attempted to strengthen hierarchical links with other firms. Most directors of those former all-Union enterprises, which are still 100 percent state property, report that the Ukrainian bodies set up to control them are inexperienced and understaffed and are simply not capable of helping them. This is now the default strategy of most managers. If they cannot think of any new ideas, their firms drift alone.

A large firm that produces consumer electronic equipment is a good example. Formerly under one of the nine central military ministries, this factory joined an interrepublican concern in 1990. However, its relations with the concern, which included all enterprises previously under one *glavk,* were much looser than its ties with the ministry. The concern did not give as many orders or decrees as the ministry and was unable to help as much in procuring inputs. After the August 1991 coup attempt, the directors of this firm were not sure what steps to take. Their membership in the concern was quickly made illegal, but they were unable to find anyone within the Ukrainian bureaucracy who was responsible for their enterprise. Independence for this enterprise was due to the lack of other perceived options.

An important aside concerns the interpretation of the formation of banks. In this case, firms apparently create a new institution and allow it some residual control rights, but these rights are strictly limited. We have encountered no case in which banks exerted effective control over either a firm that provides capital, usually in the form of equity, or a firm that obtains capital—most often as short-term debt. New banks constitute a new form of contract that does not require firms to give up existing control rights over what they do. This may be part of the reason for the current banking boom.[56]

In summary, looking at the evidence from all-Union enterprises, we see that different strategies often lie behind seemingly similar forms of spontaneous privatization. The most important distinction is between forms of spontaneous privatization that are the result of constructing new hierarchical structures and forms that are used to free firms from the remnants of old hierarchies.

What sets former all-Union enterprises apart is the permanent break in previous links with their supervising bureaucrats, such as those officials in Moscow who no longer have power in Ukraine. It is impossible for these enterprises to follow a strategy of rebuilding the former hierarchy. At the same time, many of these firms are large, have modern equipment, and produce a wide range of goods. For managers of these firms, nearly all forms of spontaneous privatization offer remunerative new opportunities.

Former Republican Enterprises
Republican enterprises—that is, firms that were always under the jurisdiction of Ukrainian ministries—now face a similar situation to that experienced by all-Union enterprises in 1990–1991. Ukrainian ministries have lost some control, but in many cases the bureaucracy retains power over important aspects of enterprise operation, such as the way in which control rights are reallocated. Furthermore, almost all Ukrainian ministries have become state committees or concerns and are trying desperately to find ways in which they can remain viable, even after the full privatization promised by the government. Clearly, for these enterprises, the previous owners—that is, the bureaucrats who formerly had residual control—are still trying to exercise their property rights.

In addition to the two options for all-Union enterprises, there is a third strategy for republican firms: Some managers are choosing (or being compelled) to rebuild the previous hierarchies that governed their firms. Other managers pursue the independent strategies discussed in the context of all-Union enterprises, but we have not encountered any republican enterprises trying to build new hierarchies for themselves. It is possible that the strategy of restructuring the old hierarchy dominates the strategy of constructing a new hierarchy.[57]

One republican enterprise strategy involves building a hierarchy that is essentially a renamed *glavk* and in which previous ties are maintained and cross-subsidies are still very evident. In these cases, the key appears to be that the ministry has been able to keep its enterprises united by continuing to provide them with inputs. An excellent example is the Ukrainian River Fleet, which is a new organization of enterprises that were previously under one ministry. Legally, this new organization is an MGO[58] that controls the most important products—cargo transport and fleet maintenance—and leaves decisions about other products to the enterprises, which are allowed to keep a much larger share of their profits than when they were under the ministry. The MGO has access to hard currency and has subsidiary organizations that supply raw materials, consumer goods, and imported machinery and that can find customers and sell abroad. In this case, the entire previous system of input provision and output coordination seems to have held—the only change is that some direct links with Moscow-based enterprises have been broken.[59]

Other hierarchies have been forcibly created from above, but the other cases we encountered are not as successful as the Ukrainian River Fleet. For example, we interviewed the manager of a factory that had joined the Uksotzhilmash concern.[60] The enterprise pays dues, and in return the concern has promised to provide contacts both with suppliers and customers. However, the manager reported that these promises are not being fulfilled. The manager believes his firm does not need the concern, but he fears that leaving the concern may bring some form of retribution. This is a clear case of an unwelcome ministerial strategy being forced on a firm, with the result that managers are unable to choose their own strategy.

The Ukrmestprom concern is a similar case. Several interviewees said they still are being helped by this concern and there is no need to leave the organization. However, managers from other factories that belong to this concern, including a firm that is near total collapse, complained they were forced to join the concern against their wishes, and, since the concern has not been able to fulfill any of its commitments, they do not wish to continue paying dues. According to the managers, nothing can be achieved through working with the concern. In sum, like many similar organizations, Ukrmestprom seems to have promised a great deal and delivered very little.

Since the beginning of 1992, many enterprises have realized that republican ministries can no longer provide inputs. Furthermore, the recent price increases have eliminated almost all shortages. Therefore many enterprises, even those that have joined new hierarchies led by the former ministries, are questioning whether working closely with former ministries is necessary. Some of these enterprises are thinking about another strategy— choosing to build their own new hierarchies—but in the spring and summer of 1992, our interviews indicated that managers of republican enterprises had not yet accomplished much in that direction.

However, a significant number of enterprises are already trying to follow a strategy of more independence. Interestingly, there are some cases in which the ministry itself has pushed its enterprises towards independence. The best example is provided by the Ministry of Wood Products, which has actively encouraged entire *ob"edineniya* to go on lease and, within each *ob"edinenie,* has pressured enterprises to lease themselves from the head enterprise. The ministry is trying to change its own strategy by formally giving away control rights that it cannot exercise in the hope of being able to establish better contractual relationships with firms.[61]

An interesting result of such changes is that the strategy of independence often involves breaking ties within an *ob"edinenie*. This fact became evident when we interviewed several managers from different enterprises of one large *ob"edinenie*. By the spring of 1992, all the "daughter" enterprises were breaking away to become independent. This trend countered the wishes of managers in the head enterprise, but, because they no longer effectively control the supply of inputs, there is nothing they can do to prevent the breakup. The managers of the head enterprise were angry and extremely bitter, partly because they had helped the affiliate enterprises obtain modern equipment, while their own firm has only outdated machines. The break-up of *ob"edineniya* appears to be occurring throughout Ukraine because many affiliates no longer want or need to allow the head enterprise to exercise residual control rights. These head enterprises no longer have access to state orders (*goszakazy*) and state-controlled supplies, and without these they have no power. From our interviews, it appears the stronger bargaining power in the breakups lies with managers who are in direct control of production.

As ministerial power in Ukraine continues to disintegrate, it seems likely that republican firms will develop strategies more similar to those of the previous all-Union enterprises. Specifically, we would expect them to introduce further reorganizations of contracts and property rights that will facilitate the creation of new hierarchies in some cases and newly independent firms in others.

Local Enterprises
We also conducted interviews with six enterprises controlled by the Kiev City Council and involved in a range of activities.[62] For these enterprises, changes in the previous hierarchy have been minimal, and they are still funded directly by the city council. By the summer of 1992, despite extremely adverse conditions, most of these firms still exhibited no managerial strategy other than trying to persuade bureaucrats in the old structure to do their job "better."[63]

For example, managers in several construction materials firms reported almost no change in the substance of their supervisory organizations in recent years, although some names have been altered. They all have few suppliers and still receive production orders and supplies through the city council. As a result, they are now in a difficult situation—there was no money in the local government budget for construction between January and March 1992, which brought the firms to a near standstill.

The firms also report a very low level of barter deals; apparently they are not allowed to barter because bartering remains the jurisdiction of supervisory bureaucrats. Consequently, there is a clear difference between these firms and another firm with the same production profile that was previously under republican jurisdiction control. The latter pays for up to 40 percent of its supplies through barter and demands that 25 percent of its customers pay with barter goods. In this case, the Ukrainian ministry is now less powerful than its republican predecessor and has been replaced to some extent by "market relations," that is, by barter.[64]

The locally controlled construction materials firms can now sell goods directly to the population. Two of the interviewed firms sell 15 percent of their goods directly, while one sells 10 percent of its goods, and the other three sell less than 4 percent. However, these firms apparently do not view this new activity with enthusiasm. One interviewee stated that his firm was not interested in direct sales because its managers had to find for themselves where to sell the products, as the city council did not help in this regard. Unfortunately, even the more aggressive firms have found little demand for their products since January 1992.[65]

Managers in locally controlled firms have not expressed a desire to leave or reorganize the existing hierarchical structures. In one firm, the interviewee was afraid that if orders from the city were to stop, the entire enterprise would have to close. Another manager was completely happy with the old arrangements, and in several cases, a manager said that while his supervisory organization had not lived up to its promises, he did not want to leave. This is a striking contrast to the attitudes and actions of managers both in former all-Union and republican enterprises.

Managers in the city-controlled firms have not had time to develop a strategy, and they have no idea how spontaneous privatization could help them survive. These enterprises are smaller than all-Union or republican firms; they are dependent on state orders and now face serious problems. Unless they are lucky enough to be in a sector that continues to receive large subsidies, the firms will struggle. At this time, their managers appear unable to cope with their massive problems.

Conclusion

Perestroika implied a move toward significant change in the structure of industrial firms in the former Soviet Union. The reformers' original intention was to decentralize decision-making and to improve the efficiency of resource use, but in practice central control over scarce goods weakened rapidly and there was significant disruption throughout the economy. Enterprises faced structural changes that allowed, encouraged, and perhaps even forced managers to develop new strategies. These strategies in turn involved further changes in firms' structures and contributed to the destabilization of the macroeconomy and the weakening of the supervisory bureaucracy.[66] This series of events was the origin of the process known as spontaneous privatization.

The evidence presented in this chapter indicates that spontaneous privatization takes many different forms. There is an important link between the initial structure of a firm—meaning how it was governed under the old system of bureaucratic control—and the subsequent development of new managerial strategies and further structural changes. Recent changes in firms' structures further indicate that the reassignment of residual control rights is an essential part of the process through which managers revise the structures of their firms. Spontaneous privatization is much more than the acquisition of property by managers.

Although our findings are tentative, we find strong evidence that managerial strategies differ systematically across various types of firms in Kiev. Managers of former all-Union enterprises seem more likely to pursue independent strategies, probably because they are completely cut off from their former bureaucratic supervisors. Managers in republican enterprises are frequently involved in rebuilding hierarchical relationships, often involving erstwhile bureaucrats in some form. Managers in local government–controlled firms seem to have no new ideas and no strategy beyond maintaining their previous relationships. The differences in strategies can be attributed to variation in enterprises' endowments and prior experience.

Previous all-Union enterprises encountered new operating conditions earlier than other firms and have used their longer experience to devise new strategies. These enterprises also tend to be bigger and better endowed with a wide variety of resources. Republican enterprises have some advantages as well because they produce consumer goods and are less dependent on trade with Russia. Enterprises under local government authority are probably in the worst position. They are relatively small, not well endowed with resources, and have very little experience in coping by themselves with difficult economic circumstances.

On the whole, our evidence offers a positive message. Despite the continued instability of the macroeconomy and the lack of a clear legal framework for state firms, our interviews reveal that managers are finding ways for their firms to survive—often by altering the structure of their firms to suit their changed circumstances. Given time, many of these managers will probably be able to do well. The lack of independent thinking in republican and local enterprises may be due more to a lack of experience than to a lack of ability.

However, there are dangers in the current situation. The new Russian and Ukrainian privatization laws will reduce the scope for spontaneous privatization, with the intention of establishing a process better controlled by the government. The primary motivation for this legislation is that spontaneous privatization provides direct benefits only to a privileged set of people—those who already work in good state enterprises. But if government-led privatization does not work, or if it proceeds slowly, then the ability of firms to continue their adjustments would be weakened. If the reallocation of control rights is not allowed, this restriction will severely limit the ways in which managers can rewrite contracts, and it will probably rule out some of the best strategies.

Furthermore, the attempt to impose uniform government privatization plans on all firms will likely meet with opposition. Managers have their own ideas about how privatization should proceed. If managers and workers already have entrenched positions in firms, the most probable outcome would be a standoff in which neither managers nor the government can take positive action. In that situation, the future of the state sector would be bleak.

Most likely—in order to get results—government-directed privatizations eventually will validate what has occurred at the firm level, with the result that managers will be strengthened and further entrenched. If this validation occurs, there would not be effective outside control over the operation of firms, and managers would receive all control rights. What will be the production and investment decisions of managers who cannot be replaced? Will they behave more like owners or like unsupervised agents? Only time and further research will tell.

Notes

This paper is the product of a research project funded by a grant to Simon Johnson from the National Council for Soviet and East European Research. Santiago Eder's participation was made possible by financial support provided by the Soros Foundation to the Project on Economic Reform in Ukraine at Harvard University's Kennedy School.

1. Leyla Boulton, "Privatization Chief Takes on Nomenklatura," *Financial Times,* January 23, 1992, p. 3.

2. Louis Uchitelle, "Stealing Toward Russian Capitalism," *New York Times,* March 8, 1992, section 3, pp. 1, 6.

3. Sanford Grossman and Oliver Hart, "The Costs and Benefits of Ownership: A Theory of Vertical and Lateral Integration," *Journal of Political Economy* 94 (1986): 691–719.

4. This fact does not imply that the form and content of contracts are imposed arbitrarily. Instead, selection of contract form and the allocation of residual control rights should be viewed as interconnected decisions made by those involved, particularly by managers.

Note that our terminology is slightly different from that of Grossman and Hart, who refer both to residual control rights and ex ante specified rights as contracts. However, the basic conceptual framework is the same.

5. Oliver Hart and John Moore, "Property Rights and the Nature of the Firm," *Journal of Political Economy* 98 (1990): 119–158.

6. In most cases these rights are acquired also in the name of workers. As there appear to have been few cases of open conflict between managers and workers over spontaneous privatization, it is not misleading to use the term "managers" as

an abbreviation. In addition, the available evidence suggests managers are the driving force behind spontaneous privatization.

Note that our definition in no way considers the price managers pay to obtain assets. This is because under present circumstances it is all but impossible to determine the "true" value of assets, so a value-based definition cannot help clarify what is occurring.

7. The issue of who precisely exercised residual control rights under the old system remains controversial. Clearly managers did have some discretion, and the precise allocation of control rights fluctuated over time. Nevertheless, it does appear true that the old system was characterized by a great deal of ad hoc bureaucratic interference in firms. Put differently, when unforeseen contingencies occurred, it was the bureaucrats who had the right to make decisions. For further discussion of these points, see Peter Rutland, "Order Out of Chaos? The Corporatization of Russian Industry," unpublished manuscript, 1992; and Simon Johnson and Heidi Kroll, "Managerial Strategies for Spontaneous Privatization," *Soviet Economy* 7, 4 (July–September 1991): 281–316.

8. These concepts are present but not emphasized in the streamlined analysis of Grossman and Hart, "The Costs and Benefits of Ownership."

9. Alfred D. Chandler, Jr., *Strategy and Structure: Chapters in the History of the Industrial Enterprise* (Cambridge, Mass.: The MIT Press, 1990), p. 13.

10. We are using the term *strategy* in the broader but more vague form found in the empirical literature analyzing corporate decision-making, such as Michael E. Porter, "How Competitive Forces Shape Strategy," *Harvard Business Review* (March–April 1979): 137–145, rather than the more formal definition of game theory. There is a large gap between the two.

11. Chandler, *Strategy and Structure.*

12. Internal changes were discussed at more length in Johnson and Kroll, "Managerial Strategies for Spontaneous Privatization."

13. In effect, we have broadened the scope of phenomena that can be studied using the framework of Grossman and Hart, "The Costs and Benefits of Ownership," although at the cost of some loss of precision.

A formal model of spontaneous privatization in the former Soviet Union would need to alter at least two assumptions of Grossman and Hart. The first is that there is already an initial endowment of assets, so it is only necessary to determine the efficient selection of contracts and residual control rights. The second is that de facto control rights are allocated in line with de jure ownership. Neither of these assumptions is appealing in the context of the former Soviet Union: Part of the spontaneous privatization process concerns the acquisition of an initial endowment, and the current legal situation is such that there is often an important difference between de jure and de facto rights.

14. Note that this survey includes construction firms but excludes agriculture, trade, and other "nonmaterial" services. However, we have conducted a separate study of banking in Kiev (Simon Johnson, Heidi Kroll, and Mark Horton, "New Banks in the Former Soviet Union: How Do They Operate?" in Anders Aslund and Richard Layard [eds.], *Changing the Economic System in Russia* [New York: St. Martin's Press, 1992]), and we are currently writing a study of farming.

15. We have also conducted interviews with managers from elsewhere in Ukraine and from other former republics, and a great deal of our understanding of spontaneous privatization is based on conversations with local privatization consultants. However, the examples used in this paper were all encountered during our interview work in Kiev.

16. We now have interviewers operating in four other Ukrainian cities.

However, it is still too early to draw any conclusions from this extension of our project.

17. Our research also finds that spontaneous privatization can be a way to achieve changes within firms. We have reported at length elsewhere on this aspect of the process (Johnson and Kroll, "Managerial Strategies for Spontaneous Privatization"). We should note that in the spring and summer of 1992 in Ukraine the only real path for de jure transfer of assets to private hands was through the creation of "small enterprises," but many managers do not like this strategy because it also involves internal decentralization.

18. Ronald Coase, "The Nature of the Firm," *Economica* 4 (1937): 386–405.

19. Oliver Williamson, *The Economic Institutions of Capitalism* (New York: Free Press, 1985).

20. Johnson and Kroll, "Managerial Strategies for Spontaneous Privatization."

21. The description of the various forms of spontaneous privatization draws generally on Johnson and Kroll, "Managerial Strategy for Spontaneous Privatization"; Sergei Shatalov, "Privatization in the Soviet Union: The Beginnings of a Transition," Policy Research Working Papers, The World Bank, Washington, D.C. (November 1991); Uchitelle, "Stealing Toward Russian Capitalism"; and Andrei Shleifer and Robert W. Vishny, "Privatization in Russia: First Steps," National Bureau of Economic Research Conference on Transition in Eastern Europe, February 1992. For insight into a similar process in Poland, see David Lipton and Jeffrey D. Sachs, "Privatization in Eastern Europe: The Case of Poland," *Brookings Papers on Economic Activity* 2 (1990): 293–341.

22. Over 86 percent of the 10,696 small enterprises established in the Russian Federation by October 1991 were owned by the state; almost 13 percent were based on some form of collective ownership; and only 39, or less than 1 percent, were owned by private citizens (*Ekonomika i zhizn'* 49, supplement [December 1991]: 1).

23. For more detailed discussions of this process, see Heidi Kroll, "Monopoly and Transition to the Market," *Soviet Economy* 7, 2 (April–June 1991): 143–174; Rutland, "Order Out of Chaos?"; Bruce G. Knecht, "From Soviet Minister to Corporate Chief," *New York Times Magazine,* January 26, 1992, pp. 24–28; and Stephen Fortescue, "The Restructuring of Soviet Industrial Ministries Since 1985," in Anders Aslund (ed.), *Market Socialism or the Restoration of Capitalism* (Cambridge: Cambridge University Press, 1992), pp. 15–18.

24. Merton J. Peck and Thomas J. Richardson (eds.), *What Is to Be Done? Proposals for the Soviet Transition to the Market* (New Haven: Yale University Press, 1991), p. 160.

25. See, for example, Jeffrey D. Sachs, "Spontaneous Privatization: A Comment," *Soviet Economy* 7, 4 (July–September 1991): 317–321; János Kornai, "The Principle of Privatization in Eastern Europe," Harvard Institute of Economic Research, Discussion Paper no. 1567 (September 1991), p. 20; and Shleifer and Vishny, "Privatization in Russia." In a seminar presented at Harvard in 1992, Leszek Balcerowicz, former finance minister of Poland, endorsed insider privatizations as a means of speeding up privatization in Poland, although he acknowledged that this approach was not politically feasible in the early stage of the Polish reform process.

26. Unlike Sachs, "Spontaneous Privatization" (p. 320), or Shleifer and Vishny, "Privatization in Russia," Kornai, "The Principles of Privatization" (p. 22), does not advocate partial employee ownership as a strategy for regularizing spontaneous privatization, though he does not have any particular objection to a moderate form of it.

27. "O privatizatsii gosudarstvennykh i munitsipal'nykh predpriyatii v

RSFSR" (On the privatization of state and municipal enterprises in the RSFSR), *Ekonomika i zhizn'* 31 (July 1991): 15–17.

28. "Osnovnye polozheniya programy privatizatsii" (Basic provisions of the privatization program), *Rossiiskaya gazeta,* January 10, 1992, pp. 13–14.

29. The elements included methods for the valuation of enterprises ("Vremennye metodicheskie ukazaniya po otsenke stoimosti ob'ektov privatizatsii" [Temporary methodology for estimating the value of the objects of privatization], *Ekonomika i zhizn'* 7 [February 1992]: 18–19) and regulations for converting enterprises into open joint stock companies ("O preobrazovanie gosudarstvennykh i munitsipal'nykh predpriyatii v otkrytye aktsionernye obshchestva" [On the conversion of state and municipal enterprises into open joint stock companies], *Ekonomika i zhizn'* 8 [February 1992]: 19).

30. "O vnesenii izmenenii i dopolnenii v Zakon RSFSR 'O privatizatsii gosudarstvennykh i munitsipal'nykh predpriyatii v RSFSR'" (On the insertion of amendments and additions to the law of the RSFSR 'On the privatization of state and municipal enterprises in the RSFSR'), *Ekonomika i zhizn'* 29 (July 1992): 13–15.

31. "Gosudarstvennaya Programma privatizatsii gosudarstvennykh i munitsipal'nykh predpriyatti v Rossiiskoi Federatsii na 1992 god" (State program for the privatization of state and municipal enterprises in the Russian Federation for 1992), *Ekonomika i zhizn'* 29 (July 1992): 15–18.

32. Chairman of the State Property Committee Anatolii Chubais stated bluntly that the government intends "to change the nature of the process and to move away from the theft of state owned property" (Celestine Bohlen, "Russia Outlines a Program to Sell State-Owned Shops," *New York Times,* February 8, 1992 p. 4). Deputy Prime Minister Yegor Gaidar likewise characterized the spontaneous process already taking place as "privatization by robbery" (Moscow TASS International Service, 1100 GMT, December 30, 1991, translated in Foreign Broadcast Information Service, Daily Report: Soviet Union, December 30, 1991, p. 36). See also Boulton, "Privatization Chief Takes on Nomenklatura."

33. In an article published in the newspaper *Izvestiya* in February 1992, a group of prominent economists criticized the government program and proposed as an alternative the idea of giving away state enterprises to their workers free of charge up to a certain limit, and supplying them with credit to purchase the rest. L. Piyasheva et al., "Otday' besplatno: dokladnaya rossiiskomu prezidentu o naibolee razumnom sposobe privatizatsii" (Give it away free of charge: Report to the Russian president on the most rational method of privatization), *Izvestiya,* February 14, 1992, p. 3. Chairman of the State Property Committee Anatolii Chubais responded to the attack in a subsequent interview, "Daarovaya sobstvennost' ne sdelaet cheloveka khozyainom" (Free property does not make a person an owner), *Izvestiya,* February 26, 1992, p. 2.

34. Temporary statutes regulate auctions ("O privatizatsii gosudarstvennykh i munitsipal'nykh predpriyatii v Rossiiskoi Federatsii na auktsione" [On the privatization of state and municipal enterprises in the Russian Federation at auction], *Ekonomika i zhizn'* 9 [February 1992]: 17) and sales by competitive tender ("O privatizatsii gosudarstvennykh i munitsipal'nykh predpriyatii v Rossiiskoi Federatsii po konkursu" [On the privatization of state and municipal enterprises in the Russian Federation by competition], *Ekonomika i zhizn'* 10 [March 1992]: 18–19).

35. The use of enterprise profits and incentive funds for privatization is regulated by a temporary statute. "O poryadke ispol'zovaniya v 1992 godu pri privatizatsii sredstv fondov ekonomicheskogo stimulirovaniya i pribyli gosudarstvennykh i munitsipal'nykh predpriyatii" (On the procedure for using the incentive funds and

profits of state and municipal enterprises for privatization in 1992), *Ekonomika i zhizn'* 11 (March 1992): 17.

36. *The Economist,* April 11, 1992, p. 72. In Moscow, where the city government was given special dispensation to develop its own privatization program, auctions have been rejected in favor of selling shops to those who work in them for a nominal price. See "Privatizatsiya: pervye shagi" (Privatization: The first steps), *Economika i zhizn'* 14 (April 1992): 6–7; and Louis Uchitelle, "Attention Moscow Shoppers: Everything's on Sale," *New York Times,* July 26, 1992, p. 3. This approach amounts to simply rubber-stamping the process of spontaneous privatization.

37. *Kommersant'* 15 (April 6–13, 1992): 22.

38. Legislation enacted in July 1992 provides for the mandatory corporatization of every enterprise with more than 1,000 workers or a book value greater than 50 million rubles (with some exceptions) by November 1, 1992. "Ob organizatsionnykh merakh po preobrazovaniyu gosudarstvennykh predpriyatii, dobrovol'nykh ob"edinenii gosudarstvennykh predpriyatii v aktsionernye obshchestva" (On organizational measures for the conversion of state enterprises and voluntary amalgamations of state enterprises into joint stock companies), *Ekonomika i zhizn'* 28 (July 1992): 21; "O kommertsializatsii gosudarstvennykh predpriyatii s odnovremennym preobrazovaniem v aktsionernye obshchestva otkrytogo tipa" (On the commercialization of state enterprises with their simultaneous transformation into joint stock companies of the open type), *Ekonomika i zhizn'* 28 (July 1992): 21–23.

39. Legislation providing for a voucher scheme in the form of personal privatization accounts and deposits that citizens can use to purchase shares was enacted along with the July 1991 law on the privatization of state enterprises. "Ob imennykh privatizatsionnykh schetakh i vkladakh v RSFSR" (On personal privatization accounts and deposits in the RSFSR), *Ekonomika i zhizn'* 31 (July 1991): 15. Initially, the Yeltsin government postponed the voucher program until the end of 1992 on the grounds that it was too costly and administratively difficult to prepare and implement, but this decision was subsequently reversed, and distribution of the first tranche of vouchers was moved forward to the fourth quarter of 1992.

40. Apart from the text of the program itself, the description of the Russian privatization program draws on *The Economist,* July 18, 1992, p. 70.

41. As Uchitelle ("In Russia, Power to the Managers," *New York Times,* July 14, 1992 p. D2) emphasizes, since only one of every 3.5 shares going to workers has voting rights, while all of the managers' shares give them voting rights, the initial distribution of shares in the newly formed joint stock companies gives management effective control over company policies.

42. The division of state property among different levels of government is regulated by a decree of December 1991. "O razgranichenii gosudarstvenoi sobstvennosti v Rossiiskoi Federatsii na federal'nuyu sobstvennost', gosudarstvennuyu sobstvennost' respublik v sostave Rossiiskoi Federatsii, kraev, oblastei, avtonomnoi oblasti, avtonomnykh okrugov, gorodov Moskry i Sankt-Peterburga i munitsipal'nuyu sobstvenost'" (On the delineation of state property in the Russian Federation into federal property, state property of the republics within the Russian Federation, krais, oblasts, the autonomous oblast, autonomous regions, the cities of Moscow and St. Petersburg and municipal property), *Rossiiskaya gazeta,* January 11, 1992, p. 5.

43. A striking example is the dispute that arose between Russia and the republic of Tatarstan over ownership of KamAZ, Russia's largest truck manufacturer and one of the first state enterprises in the former Soviet Union to be converted into a joint stock company. The government of Tatarstan, where KamAZ is located, insist-

ed on being given a controlling stake of 25 percent of the joint stock company's shares, out of the 38 percent that belonged to the former Soviet Union. "Oksana Andreeva and Lev Ambinder" (Russia and Tatarstan fight over company's stock), *Commersant,* May 19, 1992, p. 13.

44. See Shleifer and Vishny, "Privatization in Russia," pp. 26–30, for an interesting discussion of the pitfalls inherent in local control of privatization.

45. For example, 50 percent of the proceeds from the sale of municipal property goes to local budgets. "Velikii peredel, ili o reforme sobstvennosti v SNG" (The great redistribution, or, on the subject of property reform in the CIS), *Ekonomika i zhizn'* 8 (February 1992): 1.

46. Law of Ukraine, "On privatization certificates"; "On the privatization of assets of state-owned enterprises"; and "On the privatization of small state enterprises (small privatization)," translated by the Project on Economic Reform in Ukraine, Harvard University (April 1992).

47. "State Program for the Privatization of the Property of State Enterprises," translated by Santiago Eder (July 1992).

48. Simon Johnson and Santiago Eder, "The Design of Small-Scale Privatization in Ukraine," revised version of paper presented at the Small-Scale Privatization, organized by the Institute for East-West Studies, Prague, June 11–13, 1992.

49. Johnson and Eder, "The Design of Small-Scale Privatization."

50. In principle, it should be possible for a multiproduct firm to pursue a hierarchical strategy for some goods and an independent strategy for others. However, we have not yet been able to identify this phenomenon empirically, and this may be because interviews with managers tend to bring out only what is foremost in the manager's mind. This issue needs further investigation.

51. This list is probably not exhaustive, but it reflects the extent of this phenomenon that we have observed so far.

52. The exact future role of these industry-wide organizations is rather unclear. The ability of any hierarchy to secure supplies and orders is rapidly waning and will probably continue to decline if the economic reform program succeeds and market clearing prices emerge for most types of inputs. It is probable that unless these broad intrasector alliances of the "unite-to-survive" type find a new role for themselves, they will prove to be only a passing phenomenon.

53. The future of such organizations will depend on the effectiveness of Ukrainian government antimonopoly policy. An antimonopoly law already exists, and there is a minister responsible for "destatization and antimonopoly," but there have not yet been any concrete results.

54. When the managers initially obtained a lease, they did not speak about their ultimate intention to purchase the firm because they feared the ministry would not cooperate.

55. The managers had to receive special permission from the Ukrainian government because of the general moratorium on property form changes. It probably helped that they wanted to break the firm's hierarchical ties with Moscow.

56. Johnson, Kroll, and Horton, "New Banks in the Former Soviet Union."

57. The reasoning behind this statement is that the costs of forming a new hierarchy may be higher than the costs of restructuring the old hierarchy—assuming it is costly to find new partners and negotiate new contractual agreements and control rights allocations. This theory seems reasonable. But another, stronger assumption is also required: that the benefits from new hierarchies are not much greater than the benefits from old hierarchies. This assumption needs further empirical investigation.

58. This choice of legal form is a little strange, because an MGO was supposed to be an appropriate de jure structure for an interbranch organization, which the River Fleet strictly is not. However, given the current legal confusion in Ukraine, this aberration represents only a minor curiosity.

59. How did this MGO succeed? This question requires further study, but it appears important that the director of each enterprise is a member of the MGO board, and through this board a real consensus has been built among directors. Furthermore, these enterprises together can constitute a powerful cartel that will control river cargo transport in Ukraine. The MGO also differs from other similar organizations because it appears to have more hard currency. Furthermore, there is support for this MGO at the highest political levels, and it appears likely parliament will give special permission to allow this MGO to be privatized de jure without being broken up.

60. This concern is one of the most blatant examples of an attempt to preserve the old power structure. In this case even the name did not change—the ministry was also Uksotzhilmash.

61. However, this is an unusually far-sighted ministry. As a further indication that this ministry has being doing something special, in March 1992 the first deputy minister was made minister for destatization and demonopolization in Ukraine.

62. This number is relatively small because local government never had a major role in controlling industrial enterprises with more than 250 employees—the main focus of our study. However, because they represent a previously sheltered part of the economy, these local firms do provide some interesting evidence.

63. We did interview a city council–controlled meat factory that has decided to pursue a more independent strategy. But this choice appears to be attributable to the fact that the factory has a local monopoly and is virtually guaranteed "state orders," which mean an implicit subsidy in the form of cheap inputs. Therefore the factory's managers decided they would do better by dealing directly with the state, that is, by cutting out the previous intermediary organization. As a result, they are no longer subject to direct control by bureaucrats. At the same time, however, because meat processing is so politically sensitive it is unlikely this firm will become de jure private.

64. None of the city council enterprises that we interviewed had changed its property form. In contrast, this republican firm reported a significant change in its structure.

65. Some of these firms have their own "small enterprises," which were set up to sell directly to final consumers. All of these firms reported a massive fall in demand in the first quarter of 1992.

66. See Simon Johnson, "Did Socialism Fail in Poland?" *Comparative Economic Studies* 33, 3 (Fall 1991): 127–151, for a model in which decisions made by newly independent state managers cause an acceleration of inflation and for an analysis of this process in Poland during 1988–1989.

■ 8 ■

Private Sector Manufacturing in Eastern Europe: Some Cross-Country Comparisons

LEILA WEBSTER

When the Communist governments fell in Eastern Europe in 1989 and the new governments publicly embraced capitalism, questions arose about in what ways and how quickly private sectors could be built. Policymakers debated which reforms were most essential to set the stage for private sector development and in what order they should be enacted. Observers wondered whether the spirit of entrepreneurship that was needed to spark large-scale private enterprise had survived 40 years of suppression. Those who knew Poland, Hungary, and Czechoslovakia speculated about how private sector development would differ across the three countries. Almost three years later, a variety of research efforts are beginning to produce answers to these questions.

This study employs findings from firm-level surveys of private manufacturers conducted in 1991 and early 1992 in Poland, Hungary, and Czechoslovakia to shed light on these questions.[1] Cross-country comparisons are used to highlight important similarities and differences among sample entrepreneurs and their firms. Specifically, there are five conclusions:

- Reform programs in all three countries had similar objectives and components, but the business environments facing entrepreneurs at the time of the surveys differed substantially;
- Similarities in entrepreneurs' ages, employment histories, and motivations masked tremendous differences in the levels and types of experience these individuals brought to their companies;
- Manufacturing enterprises came into the private sectors via very different routes, depending mainly on prereform enterprise structures and the strategies and effectiveness of privatization programs;

175

- Major constraints to firm-level growth differed, depending mainly on firm histories and differences in the business environments;
- The characteristics of successful firms were remarkably similar across the countries, but the number of successful firms in each country differed.

This chapter is organized into seven sections. The first section introduces the research project and briefly describes research objectives and methodology. The second section outlines aggregate trends in private sector development in each country to provide a context for survey findings. Sections three through seven discuss each of the above conclusions.

Research Objectives and Methodology

Aggregate figures convey relative size and growth rates of the new private sectors but little about the major actors: entrepreneurs and their firms. To learn more about firm-level response during the transition, the World Bank financed three firm-level surveys in Eastern Europe: one each in Poland, Hungary, and Czechoslovakia. Specific objectives of the research were to develop a profile of entrepreneurs and their firms, assess firm-level constraints and prospects, and formulate recommendations for actions to support the firms' growth.

The research methodology focused on maintaining a firm-level approach and selecting stratified, random samples that were national in scope. To be eligible for inclusion in the population from which samples were drawn, firms had to be (1) registered companies; (2) at least 51 percent privately and domestically owned; (3) engaged primarily in manufacturing; and (4) employers of seven or more workers. The population was limited to registered firms (limited liability and joint stock companies) because they tended to be larger and more formally organized. Self-employed sectors, where enterprises averaged fewer than two workers and turnover was high, were excluded, as were joint ventures and other registered companies whose main activities were trade and services.

Samples were selected in two phases. First, relatively large random samples were drawn from national registers of industrial companies. They included stratified samples of companies in five preselected industries common to all three countries (knitting, clothing, plastics, metals, and machinery). Second, letters were sent to those selected asking them to verify their eligibility and inviting them to join the survey. Response rates were high, and second samples were drawn randomly from the pool of eligible respondents. Final samples consisted of 93 firms in Poland, 106 firms in Hungary, and 121 firms in Czechoslovakia.

Entrepreneurs were located throughout the countryside. Two-person teams led by World Bank staff and consultants interviewed each entrepreneur for three to four hours, using a standardized survey instrument designed to obtain a mix of quantitative and qualitative data. Surveys were completed in Poland in May 1991, in Hungary in September 1991, and in Czechoslovakia in January 1992.[2]

An Overview of Private Sector Trends

Fledgling governments in Poland, Hungary, and Czechoslovakia anticipated that new private sectors would arise from three sources: new domestic enterprises, privatized state enterprises, and foreign investors. In 1989 and early 1990, each government passed legislation permitting registration of private companies, spelling out their corporate forms, and removing decades-long restrictions on their activities and numbers of employees. Foreign investment laws laid out the regulations under which foreign companies and joint ventures would operate. Each government formulated privatization strategies, typically dividing state-owned enterprises into two groups: smaller retail and service units, to be transferred quickly into private hands in "small privatization" programs, and larger, mostly industrial enterprises, to be privatized in "large privatization" programs through a wide variety of mechanisms.

Poles, Hungarians, Czechs, and Slovaks responded immediately to this legislation by setting up thousands of private enterprises, confirming that revival of entrepreneurial ambitions was not a problem. Entry rates soared in the major legal forms: sole proprietorships (the self-employed sector), domestic registered companies (mainly limited liability and joint stock companies), and joint ventures (see Table 8.1). Between 1989 and 1991, the numbers of registered companies grew fourfold in Poland to 45,000 units and eightfold in Hungary to 42,000 and jumped from virtually none in 1989 to almost 40,000 in 1991 in Czechoslovakia. Self-employed sectors boomed, particularly in Poland, where full access to foreign exchange resulted in hundreds of thousands of individual traders. Similarly, the numbers of joint ventures grew quickly, most notably in Hungary and Czechoslovakia.

Growth in the number of registered companies was first led by the trade sector and second by the industry sector. Between 1989 and 1991, the number of registered companies engaged in trade increased in Poland from 1,759 units to 15,952; in Hungary from 1,450 units to 16,670; and in Czechoslovakia from virtually none to more than 13,000. For the same period, registered industrial companies rose in Poland from 2,769 to 8,676; in Hungary from 2,000 units to 9,500; and in Czechoslovakia from virtually none to almost 7,000.

In the large self-employed sectors, growth was led first by traders and second by small-scale industry (mostly workshop production and repair). In response to shortages and full access to foreign exchange, the number of

Table 8.1   Numbers of Enterprises

	1989	1990	1991[a]
Registered Companies[b]			
Poland	11,693	29,650	45,077
Hungary[c]	5,091	18,336	42,211
Czechoslovakia[c]	130	11,565	39,434
Sole Proprietorships			
Poland	813,500	1,135,500	1,420,000
Hungary	186,291	233,984	300,000
Czechoslovakia	8,179	381,303	1,175,716
Joint Ventures			
Poland	429	1,645	4,796
Hungary[c]	1,349	5,693	11,335
Czechoslovakia[c]	100	363	5,446

Source: Central and Federal Statistical Offices in each country.
Notes: a. 1991 figures for Polish registered companies are inflated by the inclusion of large numbers of cooperatives.
b. Excludes joint ventures.
c. Hungarian and Czechoslovak official statistics are classified by legal form and not by ownership. Therefore, the figures for registered companies and joint ventures include some state-owned enterprises, although the state share reportedly is a minority share. In addition, many sole proprietors in Czechoslovakia reportedly are either not yet operational or are working for registered companies as self-employed contract workers exempt from labor taxes.

companies in the self-employed trading sector in Poland shot up by a record 750 percent—from 72,000 in 1989 to 550,000 in 1991. Governments in Hungary and Czechoslovakia restricted full access to foreign exchange to registered companies, and as a result, the numbers of self-employed traders in these countries grew far more slowly.

Reform: Similar Strategies, Different Results

While the objectives of reform were the same in each country (stabilization in the short run; transformation to market economies and renewed growth in the long run), private manufacturers in Poland, Hungary, and Czechoslovakia faced very different economic environments 18 months into reform, when these surveys were conducted. Without question, the degree to which the macroeconomic setting was conducive to private manufacturing was a key predictor of the success of sample firms.

Polish private producers operated within a very difficult economic environment in May 1991. In January 1990, almost all prices were freed, the zloty was devalued, the trade regime was liberalized, full access to foreign exchange was established, and the banking sector was commercialized. In May 1991, recession was in full swing and was fed by falling real incomes, hard budget constraints on state enterprises, full exposure to import competition, and the collapse of Council for Mutual Economic Assistance (CMEA) trade. By the end of 1991, the gross domestic product (GDP) had declined by about 20 percent since January 1990. Industrial production in mid-1991 was 56 percent of mid-1989 levels. Inflation slowed to about 80 percent in 1991, but by the end of 1991 deflated wages had fallen by about 40 percent since the end of 1989. Despite massive devaluations, the zloty had appreciated by about 20 percent in May 1991. Unemployment was about 11 percent. Private producers faced an onslaught of competition. Full access to foreign exchange had brought a flood of imports that were bought and sold by hundreds of thousands of small, private traders and retailers. Small privatization had progressed quickly, but transfer of large enterprises into private hands had stalled. In sum, Polish manufacturers interviewed in May 1991 faced continuing inflation, weak domestic demand, an appreciated zloty, a collapsing state sector, and a massive influx of competing imports.

The Hungarian business environment in September 1991 was less difficult than Poland's but could not be described as positive. At the time of the survey, 90 percent of prices were market determined; the forint was devalued to near-market levels; the banking sector was commercialized but not privatized; and the trade regime was liberalized. Access to foreign exchange was granted to registered companies, but limitations were maintained on the amounts of hard currency available to individuals, including self-employed persons. During 1991, the GDP fell by almost 10 percent (following a fall of 4 percent in 1990), and CMEA trade collapsed. Average inflation in 1991 was 35 percent. Import penetration was increasing but lower than in Poland, due in part to the slower development of a private trading sector. Spontaneous privatization was rampant in 1989 and 1990, but privatization slowed considerably when the government took control and established the State Property Agency (SPA) to oversee the process. In short, Hungarian entrepreneurs operated in a challenging environment in September 1991, one that was hampered by continuing inflation, a stagnant economy, and a stalled privatization program but that was helped by the absence of serious import competition, growing social acceptance of private enterprise, and booming foreign investment.

By comparison, Czech and Slovak entrepreneurs were operating under positive conditions in January 1992, especially because many had started after the initial effects of the large reforms of 1990 and 1991 were felt. The reforms of January 1991 freed 85 percent of prices, devalued the crown to near-market rates, minimized trade barriers, permitted access to foreign exchange for registered companies, and laid out strategies for privatization. Consumer prices jumped 41 percent in the first quarter of 1991 but leveled

off quickly, for an annual increase of 59 percent. The GNP fell by an estimated 16 percent over the course of 1991, with almost half of the fall
attributable to the collapse of CMEA trade. Industrial output, excluding
construction, fell by about 25 percent, and retail turnover was down by
about 40 percent. Real wages declined by 26 percent over the year, and
unemployment rose to 7 percent. The "small privatization" of retail trade,
services, and small factories progressed gradually throughout 1991, and
"large privatization" was on the agenda for 1992. In short, conditions facing private producers in January 1992 were mostly positive: Inflation was
minimal, wages had stabilized, assets were becoming available through the
small privatization auctions, trade flow with the West was increasing, and
the shock of the collapse of CMEA trade had passed. The crucial questions
centered on the fate of the large state sector, upon which many private producers depended.

The Entrepreneurs: Similarities and Differences

Entrepreneurs in all three countries were almost identical in terms of age,
gender, education, motivation, and employment histories. The average age
was 42–43 in each country, a decade older than average new entrants in
most countries. They were overwhelmingly male—just over 10 percent
were women in Poland and Hungary, and only 4 percent were women in
Czechoslovakia. Entrepreneurs were highly educated; the vast majority had
trained as engineers. Almost 70 percent of Poles and almost half of
Hungarians, Czechs, and Slovaks had completed a university education,
and most of the remainder had completed secondary or college-level vocational programs. Entrepreneurs in Czechoslovakia were more likely to have
received vocational training, and Hungarian entrepreneurs were more likely
to have had postgraduate training. Only 15 percent in each country had
received any training abroad, but entrepreneurs in Hungary and Poland
were far more likely than their counterparts in Czechoslovakia to have trav-
eled extensively in the West.

The great majority of entrepreneurs in all three countries (almost all in
Czechoslovakia, 80 percent in Hungary, and 60 percent in Poland) came to
private business from employment in state enterprises, government, and
universities. Some were skilled workers, but most came from the ranks of
managers, directors, and other high-level administrators. In each country,
these former managers were evenly divided between bureaucrats and directors of technical divisions. Many Hungarians came from management positions in quasi-private enterprises: small cooperatives and economic work
partnerships that operated within state enterprises (GMKs and VGMKs).[3]
Ten percent of Polish entrepreneurs had previously worked for a foreign
company, and another 12 percent were prereform craftsmen. Few in any
country came from the ranks of blue-collar workers.

In a rough attempt to compare East European entrepreneurs' personal qualities with classic personality traits of entrepreneurs, respondents were asked to characterize themselves. Results were interesting. All described themselves as practical, disciplined, needing to feel in control, high achievers, and risk-takers. Slight differences in character were seen in the fact that Poles, Czechs, and Slovaks described themselves first as practical and disciplined, whereas the Hungarians described themselves first as high achievers and risk-takers.

Similarities in background and personality, however, masked dramatic differences in the degree and types of experience entrepreneurs brought to their new businesses. Without question, the Hungarians held the advantage of experience. Almost half owned or had owned another private business; a quarter owned more than one. Three-quarters of the Hungarian firms surveyed had operated as crafts enterprises, state firms, economic work partnerships, and cooperatives before 1989, and most current owners had worked as managers or employees in these enterprises. These individuals brought considerable know-how to their newly privatized companies. In addition, many Hungarian entrepreneurs had the advantage of having had extensive exposure to the West over the past decade as the Hungarian government focused on expanding hard-currency exports—exposure that entrepreneurs had deftly transformed into trading and investment partnerships.

Many Czechs and Slovaks also entered private business from strong, if slightly different, positions. Almost all were inexperienced because only a handful had worked as private craftsmen before the reforms of 1990. But entrepreneurs in Czechoslovakia were quick to translate their experience in the state sector into private enterprise. More than a third already owned more than one private business. Nearly half of sample firms in Czechoslovakia were former state enterprises that had been privatized and, with the exception for firms restituted to their pre-Communist owners, most current owners had worked as managers in these enterprises and were entirely familiar with all phases of operations. The relatively high levels of technical efficiency in the state sector in Czechoslovakia meant that many Czech and Slovak entrepreneurs entered private business with relatively higher technical skills than did their counterparts in Hungary and Poland. Entrepreneurs in Czechoslovakia also were more likely to exploit in-hand expertise. Over three-quarters were manufacturing products that were the same or related to products they had made before, compared to just over half of Polish and Hungarian entrepreneurs.

The Poles were the least experienced of the three groups. Although 12 percent were prereform craftsmen and many reported part-time involvement in informal sector activities, 89 percent reported that their current business was their first and only business. Only 11 percent of sample firms derived even indirectly from the state sector, so few Polish entrepreneurs had the advantage of taking over functional factories or of continuing to manage their old firms. Instead, almost all had to build their companies from scratch—leasing space, buying used equipment piecemeal, assembling a work force, and finding new markets. In addition, 40 percent chose to manufacture products that were entirely unrelated to those manufactured in their former jobs.

Origins of Private Manufacturers

As cited above, the number of registered manufacturers at the end of 1991 was about 8,700 in Poland, 9,500 in Hungary (some in repair and some with state ownership), and 7,000 in Czechoslovakia (25 percent estimated as state owned). What are the origins of these firms, and how do they differ across the three countries? This section addresses questions about origins of firms, first by identifying differences in their histories and second by summarizing differences in the sources of their physical assets. In both discussions, particular emphasis is given to the contribution of privatization programs to the new private manufacturing sectors.

Histories of Firms
Sample histories of firms reveal fundamental differences in the composition of the new private manufacturing sectors. In Poland, we see that almost all sample firms started as private firms, with few coming from the state sector (see Table 8.2). Specifically, 89 percent had been private since start-up—mostly as new firms initiated after 1989, along with a handful of prereform craftsmen who had transformed their enterprises into limited liability companies. Only 11 percent of sample firms traced their origins to the state sector—7 percent as former state enterprises and 4 percent as former cooperatives. In-depth examinations of the histories of these firms show that almost all had purchased or leased state enterprises and cooperatives that were failing or had folded. These findings indicate that few state-owned enterprises were available for purchase or lease by private agents before May 1991, and those that were available were functioning poorly or were closed.

Reflecting the complex structure of the prereform Hungarian enterprise sector, the origins of sample firms in Hungary were much different from the origins of firms in Poland. Only a quarter of sample Hungarian firms were new entrants. Hungary's decade-long experimentation with liberalization of private enterprise was reflected in the fact that the other three-quarters of sample firms were transformed into private registered companies from various pre-1989 private enterprise forms, including traditional craftsmen, state firms, small cooperatives, industrial divisions of agricultural cooperatives, and economic work partnerships (GMKs and VGMKs). Only 12 percent of the sample firms were privatized state enterprises. The first implication of these findings is that the private manufacturing sector in Hungary contains many enterprises that are well over five years old and

Table 8.2 History of Firms (percent of firms)

	Poland	Hungary	Czechoslovakia
Private since start-up	89	37	55
Craftsmen	12	12	3
New start-ups[a]	77	25	52
Former state enterprises	7	12	31
Former economic work partnerships[b]	—	18	—
Former cooperatives	4	33[c]	12
Other	0	0	2

Notes: a. New start-ups are defined as enterprises with new products and markets, irrespective of the source of the buildings and equipment.
b. VGMKs and GMKs.
c. These firms derived from two forms of cooperatives: small cooperatives that functioned mostly as private enterprises (18 firms) and industrial divisions of agricultural cooperatives (11 firms). It should be noted that about half of the former cooperatives in the sample previously were GMKs and VGMKs.

therefore presumably have better odds of surviving than most new firms. The second implication is that, as in Poland, the official privatization program in Hungary had contributed very few enterprises to the new private sector by September 1991, due mainly to delays caused by the SPA and the unavailability of long-term financing from the banks. The third implication is that Hungary's second-economy enterprises have become major contributors to the first economy.

The origins of sample Czech and Slovak firms revealed yet another pattern. A little more than half (55 percent) of sample firms in Czechoslovakia had purely private origins, mostly as new start-ups, with only four (3 percent) prereform craftsmen. The remainder came from the state sector—all through official channels, that is, direct sales (56 percent), the small privatization auctions (30 percent), and the restitution program (14 percent). As in Hungary, the new manufacturing sector in Czechoslovakia was almost an equal mix of new and older firms. But unlike Poland and Hungary, the official privatization program in Czechoslovakia had contributed significantly to the number of firms in the private manufacturing sector.

Sources of Property
Exploring the avenues by which entrepreneurs obtained their land and buildings adds insight into the origins of sample firms. In all three countries, most factory buildings were purchased or leased from state enterprises, but ownership rates and the routes to ownership differed.

Only 12 percent of Poles purchased their production facilities (see Table 8.3). The availability of industrial property was limited by the state's failure to release state-owned land and buildings for purchase by private agents. The abilities of entrepreneurs to purchase available real estate were further curtailed by lack of access to long-term loans. Most had multiyear leases on their production space, which afforded them sufficient security to undertake the substantial renovations suitable to their needs.

Table 8.3　Source of Factory Buildings (percent)

	Poland	Hungary	Czechoslovakia
Owned	12	28	45
Leased	88	72	55

About twice as many Hungarians (28 percent) as Poles had purchased their factories, mostly from state enterprises. Most entrepreneurs who owned their buildings had purchased them in the early days of reform in 1989 and 1990, when spontaneous privatization was rampant but before the government clamped down on state managers' practices of buying divisions of their own enterprises. In-house deals appeared common. Those who leased did so either because they lacked the capital to purchase or because they were waiting for the SPA (which reportedly was very slow) to approve a sale. It was clear that substantial assets had passed from state to private hands in Hungary, although most transfers appeared to have taken place through informal arrangements rather than through official routes, and widespread leasing was common.

A surprising 45 percent of Czech and Slovak entrepreneurs had purchased their factory buildings, virtually all through official channels as part of the "small privatization program." Fifty-six percent bought their real estate directly from the state (including municipal governments), 30 percent through the network of "small privatization" auctions, and 14 percent through the restitution program. Four characteristics of Czechoslovakia's small privatization program were distinctive: (1) Small factories were included along with enterprises involved in trade and services; (2) the possibility of in-house deals cannot be entirely ruled out, but transparency appeared to be exceptionally high; (3) factories were usually transferred intact, including equipment and workers; and (4) widespread availability of long-term financing was crucial to entrepreneurs' abilities to purchase their property.

To summarize, private manufacturing enterprises in each country were distinctive. Polish firms typically were new companies, managed by owners who were well educated but inexperienced in private business. Their asset base was thin, usually made up of cast-off equipment from the state sector and long-term leases on factory space typically in need of substantial renovation. New start-ups in Hungary looked much like their counterparts in Poland, but pre-1989 Hungarian firms were distinctive because most originated as quasi-private enterprise forms. Their managers were seasoned, and sales in these enterprises were twice the sample average. In Czechoslovakia, new start-ups and privatized state firms were more similar than dissimilar. Both were managed by inexperienced but technically proficient owners, many of whom had amassed substantial assets in their short time in business. The availability of investment capital in Czechoslovakia enabled many new entrants to purchase factory buildings and/or new equipment; it also enabled owners of privatized companies to purchase fully functional factories through the auctions.

Constraints

When asked to name the single largest problem affecting their businesses, entrepreneurs in all three countries spoke first of problems with demand and finance. Analysis of the roots of these problems showed that, however similarly problems were framed, their sources were quite different from one country to another.

A quarter of Polish entrepreneurs complained that demand for their products was inadequate due to reduced real incomes associated with the Polish recession. A closer look, however, showed that soft demand stemmed not only from declining real incomes and decreasing orders from the state sector but also from a tremendous expansion in the supply of goods from new domestic entrants and an influx of highly competitive imports. Close scrutiny of firms with decreasing orders disclosed that at least 60 percent were competing, or failing to compete, with large numbers of other new entrants and imports. This finding is not surprising in light of the lack of competitiveness of many Polish goods and pent-up consumer preferences for foreign goods—made cheaper by the appreciated zloty and readily available due to the rapid development of the private retail sector.

Other constraints cited by Polish entrepreneurs concerned inadequate finance. Sixty-eight percent of Polish entrepreneurs had received bank loans since 1988, almost all short-term credits with terms of 12 months or less. Nevertheless, Polish firms were chronically short of working capital for several reasons. First, most entrepreneurs refused to borrow further at nominal interest rates of about 70 percent because they considered the rates exorbitant. Second, most Polish entrepreneurs relied on state enterprises as their main suppliers and customers. Many were caught in the bind of having to pay cash for their inputs but having to wait months to be paid for goods delivered. The result was severely eroded working capital. Third, inflation remained high in the first half of 1991, and entrepreneurs faced rising prices for their inputs but could not pass costs through to consumers because of competition.

Finance problems topped the list among Hungarian entrepreneurs. These constraints were alternately described as the banks' unwillingness to extend loans, nonpayment or slow payment for goods by state enterprises, and high interest rates. One in five Hungarian entrepreneurs cited lack of access to credit as the single largest problem affecting his or her business. Since start-up (going back to 1982 in many cases), 43 percent of entrepreneurs had received short-term loans, 17 percent had gotten long-term loans, and 14 percent had received both. Besides the lack of access to loans, finance problems were exacerbated by slow payments from state clients, which robbed entrepreneurs of their working capital.

Hungarian entrepreneurs were stretching scarce capital as far as possible, but the costs of inadequate capital were evident everywhere. Common strategies for minimizing capital requirements included shifting into subcontracting, which covered raw material costs but cut into profits; using home workers with their own machines to avoid capital expenditures and save labor taxes; pursuing foreign partners who could contribute capital; participating in interenterprise credit networks; and extensive use of equipment leasing. The obvious drawback was that entrepreneurs often had to settle for less than optimal arrangements to get the capital they needed. Sometimes they failed. Researchers met a number of Hungarians who were unable to fill in-hand orders because they could not finance the raw materials. Others paid higher prices for their inputs because they could afford only very small quantities at a time.

The second most prevalent complaint among Hungarians was inadequate demand. An analysis of firms with demand problems, however, shows a different pattern than the one seen in Poland. Hungarian firms with demand problems faced little competition. Rather, their problems stemmed from their dependency on orders from a declining state sector. Many were privatized firms with historical structures geared to meet the demands of long-time state customers that were now in trouble. Survival of these firms depended on their owners' abilities to restructure their production to meet the demands of the new economy.

Czech and Slovak entrepreneurs differed from their Polish and Hungarian counterparts in that no single constraint dominated the others. The most frequent complaints concerned slow payment by state-owned customers and weak demand. These problems were intertwined because they both stemmed mainly from a slowdown in the state sector. The relatively small size of the private sector in Czechoslovakia and the overwhelming dominance of the state sector meant that entrepreneurs who sold nationally in domestic markets relied on state firms as primary customers. Many managers of state enterprises in Czechoslovakia reportedly were uninterested in buying from private firms: Some were "frozen" until they saw what privatization would bring, and others were unwilling to do business with private entrepreneurs. Sample entrepreneurs were in the difficult position of first persuading managers to buy from them, and then persuading managers to pay for goods delivered. As discussed in the next section, almost half of Czech and Slovak entrepreneurs avoided this problem by exporting, and 10 percent restricted their sales to local markets.

Prospects

Successful firms shared common characteristics across the three countries, but the frequency with which they were encountered in each country differed. Three questions are relevant here. The first is how successful firms differed from unsuccessful firms, with the objective of identifying key variables for success in transition economies. The second questions the role of firms' origins in their performance; that is, do privatized firms have better prospects than new start-ups? The third asks why more strong firms and fewer weak firms were located in Hungary and Czechoslovakia than in Poland.

Strong Firms Versus Weak Firms

To isolate key variables for success, the strongest and weakest firms in each sample were separated from the larger samples. The firms were compared first with one another and second across the three countries. Firms were classified as strong if they met three criteria: Production was increasing; profits were rising; and interviewers ranked their prospects as positive based on having interviewed their owners, toured their facilities, examined trends in their businesses, and applied knowledge from other firms in the same activities. Firms were classified as weak if production was decreasing, profits were declining, and interviewers judged that their prospects were poor.

Of the 320 firms surveyed, 70 were classified as strong and 34 as weak (see Table 8.4). The Polish sample contained 18 strong and 18 weak firms. Among the Hungarian firms, 27 were strong and 12 were weak. In Czechoslovakia, 25 firms were strong and 4 were weak. Firms classified as neither strong nor weak ranked positively on some criteria and negatively on others.

What did each group have in common? The numbers of firms in each group were too small to be statistically significant, but analysis of these firms provides information about what it takes for private manufacturers to survive and grow in transition economies.

Strong firms had six important characteristics in common in all three

Table 8.4   Strong and Weak Firms (number of firms)

	Poland	Hungary	Czechoslovakia
Strong firms	18	27	25
Weak firms	18	12	4
Total firms in sample	93	106	121

Note: Firms were classified as strong if production was increasing, profits were rising, and interviewers judged that prospects were positive. Firms were classified as weak if production was declining, profits were falling, and their prospects were judged as poor.

countries. First, their owners were exceptionally competent. They were good analysts of their financial status, knowledgeable about their markets and competitors, focused on improving production efficiency and product quality, and savvy in cutting through red tape. Second, they produced highly differentiated goods, usually at the top end of the market. Third, they were larger, with average sales three times the volume of weak firms. Fourth, they occupied market niches where they faced fewer competitors than did other sample firms. Fifth, they bought their inputs mostly from the state sector, as did all sample firms, but they avoided selling their products to state enterprises by exporting them and locating niche markets. Sixth, a larger proportion of sales in strong firms than in weak firms was exported (40 percent vs. 20 percent).

Similarly, weak firms in all countries shared characteristics. First, they were more likely than other sample firms to manufacture homogeneous, mass-produced consumer products such as everyday clothing, plastic containers, and simple metal parts. Second, their equipment was worth less and was nearly twice as old as equipment in strong firms (averaging 12.2 years vs. 7.4 years in strong firms). Third, they faced more competitors, which is not surprising, since low start-up costs for simpler products ensured many new entrants. Fourth, they sold mainly to state enterprises, leaving these firms vulnerable to unreliable demand and problems with payments.

Interesting differences among the countries include the following: Strong firms in Poland were disproportionately located in the Warsaw area, whereas strong firms in Hungary and Czechoslovakia were evenly distributed by region and in urban and rural areas. A full third of strong firms in Poland and Hungary were machine manufacturers, compared to only 8 percent of strong firms in Czechoslovakia, which is perhaps a reflection of the strength of machine manufacturers in the Czechoslovakia state sector. In Czechoslovakia, strong firms were much more likely to be exporters than in Hungary and Poland.

The Role of Origins

How important is firm history in firm performance? Answers are neither uniform nor conclusive. In Poland, strong firms were represented by new start-ups and descendants of state firms in proportion to their occurance in the sample. But weak firms were about twice as likely to descend from the state sector as strong firms.[4] A number of factors account for the fact that privatized Polish firms did no better and, in some cases, did worse than new entrants. Most importantly, most privatized firms in Poland originated from divisions of state enterprises or cooperatives that had closed because they were unprofitable. In effect, the entrepreneurs had purchased from the state sector small units that already had proved troublesome. As a result, the new owners were faced with the tasks of resuscitation and restructuring, but without benefit of credits with terms of greater than 12 months and often with implicit and explicit limitations on cutting back the incumbent labor force. Production in privatized units was structured to meet the needs of the state sector. Not surprisingly, privatized firms in the Polish sample sold mainly to state enterprises and were four times more likely than other firms to list collections as their biggest problem. As expected, equipment in these firms was much older than that in new entrants (averaging 14.4 years old vs. 9.8 years).

In the case of Hungary, strong firms contained pre-1989 firms and new start-ups in proportion to the sample as a whole; that is, 25 percent were new start-ups and 75 percent were pre-1989 enterprises. But pre-1989 firms accounted for 89 percent of the total sample sales and 87 percent of the total sample exports. An obvious explanation for the overall better performance of privatized firms in Hungary is that most of these firms operated previously not as state enterprises but as quasi-private enterprises (economic work partnerships and cooperatives) that were subject to many of the demands of private business. Their managers were experienced and fully familiar with business basics. The informal network of personal connections was notably strong in Hungary, conferring an advantage on long-time players and making procurement of inputs and markets more difficult for newcomers. A hypothesis that accounts for the relative strength of these older firms is that individuals with the strongest potential as entrepreneurs may have entered private enterprise in 1982 when the laws were liberalized.

In Czechoslovakia, the opposite pattern is seen. New start-ups accounted for more strong firms than did privatized firms.[5] A similar hypothesis to that for Hungary can be posed for Czechoslovakia, namely that the first wave of entrepreneurs may have the greatest potential for success. The strong start made by many of the new start-ups in Czechoslovakia—unable to enter private enterprise until 1990—lends credence to this notion. It must be noted that, although fewer privatized firms than new firms appeared among the strongest firms in the Czechoslovakia sample, most privatized firms in Czechoslovakia were far stronger than privatized firms in Poland. Through the auctions, fully functional enterprises were purchased, and most former managers (now owners) were actively reorienting their production to meet demand in the new economy, aided by the availability of term finance from the banks. As in Poland, they inherited equipment that was older and more outdated than that in new start-ups, and they sold mainly to state enterprises with the familiar difficulties of declining orders and payment problems.

The Distribution of Strong and Weak Firms
The concluding question asks why strong firms were disproportionately located in Hungary and Czechoslovakia, while weak firms were found in greater numbers in Poland. There are many explanations, but several are outstanding. First, as summarized above, Polish entrepreneurs faced a far more difficult macroeconomic environment at the time of the Polish survey than did the other two groups of entrepreneurs. May 1991 may have been the low point of the Polish recovery, with deep recession, a collapsing state sector, and the enormous impact of full trade liberalization. Drops in output have been similar in Hungary and Czechoslovakia, but entrepreneurs in those countries received some respite from intense import competition. In addition, private producers in Hungary and Czechoslovakia had managed to obtain critical assets from the state enterprise sector to a far greater extent than their Polish counterparts—in Hungary through spontaneous privatization and widespread leasing and in Czechoslovakia through the small privatization program. In short, the Poles operated in a more difficult macroeconomic environment with fewer assets and far more competition than did the Hungarians, Czechs, and Slovaks. Since 1991, indications are that the Polish economy has begun to recover and that the engine of growth is a growing private sector.

Second, an outstanding weakness among Polish entrepreneurs was their inability to enter export markets. Hungarian, Czech, and Slovak entrepreneurs were far more proficient in entering export markets: 42 percent of sample firms in Czechoslovakia and 45 percent in Hungary were exporting, compared to only 23 percent in Poland. More telling, a third of total sales from Czechoslovak and Hungarian firms were exported compared to only 17 percent of Polish sales. As domestic markets in transitional economies decline with collapsing state sectors, many private producers rely on export markets to secure their sales. In May 1991, Polish producers had made few inroads in export markets. As a result, many private producers were pulled down with the larger economy. Fortunately, recent evidence points to increasing large-scale private sector exports in Poland, a phenomenon that can be attributed to time, experience, and a more correctly valued currency.

Third, the experience of enterprise managers made a big difference. As discussed above, much of the strength of the Hungarian private manufacturing sector lay with the substantial experience of Hungarian entrepreneurs, many of whom had been operating for a decade in quasi-private economic work partnerships and cooperatives. A major dividend of Hungary's decade of partial reform of the state sector is this cadre of highly seasoned manufacturers who are accustomed to many aspects of business management. The strength of many Czech and Slovak firms was found in the developed technical skills of their managers who were able to exploit quickly the assets made available to them by the state sector and the banks.

Notes

1. These surveys were conducted under a World Bank research project financed by the Research Committee of the World Bank. Research results are presented here with no attempt to place them within the general literature on private sector development.

2. Country-specific reports were written following each survey, and this chapter builds on data originally presented in these three papers.

3. Economic work partnerships (GMKs) and enterprise economic work partnerships (VGMKs) were established by workers in cooperation with state enterprises under a set of guidelines established in 1982. Many operated as private enterprises under the umbrella of state firms.

4. Analysis of firms descending from the state sector in Poland is only suggestive, as just 11 percent of sample firms in Poland originated in the state sector.

5. Because there are only four weak firms in the Czechoslovakia sample, only strong firms are analyzed.

■ Part 3 ■
Restructuring and Soft Budget Constraints in Post-Communist States

■ 9 ■

Restructuring Programs in Transitional Economies

IZAK ATIYAS

Manufacturing industries in Eastern Europe need major restructuring.[1] Industrial restructuring is defined here as a set of discrete, or fundamental, actions that either reorganize the assets and liabilities of enterprises to make them internationally competitive or arrange a shutdown. The latter option is not a trivial matter; plant closures are costly, even if they ultimately save resources.

Industrial restructuring entails action on two fronts. First, enterprise assets should be reorganized to increase efficiency and profitability. These actions include streamlining production, eliminating unviable units, introducing proper managerial practices, adopting new technologies, liquidating unproductive assets, and eliminating excess staffing. Second, these actions should be supported by a financial package that contains new resources; a reorganization of the liabilities of the enterprise, including redistribution of financial claims; and, often, debt relief.

Industrial restructuring faces many barriers. It requires policy and institutional actions on many fronts. These actions include eliminating state protection in order to strengthen enterprises; enhancing the mobility of labor and capital; and increasing the availability of resources such as information, skills, and finance.[2] This chapter will focus on two sets of "agency" problems, or conflicts of interest, associated with the restructuring of enterprises that are not under private ownership. The first set of agency problems is the conflict of interest between those agents that exercise effective control over assets and agents or owners who hold residual claims. Actions undertaken by those who control the assets will not necessarily increase the enterprise's value, so the ultimate resolution of this well-known "ownership" problem often requires some form of privatization. The second set of agency problems is conflicts of interest between insiders of an enterprise and actual or potential providers of external finance. This problem has been called "agency costs of external finance" in finance literature. The insiders' actions are likely to be necessary, if drastic, delaying measures to restore efficiency. If failure of the firm is imminent, insiders are likely to strip assets or assume excessive risk. The implication of the second agency problem is similar to the ownership problem, with the important addition that it hinders the flow of financial resources for restructuring, even when the ownership problem is solved.

The objective of this chapter is to examine the implications of the agency problems and to evaluate restructuring programs in some East European countries in terms of mechanisms they use to resolve them. This evaluation includes an analysis of bankruptcies and bank-led restructuring as possible decentralized mechanisms. The message is twofold: First, restructuring is a policy concern that cannot be accomplished by privatization alone. Second, governments have to rely on decentralized mechanisms to solve agency problems and encourage restructuring for the majority of the enterprises.

The rest of this chapter is organized as follows. The next section reviews the agency problems of external finance. The third section discusses the institutional responses to this problem that are used in capitalist economies. The fourth section discusses relationship between privatization and restructuring, and the fifth section reviews aspects of restructuring programs in the former East Germany, Hungary, and Poland. The final section summarizes these points and concludes the chapter.

Agency Problems of External Finance

It is well known that providing external financing to enterprises through loan contracts creates a conflict of interest between creditors and recipients of the loans.[3] If the enterprise is successful, insiders reap all the benefits, except for the fixed repayment of the loan. If the enterprise is unsuccessful, insiders do not bear all the losses, due to limited liability. This creates adverse incentives: Once a loan is obtained, insiders have an incentive to try to transfer wealth from creditors by, among other things, engaging in riskier activities.[4]

The adverse incentive effects are aggravated when the enterprise is in financial distress and has lost competitiveness. There are two reasons: First, financial distress increases the incentives for excessive risk-taking. Moreover, actions that insiders may undertake to help the enterprise survive often damage the value of the loan or the enterprise to the creditors. Second, if insiders are better informed than outsiders and perceive an imminent failure, they may engage in activities, such as asset stripping, that accelerate the demise of the enterprise. Restructuring that will produce efficient outcomes is often detrimental to insiders' interests because workers and managers may lose their jobs, so insiders are expected to resist efficient restructuring measures. Because of these problems, financing enterprise restructuring is perceived as a risky activity; this perception hinders the flow of finance for enterprise restructuring when financing is most urgently needed.

Problems associated with external debt financing are even more aggravated when there are many creditors. Enterprises in need of restructuring typically suffer from a debt overhang. That is, the adverse incentive effects of the existing stock of debt may be such that its reduction or rescheduling could improve incentives and benefit creditors as a whole. However, when the number of creditors is large, a free-rider problem arises: No single creditor has the incentive to reduce the face value of his or her claims unless other creditors do the same. Conversely, if all other creditors reduce their claims, then a single creditor may prefer to stand by and reap the benefits of the overall debt reduction, since the benefit of an additional reduction in his or her claim, in terms of the corresponding increase in the value of the debtor enterprise, is not large. This situation creates coordination problems and precludes voluntary debt reduction. Moreover, conflicts of interest exist between different types of creditors (for example, between secured and unsecured creditors). As a result, the reorganization of the debtor's liabilities, which is an essential component of industrial restructuring, becomes difficult.

What sort of mechanisms would reduce the impact of agency and coordination problems and secure the flow of financing for restructuring? First, creditors may attempt to reduce agency problems by securing adequate monitoring and/or control of enterprises going through restructuring. But monitoring alone would not be sufficient to protect the creditor's interests unless creditors can act on the basis of information revealed by the monitoring. By acquiring the right to manage and control an enterprise's assets, creditors can guarantee that funds are allocated to activities that increase the value of their claims. If that is impossible, creditors may try to delegate the control or monitoring function to a third party that they believe would protect their interests. The next section reviews institutional mechanisms established in some countries to resolve the agency and coordination problems.

Institutional Responses:
Examples from Capitalist Economies

Institutional mechanisms that have developed to cope with the agency and coordination problems vary across countries. For the purposes of this chapter, and at the risk of oversimplification, it is useful to distinguish between stock market–based economic environments; environments where commercial banks play a leading role in corporate control, finance, and restructuring; and environments in which the state has taken a direct and active part in the restructuring process.[5]

Primary examples of stock market–based economic environments exist in the United States and the United Kingdom. In these environments, ownership is widely distributed, and the problem of corporate control is mainly solved via takeover threats or actual takeovers through the stock market. However, particularly in the last decade, bankruptcy reorganizations have tended to play a prominent role in the restructuring of distressed enterprises. The bankruptcy procedures of both countries provide legal frameworks within which an agreement can be achieved between creditors and debtor through a reorganization plan that allows the restructuring of the assets and liabilities of the debtor. Nevertheless, the two countries also exhibit differences in the ways they resolve the agency and coordination problems. In the United States, Chapter 11 of the Bankruptcy Code allows the incumbent management of the debtor firm to retain control (albeit somewhat restricted) over the firm's assets during the reorganization procedure unless the court appoints a trustee. In principle, a reorganization plan must be approved by a certain percentage of every class of creditors, although there is also some room for the approval of a plan in cases where some classes of creditors dissent. In the United Kingdom, the Insolvency Act includes several mechanisms for reorganization, the most important being administration and administrative receivership. In both cases, the management of the company is taken over by an insolvency practitioner, so the incumbent managers and owners lose their control rights. In most cases, secured creditors dominate the process.[6]

The efficiency of bankruptcy outcomes is closely linked to resolution of the agency and coordination problems. For example, because Chapter 11 of the US code allows the debtor to retain significant control rights during the reorganization process, it often provides excessive bargaining power to debtors and results in delayed liquidations. By contrast, the UK legislation is likely to cause too many liquidations because secured creditors often completely dominate the process.[7]

Stock market–based systems also rely on informal reorganizations for corporate restructuring. These are out-of-court agreements reached between debtors and creditors. Sometimes these agreements are ratified by the court to decrease the chance of postagreement litigation. Because bankruptcy procedures are costly, in terms both of time and resources, informal reorganizations provide substantial savings over formal reorganizations. However, they also have an important disadvantage compared to formal bankruptcy reorganizations. While an informal reorganization requires the approval of all creditors, the consent of only a fraction of creditors is necessary for a formal reorganization. This complicates the effort to reach agreements in informal workouts.

Germany and Japan are primary examples of systems in which banks play an important role in corporate restructuring. With close ties to industry forged through debt financing and through equity participations, banks are well positioned to efficiently reduce agency problems, decrease information asymmetries through long-term relations, and provide adequate financing to industry while exerting control over management. During periods of financial distress, banks can capitalize on this long-term relationship and play a leading role in restructuring. The degree of monitoring and control that banks exercise increases during restructuring.

German banks have significant representation in companies' supervisory boards.[8] During periods of normal profitability the role of the supervisory boards is limited. They become active in monitoring and managing firms during periods of poor corporate performance or financial distress. In particular, they act under these circumstances to screen and replace managers.[9] Banks also play an important role in resolving coordination problems among creditors, especially by putting together lending consortia to rescue the distressed companies.[10]

Japanese banks identify clients in difficulty during the normal course of their monitoring process. This may take place well before any default on interest payments occurs.[11] Once such identification is made, the bank sends advisory managers to the company to renegotiate the loan and reach agreement on a restructuring program. In many instances, banks take over the higher management of the company.[12] Often, as in Germany, the bank is active in coordinating the rescue strategy with other creditors.

In both countries, the restructuring of especially large companies takes place outside the formal bankruptcy system. In fact, one of the purposes of early bank intervention is to avoid costly bankruptcy procedures altogether.

An important and common feature of institutional mechanisms discussed so far is that the role of the state in corporate restructuring is limited and does not extend beyond mediation and, in some cases, provision of loan guarantees. The components of real and financial restructuring are negotiated between creditors and enterprises. By contrast, the Korean government has intervened directly in the restructuring of individual subsectors and even of companies.[13]

During the 1970s the Korean government promoted the heavy and chemical industries. Even though these subsectors grew rapidly, by the late 1970s Korea started to lose international competitiveness. Excess capacity started to develop in the heavy and chemical industries, and nonperforming loans became a major problem in the banking system. Rather than relying on bankruptcy procedures or voluntary actions by the banking system, the government became directly involved in the restructuring process. Its intervention in industrial restructuring entailed encouraging mergers, capacity reduction programs, general support for commercial banks, and substantial financial workouts.

In the shipping industry, for example, firms willing to participate in the government's rationalization program benefited from loan moratoria and significant rescheduling with government guarantees. Through the program, the number of firms in the industry was reduced from 63 to 17.

Insolvent firms often were absorbed by those that were financially sound. Credit provided to firms that were taking over a distressed firm included a subsidy equal to the excess of liabilities over assets of the distressed firm. Banks, in turn, were provided with low-interest loans to alleviate the financial burden incurred during corporate restructuring. The government therefore designed restructuring programs for industry and used its leverage over commercial banks to force them to finance the process. In summary, the agency and coordination problems were solved by the direct imposition of restructuring measures by the government.[14]

It is important to note that control by creditors or the state is costly. In Japan, Germany, and Korea, restructuring was extensive and included significant measures such as redeployment or liquidation of assets, changes in managerial practices, and mergers. Exercise of control was predicated on the access to skills, especially managerial skills, that surpass those ordinarily required for the operation of a commercial bank.

Privatization and Restructuring

The typical ownership problem discussed in finance literature has to do with the separation of ownership and control in modern Western corporations. To summarize, especially in stock market–based economies where ownership is diffuse, owners who hold residual rights of control face significant transaction costs and free-rider problems in exercising control over management. Additional control is presumed to be exerted through takeover threats. However, recent assessments of takeovers in the United States have raised doubts about this presumption. Some economists argue that, rather than providing mechanisms to exert control over management, takeovers may have acted as a means through which management has realized its own objectives at the expense of other stakeholders.[15] As discussed in the previous section, in economies where banks have close links with enterprises, banks are also presumed to exercise additional control over management.

The ownership problem in the transitional economies of Eastern Europe is even more complicated. There, the control rights of the state are extremely limited. Control over assets is effectively exercised by insiders, that is, by workers' councils, management, or both. In some countries (especially Hungary and Poland), even though the state is the nominal owner of enterprises, it lacks authority to undertake functions that owners (or boards of directors) in Western corporations would normally undertake. Among such functions are making decisions on corporate strategy, investments, employment, managerial appointments, divestitures, or privatization. In particular, the state cannot impose restructuring measures unless they are endorsed by workers' councils (or enterprise councils in Hungary). The consequence is that the state faces the *legal* constraint of not being able to impose restructuring measures that would challenge the interests of the insiders.

There is general agreement that the resolution through privatization of the ownership problem is essential for industry in Eastern Europe to operate efficiently. Given that privatization is an overriding objective in the policy agenda, the central issue is the appropriate role of the state in industrial restructuring. In particular, can governments rely on a strategy of transformation that consists of privatization alone, in the hope that assigning assets to owners through privatization will create sufficient incentives to allow the restructuring problem to be resolved through market mechanisms? This section argues that restructuring represents a policy problem in its own right.

The first practical argument deals with administrative, political, and economic factors that limit the speed at which state-owned enterprises can be delivered to private owners. Privatization programs in most East European countries are advancing at a much slower pace than was expected.[16] For enterprises that remain under the ownership of the state, failure to implement some immediate restructuring measures (especially for stemming losses) would substantially increase the cost of restructuring in the future. Second, large loss-making enterprises present special problems. It is unlikely that large and unviable enterprises will be liquidated quickly, especially if their closure would have serious consequences for regional employment and income. In these cases, governments' role in a solution will have to be direct, even if the restructuring plans require plant closures. Finally, some components of restructuring are better undertaken before privatization, if only to prepare enterprises for sale. Enterprises that carry large financial or environmental liabilities would be difficult to sell without a prior reorganization of these liabilities. In addition, enterprises that are too horizontally or vertically integrated may need to be broken up to enhance competition. Experience has shown that demonopolization is easier to accomplish before new stakeholders join the project.

Any role that governments might play in enterprise restructuring in these cases depends on their ability to legally circumvent the control of workers' councils. Corporatization, which transforms state-owned enterprises into corporate entities, establishes the ownership rights of the state and allows the state to exercise these rights through, for example, the appointment of boards of directors. Therefore, corporatization often has been presented as a necessary (but not sufficient) step of any program that attempts to solve the restructuring problem in a systematic way. When massive corporatization has not been possible, governments in Hungary and Poland have attempted to employ bankruptcy mechanisms to wrestle control from insiders, a strategy that will be discussed in the next section.

The more substantial argument is that privatization is at best a solution to only one of the agency problems discussed in this chapter. It remains to be seen whether mass privatization schemes (such as in the Czech Republic) are likely to result in diffuse ownership structures that will create incentive and control mechanisms and allow owners or their delegates to monitor managers and encourage them to undertake efficient restructuring. However, even when privatization is successful in providing reasonable solutions to the ownership problem, restructuring will require access to financial resources, which requires resolution of the agency problem of external finance. Unless most privatized enterprises are paired with foreign counterparts that relax financing constraints, freeing resources for postprivatization restructuring will present one of the major challenges for East European countries.

Two problem areas require consideration by policymakers. The first is the restructuring of enterprises that for one reason or another are not privatized and will not be privatized in the near future. The second is the restructuring of enterprises after privatization. The appropriate role of the government in these areas is the topic of the next section.

Restructuring in Transitional Economies of Eastern Europe: Centralized and Decentralized Mechanisms

A Centralized Approach: The Treuhandanstalt

In eastern Germany, a government agency, the Treuhandanstalt, is assigned the task of restructuring and privatization. As in the Korean case, the state has played a primary role in restructuring, but on a more massive scale. The functions of the Treuhand include creating supervisory boards; monitoring management; evaluating the viability of enterprises; and undertaking financial and real restructuring, including closures. The Treuhand also finds buyers and negotiates employment and investment targets with them.[17] Compared to other countries in Eastern Europe, privatization in eastern Germany has advanced at a fast pace. The Treuhand is also a mechanism that allows for an efficient transfer of control from the state to managers of individual enterprises in the private sector. The Treuhand is able to deal with externalities and social objectives such as employment, industrial/ regional and competition policy, and problems of control that arise during the transition.[18]

The Treuhand assumes the ownership of the companies to be privatized but grants some functions to supervisory boards, most of which (60 percent to 70 percent) consist of managers from west German firms; representatives of west German banks make up about 20 percent to 25 percent of the boards.[19] Often, banks' representation on supervisory boards has not been accompanied by flows of funds. In fact, monitoring and control and evaluation of restructuring plans have been the main contributions of the banking system to the restructuring process. Banks have been unwilling to finance the process, except when guarantees are provided by the Treuhand.[20] The contribution by the stock market to the restructuring process has also been minimal.

What are the implications of the Treuhand experience for the rest of Eastern Europe? Carlin and Mayer argue strongly for a "top down" approach, as in the Treuhand model, in Eastern Europe.[21] Counterarguments emphasize the high costs incurred by the Treuhand during the process and the poor finances of East European states. It has also been argued that the credibility the Treuhand commands in the German economy would be difficult to replicate elsewhere.[22] Perhaps as important, however, is the problem of economic and managerial skills. The Treuhand had access to managerial skills and supervision from western Germany, and by 1991, the Treuhand was employing about 3,000 people. The rest of Eastern Europe is much more constrained by the shortage of such skills.[23]

To economize in states' resources, especially skills, countries in Eastern Europe have to rely on decentralized mechanisms to restructure most enterprises. The decentralized mechanism has to address both the restructuring of enterprises that will not be privatized in the near future and postprivatization restructuring. In the case of enterprises that have not been corporatized, the mechanism has to include a method for dislodging control rights from insiders. In the case of postprivatization restructuring, it has to create an environment that encourages the flow of finance to private restructuring activities. In addition to the decentralized mechanism, governments also need to address the restructuring problems of large losing enterprises as well as regional issues. A primary objective of assigning the greater part of the restructuring problem to a decentralized mechanism is to allow governments to focus their resources on these policy areas.[24] The rest of this section reviews bankruptcy and bank-led restructuring as potential decentralized mechanisms for restructuring.[25]

Bankruptcy
Can bankruptcy procedures play the main role in enterprise restructuring? The answer is probably not. Bankruptcy procedures are not well suited to deal with *systemic* restructuring problems. Bankruptcy is a costly legal procedure; it easily can be delayed, if not paralyzed, by backlogs in the judicial system. In addition, the court systems in Eastern Europe are not well equipped to deal with cases that require commercial expertise, especially when they arise on a massive scale. The limitations of the judicial system are likely to prevent bankruptcy from becoming the pivotal mechanism for restructuring, as experience in Hungary shows.

Janet Mitchell identifies another problem that may limit the role of bankruptcy procedures in industrial restructuring.[26] She argues that, for several reasons, creditors in East European countries do not have incentives to initiate bankruptcy proceedings. One reason is the presence of large nonperforming loans in the banking systems. Some of these loans are inherited from the old socialist economic systems. When combined with poor regulation, poor supervision, and poor auditing of the financial system, financial distress among creditors may induce them to continue financing insolvent firms even when the firms undertake risky or speculative projects. Moreover, creditors hesitate to initiate bankruptcy proceedings against their debtors for fear of signaling their own financial distress.[27] The growth of interenterprise debt is another reason for creditor passivity because it has made trade credit an important portion of enterprise liabilities.[28] First, trade creditors may be unwilling to initiate bankruptcy proceedings for fear that they would disrupt their own businesses.[29] Second, since interenterprise debt has created a complex web of cross-claims and liabilities among enterprises, creditors fear that disruption of business would be contagious and would result in an unnecessarily large number of bankruptcies.

Nevertheless, an interesting aspect of bankruptcy policies in Poland and Hungary is that they also have been used to circumvent the ownership problem in the case of enterprises in default. In both countries, bankruptcy includes trigger mechanisms that deliver control of enterprises to outsiders. In both cases, entering bankruptcy eliminates or limits the control rights of enterprise insiders and allows outsiders (the state, the court, or creditors) to take some action.

In the Polish case, bankruptcy was triggered if the dividend tax was not paid for three months. This trigger mechanism was extended in September 1991 to include defaults on any taxes.[30] Once bankruptcy was initiated, the Ministry of Industry or another founding organ appointed a liquidator to the enterprise and took over its management. The process was an administrative rather than a legal one. An enterprise that enters bankruptcy can be restructured or liquidated. However, these procedures so far have not played a significant role in Poland. Brian Pinto[31] reports that, as of September 1991, 718 enterprises were identified as in arrears to the budget. However, the Ministry of Industry was involved in only 126 restructuring cases. Hence, even though the legislation endowed the government with the ability to take over control rights, in practice this right was not usually exercised.

In Hungary, amendments to the old bankruptcy law, and the new bankruptcy law that has been in effect since January 1992, have introduced trigger mechanisms for *automatic* bankruptcy. According to this measure, a debtor is compelled to petition the courts for bankruptcy if the debtor is in default of payments for over 90 days. Hence, the government was not involved in initiating the bankruptcy procedure, and recourse to bankruptcy has been more prominent in Hungary than in Poland.[32] Automatic bankruptcy proved an effective way of initiating bankruptcies and resulted in a massive number of applications in 1992 (about 3,800 between January and September, about two-thirds of which occurred in the month of April, when the 90-day period first became effective). As of August 1992, based on 1991 balance sheets, employment at enterprises affected by bankruptcy or liquidation[33] was in excess of 750,000. Most of the enterprises under bankruptcy or liquidation are cooperatives or small business organizations; industrial enterprises make up about 10 percent of the total. As of August 1992, 37 percent of the bankruptcy cases were resolved; 60 percent of the concluded procedures ended with a settlement, involving reductions in debtors' liabilities. Whether these agreements have actually been carried out is not yet known.

Provisions for automatic bankruptcy seem to have ameliorated somewhat the problem of passivity. However, whether the automatic bankruptcy system has created an efficient selection mechanism is not clear. The trigger mechanism is unavoidably crude; it may result in an unnecessarily high number of bankruptcies. On the other hand, when there is a great need for restructuring in the economy, and the number of losing enterprises is large, a crude selection mechanism may be better than complete inaction or passivity. It has been estimated that about one-fifth of the declared proceedings in Hungary involve enterprises with continuous losses. Provisional assessments also suggest that many enterprises with continuous losses have avoided bankruptcy or liquidation. An accurate judgment clearly requires more data. What is apparent, however, is that the massive increase in applications has significantly overloaded the judicial system. There are substantial delays caused by the limited capacity of the courts, lack of appropriate personnel, and incorrect and deficient petitions.

These observations are not intended to understate the importance of bankruptcy procedures in Eastern Europe or their likely contribution to industrial restructuring. In fact, whatever institutional solution is adopted to resolve the agency problems in restructuring, its effectiveness would depend on the existence of a credible threat of bankruptcy. The argument here is that bankruptcy procedures cannot be expected to act as the main forum in which the restructuring problems of most enterprises can be resolved.

Bank-led Restructuring in Poland

Can the banking system assume a leading role in restructuring? Takeo Hoshi, Anil Kashyap, and Gary Loveman have reviewed the main bank system in Japan and suggest that it may provide a useful model for the development of the financial sector in Poland.[34] The argument is that equity markets in Poland are not likely to provide significant financing for industry in the near future.[35]

Regarding the specific problem of restructuring, evidence from Japan shows that firms that have close relations with banks are better able to grow out of financial distress.[36] As discussed earlier in this chapter, this evidence demonstrates the close relations between banks and industry and also the banks' influence on and participation in managerial decisions, which help alleviate agency problems that are aggravated when enterprises experience financial distress. Moreover, the main bank also organizes lending consortia, a mechanism that helps relieve coordination problems among creditors.

The Polish government's program of bank-managed industrial restructuring relies on the Enterprise and Bank Restructuring Law, which was submitted to the parliament in August 1992. Basically, the law allows banks and a state agency (the Industrial Development Agency, or IDA) to hold out-of-court conciliatory proceedings with troubled debtor enterprises. These proceedings are expected to result in a financial restructuring program for enterprises, based on a reorganization plan that includes closure of loss-making units, divesting of nonproductive or underused assets, and shedding of excess employees. The conciliation requires the agreement of creditors representing 50 percent of an enterprise's liabilities. The important feature of the legislation is that even though it prescribes out-of-court conciliation procedures, it does not require the unanimous consent of the creditors for the validation of an agreement. In that way, it overcomes one of the drawbacks of informal workouts as they exist in, for example, the United States and facilitates conciliation. The court system gets involved in the procedures only if minority creditors appeal. The program is also linked to privatization. Under the legislation, creditors holding at least 30 percent of the enterprise's debt will be allowed to ask the Ministry of Privatization for the conversion of their claims into equity. Banks also will seek to find buyers for enterprises during the process, which tries to avoid the ownership problem as follows: The initiation of proceedings requires the endorsement of management and workers' councils. Conciliatory proceedings can be concluded only when the enterprise is commercialized, meaning the transformation of a state-owned enterprise into an independent legal entity and the institution of the state as the clear holder of the residual control rights. If conciliation proceedings fail, banks will petition for bankruptcy.

Banks can play a useful role in restructuring only if they have proper incentives. Existence of nonperforming loans in bank portfolios distorts incentives and encourages excessive risk-taking.[37] To reduce adverse incentives, the Polish program includes the recapitalization of banks on an ex ante basis. Once the recapitalization is done, banks are expected to be fully responsible for their actions in their exposure to the enterprise sector and outcomes of restructuring. Ex ante recapitalization dominates an approach in which banks' recapitalization is based on actual losses incurred as a result of financial restructuring of the debtor enterprises. The latter approach creates a morally hazardous problem and reduces banks' incentives to act vigilantly to collect their debts or initiate bankruptcy if necessary. Ex ante recapitalization may also help alleviate the problem of creditor passivity.

There are two potentially serious constraints that may limit the effectiveness of this mechanism. The first is that workouts require financial and managerial skills beyond those necessary for more straightforward lending decisions. In order to be effective, banks' skill endowments will have to be enhanced. Augmenting bank personnel with (possibly foreign) workout specialists may provide a solution. A complementary solution would be to promote market-based workout skills. These skills would be exercised by companies that possess both financial and managerial skills and that may be hired by commercial banks to help them design and implement restructuring plans. In order to create correct incentives, these companies' remuneration should be tied to the success of restructuring, for example, by linking payments to the eventual sale price of the enterprise or by making part of the payments in terms of equity.[38]

Perhaps more important, the proposed mechanism by itself runs the risk of concentrating only on financial restructuring and organizational changes and of lacking an industry focus. In that case, the benefits of financial restructuring are likely to be eroded rather quickly over time. Whether making privatization an explicit objective of the process would ameliorate this problem depends on who the buyer is. If the enterprise is sold to a foreign buyer after the reorganization, one may expect that the buyer would also bring in expertise to restructure the enterprise. If the enterprise is privatized through a management buyout, real side problems are likely to remain.

Often, an exclusive focus on financial restructuring is due to lack of information on products, standards, technology, foreign demand, and markets. Information has a public-good nature and suffers from problems of appropriation. The government may provide a useful function by collecting and disseminating information relevant for restructuring, especially on technology and foreign markets, either by actually providing information services or by subsidizing the acquisition of such information.

Finally, in order to be effective, these procedures must be supplemented by others that would take the enterprises over from the banks if the conciliatory proceedings fail. The purpose of these complementary proceedings would be either slow or immediate liquidation, depending on the social feasibility of the former. Preferably, management should be removed automatically if conciliation fails; moreover, the transition from the conciliatory proceedings to liquidation proceedings should also be automatic. This system would provide incentives to management to adopt a cooperative attitude toward the conciliatory proceedings.

Conclusion

This chapter has focused on agency problems that hinder industrial restructuring in the context of East European economies. While privatization may help alleviate the ownership problem, it does not address agency problems associated with acquiring external financing. Moreover, in some countries (especially Poland and Hungary) privatization is not likely to occur fast enough to transfer most assets to private agents in the near future, so restructuring remains a policy concern in its own right.

In addition, the chapter has reviewed the main types of institutional responses to the agency problems of external finance in capitalist economies, namely bankruptcy, informal workouts, bank-led rescues, and direct government intervention. East European economies have to rely on decentralized mechanisms to alleviate the agency problems and accelerate the process of industrial restructuring.

Formal bankruptcy proceedings are unlikely to play a major role in East European economies because the judicial systems lack the capacity and skills to handle the cases. Bank-led, out-of-court procedures probably are a more efficient mechanism.

Notes

The views expressed in this chapter are those of the author and should not be attributed to the World Bank, its board of directors, its management, or any of its member countries.

1. Gordon Hughes and Paul Hare, "Industrial Policy and Restructuring in Eastern Europe," CEPR discussion paper no. 653, March 1992; and Claudia Senik-Leygonie and Gordon Hughes, "Industrial Profitability and Trade Among the Former Soviet Union Republics," *Economic Policy* 15 (October 1992): 353–386, show that, when evaluated at world prices, many of the industrial subsectors in formerly planned economies are not competitive; some in fact produce negative value added. Moreover, many enterprises are excessively indebted and cannot generate sufficient operating earnings to cover their debt payments.

2. For a detailed discussion of barriers to restructuring and a comprehensive policy and institutional framework to overcome those barriers, see Izak Atiyas, Mark Dutz, Claudio Frischtak, and Bita Hadjimichael, "Fundamental Issues and Policy Approaches in Industrial Restructuring," Industry and Energy Department Working Paper, Industry Series Paper no. 56, The World Bank, Washington, D.C. (1992).

3. The classic statement of this problem is in Stewart C. Myers, "The Determinants of Corporate Borrowing," *Journal of Financial Economics* 5, 2 (1977): 147–175.

4. In principle, these adverse incentives could be dealt with by detailed provisions in the contract that spell out the permissible activities of the insiders under different contingencies. However, such contracts are costly to enforce either because creditors lack the necessary information or because they cannot rely on the court system to enforce the contract on the basis of that information. In addition, writing such detailed contracts itself may be costly.

5. The reader should be reminded that this list is not necessarily the only scheme of classification that can be utilized to examine the distinguishing features of vastly varying systems of corporate finance and control that exist in capitalist economies. For example, from the perspective of mechanisms of corporate control, Jenny Corbett and Colin Mayer, "Financial Reform in Eastern Europe: Progress with the Wrong Model," *Oxford Review of Economic Policy* 7, 4 (1991): 57–75,

find it useful to distinguish between systems in which control is exercised by "outsiders" (mainly through the takeover threat in the stock market) and those in which "insiders" (such as banks, suppliers, customers, and other stakeholders who either hold equity in the firm or are represented on its board of directors) are the main agents of control. However, from the perspective of mechanisms of corporate restructuring, the classification suggested here seems more useful.

6. For a comparison of the US and UK approaches to bankruptcy, see J. R. Franks and W. Torous, "Lessons from a Comparison of the U.S. and U.K. Insolvency Codes," *Oxford Review of Economic Policy* 8, 3 (1992): 70–81.

7. For details, see Franks and Torous, "Lessons from a Comparison."

8. For the importance of bank representation in supervisory boards in Germany, see Kenneth Dyson, "The State, Banks, and Industry: The West German Case," in Andrew Cox (ed.), *State, Finance, and Industry: A Comparative Analysis of Post War Trends in Six Advanced Industrial Economies* (Sussex: Wheatsheaf Books Ltd., 1986); and Christian Harm, "The Relationship Between German Banks and Large German Firms," Policy Research Working Papers no. 900, The World Bank, Washington, D.C. (1992). Supervisory boards oversee and monitor the activities of executive boards; the latter undertake the day-to-day management of firms.

9. Wendy Carlin and Colin Mayer, "Restructuring Enterprises in Eastern Europe," *Economic Policy* 15 (1992): 311–352.

10. Perhaps the most prominent bank-led rescue in Germany was that of AEG-Telefunken in 1979. For this and other examples, see Dyson, "The State, Banks, and Industry."

11. See Jenny Corbett, "International Perspectives on Financing: Evidence from Japan," *Oxford Review of Economic Policy* 3, 4 (1987): 30–55, for a detailed overview of banks' reactions to problem loans in Japan.

12. See Paul Sheard, "The Main Bank System and Corporate Monitoring and Control in Japan," *Journal of Economic Behavior and Organization* 11 (1989): 399–422; and Masahiko Aoki, "Toward an Economic Model of the Japanese Firm," *Journal of Economic Literature* 28 (1990): 1-27.

13. On industrial restructuring in Korea during the 1980s, see D. M. Leipziger, "Industrial Restructuring in Korea," *World Development* 16 (1988): 121–135; and S. W. Nam, "Industry Promotion, Restructuring, and the Financial Sector in Korea," mimeo (Washington, D.C.: The World Bank, EDI, 1992).

14. Whereas earlier a case-by-case approach was used to restructure individual companies, the enactment of the Industrial Development Law in 1986 made designation as a "rationalization industry" a condition for obtaining government assistance. Rationalization plans for designated industries, prepared by the Ministry of Trade and Industry, lasted for two or three years and included measures such as capacity reduction, inducement of specialization, entry deterrence, and provision of credit for upgrading old capital equipment. Again, the government played a major role in providing the necessary monitoring and control functions.

15. Carlin and Mayer, "Restructuring Enterprises in Eastern Europe," present a useful summary of this vast literature. Andrei Shleifer and Robert Vishny, "Takeovers in the 60's and the 80's: Evidence and Implications," World Bank mimeo (1991), cast doubts on the traditional role ascribed to takeovers in alleviating managerial agency problems.

16. See, for example, Patrick Bolton and Gerard Roland, "Privatization Policies in Central and Eastern Europe," *Economic Policy* 15 (1992): 275–309; Carlin and Mayer, "Restructuring Enterprises in Eastern Europe"; and O.E.C.D., *Methods of Privatizing Large Enterprises* (Paris: 1993).

17. Carlin and Mayer, "Restructuring Enterprises in Eastern Europe," present a detailed overview of the Treuhand.

18. Wendy Carlin and Colin Mayer, "The Treuhandanstalt: Privatization by State and Market," paper presented at the National Bureau of Economic Research Conference on Transition in Eastern Europe, 1992.

19. Carlin and Mayer, "The Treuhandanstalt."

20. This point brings out an important distinction between the role of banks in restructuring in Germany and Korea. In Korea, banks were practically forced into financing industrial restructuring. In Germany, their participation has been voluntary.

21. Carlin and Mayer, "Restructuring Enterprises in Eastern Europe" and "The Treuhandanstalt."

22. See the comments by discussants following Carlin and Mayer, "Restructuring Enterprises in Eastern Europe."

23. For example, the state property agency in Hungary, which oversees privatization, had only 140 employees toward the end of 1992.

24. See Sweder Van Wijnbergen, "Economic Aspects of Enterprise Reform in Eastern Europe," mimeo (Washington, D.C.: The World Bank, 1992).

25. See Van Wijnbergen, "Economic Aspects of Enterprise Reform," for suggestions on restructuring large loss-making enterprises.

26. Janet Mitchell, "Creditor Passivity and Bankruptcy: Implications for Economic Reform," in Colin Mayer and Xavier Vives (eds.), *Financial Intermediation in the Construction of Eastern Europe* (Cambridge: Cambridge University Press, 1993).

27. Mitchell, "Creditor Passivity and Bankruptcy," also mentions bankruptcy costs, including uncertainty and the consequent costs of valuation of debtor firms, as a factor that may hinder individual creditors from initiating bankruptcy, even when doing so may be in the interest of all creditors. In practice, this factor is not likely to be important. Most bankruptcy costs are incurred not at the initiation stage but during the procedures. Costs incurred during the procedures, however, often are given priority over other claims and therefore are collectivized. The free-rider problem therefore is eliminated.

28. See, for example, Brian Pinto, Marek Belka, and Stefan Krajewski, "Microeconomics of Transformation in Poland," Policy Research Working Papers no. 982, The World Bank, Washington, D.C. (1992), for the importance of inter-enterprise credit in Poland.

29. In fact, costs associated with disruption of business would be among those that would not be collectivized in bankruptcy procedures; moreover, such indirect costs do not carry any corresponding financial claims on the debtor. Therefore, indirect costs are likely to create creditor passivity.

30. Pinto, Belka, and Krajewski, "Microeconomics of Transformation in Poland."

31. Pinto, Belka, and Krajewski, "Microeconomics of Transformation in Poland."

32. For a review, see Izak Atiyas, "Notes on Bankruptcy and Liquidation Procedures in Hungary," World Bank mimeo (1992).

33. In the context of Hungary, bankruptcy refers to reorganization procedures. The terms liquidation or winding up are used for liquidation procedures.

34. Takeo Hoshi, Anil Kashyap, and Gary Loveman, "Lessons from the Japanese Main Bank System for Financial System in Poland," World Bank mimeo (1992).

35. See Corbett and Mayer, "Financial Reform in Eastern Europe," for a similar argument. O.E.C.D., *Methods of Privatizing Large Enterprises,* p. 19, also emphasizes the role of financial institutions in industrial restructuring.

36. See Takeo Hoshi, Anil Kashyap, and David Scharfstein, "The Role of Banks in Reducing the Costs of Financial Distress in Japan," *Journal of Financial Economics* 27 (1990): 67–88.

37. See Michael Maresse, "Solving the Bad-Debt Problem of Central and Eastern European Banks: An Overview," World Bank mimeo (1992).

38. See Atiyas, Dutz, Frischtak, and Hadjimichael, "Fundamental Issues and Policy Approaches in Industrial Restructuring," for an example from Turkey.

■ 10 ■

Can Privatization Solve the
Problems of Soft Budget Constraints?

ZHIYUAN CUI

Privatization is high on the agenda of economic transformation in Eastern Europe. Soon after they took power, all post-Communist governments in the region announced programs for privatizing state-owned enterprises. Roughly speaking, there are two major categories of privatization strategies: (1) selling off and (2) giving away.[1] In Hungary, the former East Germany, and in Poland under the first term of the Solidarity government under Tadeusz Mazowiecki, the strategy of selling off predominates. In the cases of the former Czechoslovakia, and Poland under the second-term government led by Jan Krzysztof Bielecki, it is the giving-away strategy that seizes the attention of policymakers.

The purpose of this chapter is to evaluate the two major privatization strategies in terms of their feasibility under recessionary macroeconomic conditions and to reexamine the theoretical case for privatization as the way to harden budget constraints of firms.

The chapter is organized as follows: The next section explores whether privatization is a practical policy under current recessionary macroeconomic conditions. This section is followed by a theoretical evaluation, which concentrates on the nature of soft budget constraint (SBC). Contrary to conventional thinking, this evaluation shows that SBC does not come from state ownership but has its origin in the dilemmas caused by credit money and incomplete capital market. Therefore, some degree of SBC is unavoidable in any modern market economy. Finally, the pragmatic and theoretical evaluations are linked, and they conclude that because of the current recessionary macroeconomic conditions, and because SBC cannot be eliminated through privatization, sensible policy is not to rush into privatization but to engage in an extensive public sector reform.

The examination of privatization emphasizes the importance of monetary factors (in contrast to real factors).[2] This chapter also brings Joseph Schumpeter's often forgotten insight—that mainstream neoclassical economics is a theory of barter economy—into our discussion of economic reform in Eastern Europe and draws on that insight's implications for the theory of property rights.

Recession and Privatization

A constant theme of Schumpeter's work is that neoclassical economics has always had a bias toward real analysis:

> Real Analysis proceeds from the principle that all the essential phenomena of economic life are capable of being described in terms of goods and service, of decisions about them, and of relations between them. Money enters the picture only in the modest role of a technical devise that has been adopted in order to facilitate transactions. This devise can no doubt get out of order, and if it does it will indeed produce phenomena that are specifically attributable to its modus operandi. But so long as it functions normally, it does not affect the economic process, which *behaves in the same way as it would in a barter economy* [my emphasis]: this is essentially what the concept of Neutral Money implies.[3]

The bias toward real analysis can be seen vividly in the current discussions about the deep recessions[4] following the standard "shock therapy" type of stabilization program. The majority of neoclassical economists believe that a fall in output after shock therapy is inevitable and even desirable: The output loss after price liberalization reflects the real competitive forces in the economy—eliminating inefficient enterprises and stopping socially unwanted production. Noted Polish economist Jan Winiecki makes this point explicitly: "The change in behavior inevitably induces a fall in output but the level of welfare remains unchanged."[5] David Lipton and Jeffrey Sachs hold a similar view.[6]

I do not dispute the elements of truth contained in this real perspective on output loss. Under the traditional command economy, there were many spurious outputs that nobody wanted, and a healthy structural adjustment of the whole economy may cause temporary loss in outputs. However, even the basic intuitions of noneconomists suggest that there may be another independent monetary cause of the recession: Firms have to pay for inputs and wages *before* their outputs can be sold.[7] This can cause output losses because firms are severely credit constrained—a reason that has nothing to do with the real operational efficiency (X-efficiency) of the firms. In other words, if we consider monetary factors, "bad" firms as well as "good" firms can be forced to reduce their production.

Why is the layman's intuition ignored by current discussions about the deep recessions in Eastern Europe? Returning to Schumpeter's point, neoclassical economics is in fact a theory of barter economy. We can appreciate Schumpeter's point by reviewing the neoclassical concept of "integration of monetary and value theory," which was formulated by Don Patinkin after Schumpeter's *History of Economic Analysis* was published in 1954.[8]

This review is necessary because Patinkin's theory of neutral money is regarded as the theoretical foundation of the standard International Monetary Fund (IMF)–sponsored stabilization program.

Patinkin's central theme is the integration of monetary analysis *into* the existing framework of real analysis. Also known as the competitive general equilibrium theory, this reasoning is based on the assumption that the excessive demand function for each commodity is homogeneous of degree zero. According to Patinkin: "Assume now that an initial position of equilibrium is disturbed in such a way as to cause equi-proportionate change in all money prices. Since this does not change relative prices, the 'homogeneity postulate' implies that none of the demand functions in the real sector are thereby affected."[9]

This is the famous proposition of "the neutrality of money," which integrates monetary and real analysis by making money economy equivalent to barter economy: "Strictly speaking, such neutrality occurs if the mere conversion of a barter economy to a money economy does not affect equilibrium relative price and interest."[10]

We now have a better understanding of Schumpeter's point that neoclassical economics is a theory of barter economy, not because it fails to mention monetary factors but because money, which is claimed to be neutral, does not play an essential real role within its theoretical framework. Money's only role in Patinkin's theory is that of a "nominal anchor" of the real economy: Total money supply is the nominal variable that determines the absolute price level, and the relative prices are determined by the real competitive forces of demand and supply in the economy.

This neoclassical nominal anchor theory is extremely influential in the design of the stabilization program[11] in Eastern Europe. Much attention is devoted to determining which is the correct nominal anchor: targeting the money growth rate or fixing the exchange rate.[12] The underlying logic is that once a correct nominal anchor is chosen and the absolute price level is controlled, the rest can be left to the free play of relative prices that are determined by real forces of competition. This will result in the efficient allocation of resources. How neat a picture!

Based on the choice of nominal anchor and price liberalization, the standard IMF-sponsored stabilization programs (also applied in Eastern Europe) are a telling example of the dominance of neoclassical economics in macropolicy-making. However, it is worth noting that Kenneth Arrow, the leading figure in the area of competitive equilibrium theory (real analysis), has applied the theory to macropolicy analysis.[13] This may be because he is aware that, due to the assumption of completeness of markets, there is no place for money as a medium of exchange in this theory. Because each commodity is assumed to have a current price for every future time and possible event (this is the assumption of completeness of markets), there is no need for liquidity (money) to deal with uncertainty.[14]

The neoclassical obsession with real factors neglects the major monetary factors of the shock therapy type of stabilization program, which may be partially responsible for the deep recessions in Eastern Europe.[15] These factors are as follows.

1. Fixing exchange rate as a nominal anchor and adhering to the theory of neutral money leads to a very high real interest rate (in order to bolster the fixed exchange rate). This factor, together with the subsidy cut and the collapse of the CMEA—which caused a large increase in imported input prices—forced many firms into a severely credit-constrained situation.

2. The central bank's high discount rate and direct credit ceilings (because the money growth rate is also used as a nominal anchor) on commercial bank loans further contributed to the credit crunch of the firms. Moreover, even without a government credit ceiling, commercial banks will increase credit rationing in the face of high uncertainty.[16]

3. As a result of these factors, there is a huge increase of interenterprise debt.

Taken together, the three monetary factors imply that the output losses are not due solely to the real competitive force, because many efficient firms (capable of survival in less adverse macroeconomic conditions) also reduce their production and even go bankrupt. The relative contributions of real and monetary factors to the recessions in Eastern Europe surpass the scope of this chapter.[17] However, it is unwarranted to neglect the monetary factor in neoclassical thinking about the recessions.[18]

When we accept the existence of monetary factors in East European recessions, we can realize the implications of monetary factors for privatization strategies. Clearly, the general credit crunch and interenterprise debt makes it difficult and unreliable to evaluate firms being privatized. In the case of the selling-off strategy, buyers have no strong incentives to buy unless sale prices are extremely cheap, because so many firms have negative book values due to the general credit crunch. However, cheap sale prices contradict government objectives of increasing revenue[19] and tend to erode public support for privatization.

In the case of the giving-away strategy, all bets are put on its alleged efficiency-enhancing effect because it obviously involves short-term revenue loss. According to the advocates of this strategy, the government should distribute free shares of the state enterprises to every citizen, either directly or through holding companies. Although they initially received these shares for free, the giving-away strategy stipulates that there should be a stock market afterward. Consequently, the receivers have no way to determine which firm's share is more valuable, because the long chain of interenterprise debt makes a big noise in evaluating each enterprise. In this situation, we can expect not a stock market that monitors the managers of enterprises efficiently but only stock bubbles.[20]

In the current deep recessionary macroeconomic environment, the rush into privatization is not a sensible strategy. It is ineffective, and even counterproductive, because the revenue loss makes stabilization harder to achieve.

Soft Budget Constraint and Privatization

If we abstract from the current macroeconomic conditions, can we make a purely theoretical case for rapid privatization? Many people conceive of privatization as a means to solve the SBC problem or to make enterprise subject to hard budget constraint, thereby creating a strong incentive to perform efficiently.

According to János Kornai, "the softening of the budget constraint appears when the strict relationship between the expenditure and earnings of an economic unit (firms, household, etc.) has been relaxed, because expenditure will be paid by some other institutions, typically the paternalistic state."[21] It is the widely shared belief that the root of SBC is state ownership.[22] However, SBC could have a deeper root in any modern market economy based on credit money. Consequently, privatization itself cannot solve the problem of SBC.

Kornai's theory of soft budget constraint is closely related to the Alchian-Demsetz-North theory of property right, which states, "property rights develop to internalize externalities."[23] Kornai defines SBC as an economic unit that expects other institutions to pay for its expenditure; in other words, property rights are ill-defined, and SBC is a clear sign of the absence of internalization of the firms' own cost and benefits.

Real analysis versus monetary analysis is also central to our understanding of issues of property rights and budget constraints. The current thinking on privatization in Eastern Europe and on property rights in general is basically a real analysis because there is emphasis on the real person. Kornai talks about "flesh-and-blood person" as private owner.[24] Polish Finance Minister Leszek Balcerowicz argues that private ownership generates the "quickest improvement of the level of life of citizens. This is so because economizing costs, good organization of work, high quality of production, effective search for new markets as well as technical progress and development are in the interest of the proprietors who direct the work of enterprise."[25] North and Thomas point out that secured property rights is the central factor which fosters economic growth.[26] Alchian and Demsetz argue that private ownership is the solution to the monitoring problem in team production.[27] All these arguments neglect the possibility that monetary factors also can make SBC a central characteristic of market economy based on private ownership. When we take into account the monetary fac-

tors, the clear-cut relation between private ownership and efficiency depict-
ed by the above arguments becomes blurred. In other words, the existence
of SBC under private ownership monetary economy implies that the
Alchian-Demsetz-North theory of property right is not a correct description
of capitalist economy.

One of the complications that causes SBC in a private ownership monetary economy is the fact that modern banking systems have the ability to
create credit money. Under the fractional reserve system, the banks can
loan more money than they receive in deposits. For example, if the reserve
requirement is 20 percent, the bank with 20 dollars in deposits can lend out
100 dollars.[28] Moreover, the bank can lend out money it does not hold: It
simply opens a creditor account from which the customer may draw up to
the amount he or she promises to pay. This practice is called "loans make
deposits." Clearly, Kornai's definition of SBC—the nonexistence of a
"strict relationship between expenditure and earning"—does fit the modern
banking system based on fractional reserve.[29] Outlined below are three
sources of SBC in a modern monetary economy.[30]

Inflation and SBC
According to Schumpeter, credit money is not necessary to maintain a cir-
cular flow in perfect equilibrium, but it is indispensable for a growing
economy.[31] When an enterprise asks for bank credit, it can offer the goods
it will produce as collateral. Thus, the quantity of outstanding credit always
exceeds the quantity that is "fully covered" by collateral. Moreover, due to
the fractional reserve system, banks have the power to create money and
thereby can supply whatever volume of credit their borrowers demand. As
a result, there is always a danger of credit inflation. But Schumpeter argues
that credit inflation is temporary as long as the investment projects are successful. Because there is no way to be absolutely sure in advance which
projects will succeed, the moderate rate of inflation may be the price we
have to pay for economic growth. However, inflation expectation by enterprises causes SBC because loans will be repaid in cheaper dollars. In short,
other institutions—in this case, the society as a whole—pay for the enterprise's expenditure. This explains why entrepreneurial activities flourish
most during an expansionary period. In this case, SBC is a result of the
dilemma between monetary economy and inflation: Without moderate
inflation, there is no growth; but if hyperinflation ensues, there is no
growth either.

Lender of Last Resort and SBC
Under the fractional reserve system, the banks are subject to the risk of a
"run," in which a large number of depositors withdraw money at the same
time because they think the bank will not continue to honor its commitment. A bank run can cause serious production contraction, as shown by
the experiences of bank panics in the last two centuries. Central banks were

developed in Europe and the United States as the "lender of last resort" to provide liquidity for troubled banks.[32] After the Great Depression, the Federal Deposit Insurance Corporation (FDIC) was created explicitly to insure deposits of less than $100,000 per account. The Federal Reserve implicitly insures against almost all financial defaults, including commercial papers of corporations,[33] repurchase agreements[34] against Treasury securities, customers' assets held by stock exchange firms, pension liabilities and some life insurance liabilities, and most deposits above the $100,000 limit.[35]

The rationale for the broad explicit and implicit government insurances is the "public good" nature of the financial industry. If one bank is allowed to go bankrupt, it may adversely influence other banks and enterprises. This is an example of negative network externality. Thus, market failure is not confined to issues such as defense and pollution. If we take into account the monetary factors of our modern market economy, externality is almost everywhere. If we adhere only to the real analysis, banks are private institutions; but if we adopt the monetary analysis, we can see that banks are essentially public institutions. It is no wonder that the US Bankruptcy Code *does not* apply to banks (they can be closed only by their regulatory agency). It is also no wonder that Franklin Roosevelt's first proposed legislation, when he became president in 1933, was the Banking Act—to prevent bank runs.

However, although the lender of last resort and insurance by the central bank are necessary to maintain financial stability of the economy, this creates a moral hazard problem—a kind of SBC, since the insured expects other institutions to pay for its expenditure—on the part of issued banks and their client firms. For example, "it has been standard practice for firms to obtain a backup line of credit on commercial papers."[36]

Generally, there is a two-tier lender of last resort in the United States today: "The Federal Reserve System is the lender of last resort to member banks (particularly to giant member banks), and giant member banks are the lenders of last resort to the institutions and organizations that use the commercial-paper market."[37] Moreover, when regulation is relaxed but insurance (lender of last resort) is still there, the banks will not behave prudently, as was shown by the recent savings and loan (S&L) debacle in the United States. This crisis is a perfect example of SBC. In 1982, hundreds of S&Ls had negative net values, according to the Generally Accepted Accounting Principles (GAAP). However, the Federal Home Loan Bank Board permitted the S&Ls to overstate their net worth by using so-called regulatory accounting.[38] In this case, SBC is a result of the dilemma between a monetary economy and bank runs: Without the lender of last resort, we face the danger of financial collapse; with the lender of last resort, we cannot avoid moral hazards for financial institutions and their client firms.

Credit Rationing, Bankruptcy Code, and SBC

Although the bank has the ability to create credit money, the bank will not necessarily be willing to lend out money to borrowers indiscriminately. In fact, at any particular time the credit markets are characterized by credit rationing, by which the demand for loans may not equal the supply of loans and interest rates do not rise to clear markets. The reason is that credit market is not like a good market. As Stiglitz and Weiss noted: "Credit is fundamentally different from goods such as peanuts. When individuals exchange commodities contemporaneously, the price has a tangible meaning: it denotes the ratio of the number of units of one good that are given up in exchange for the number of units of the other good that are received. The interest rate, however, is nothing more than a promise, an agreement that a certain amount will be repaid, if possible, at some date in the future."[39]

If a bank raises the interest rate to clear the market, it will face the problem of adverse selection: Those who bid for high interest rates are mostly risk-lovers and crooks. Therefore, "The mix of loan applicants changes adversely, so much so that the expected return from those receiving loans may actually decrease as the interest rate charged increases."[40]

Because credit market equilibrium is characterized by credit rationing—that is, because the credit market is not perfect—many good firms may not be able to get credits.[41] This is another example of monetary factors, rather than the real forces of competition, getting enterprises into trouble.[42] The concern about an imperfect credit market motivated the adoption of Chapter 11 of the US Bankruptcy Code during the New Deal era.[43] Chapter 11 is a device for saving the good—but credit-constrained—enterprises by "reorganization." In contrast, Chapter 7 deals with the "liquidation" of firms that should be shut down because their economic future looks bleak. Chapter 7 stipulates that the bankruptcy court appoint a trustee who sells the firm's assets and turns the proceeds over to the court for payment to creditors; whereas, according to Chapter 11, the existing managers of the enterprise remain in control and the enterprise continues to operate. More importantly, firms filing for Chapter 11 have the right to terminate underfunded pension plans, and the government assumes the uncovered pension costs. Also, the firms' obligation to pay interest to prebankruptcy creditors ceases. All these subsidies are intended to provide breathing space to the "supposedly viable firms that are in temporary financial distress."[44] However, even though Chapter 11 is justifiable because of imperfect credit markets (credit rationing), it also creates the problem of SBC because many firms file for Chapter 11 to get subsidies when they should file for Chapter 7 or not file for bankruptcy at all. SBC is again the result of the dilemma in monetary economy: Without Chapter 11, good firms may go bankrupt; with Chapter 11, bad firms can survive by relief and subsidy. A telling example of SBC in the bankruptcy process is the story of the Texaco-Pennzoil dispute. Texaco filed for bankruptcy under Chapter 11 in April 1987 to avoid paying $10 billion in damages to Pennzoil for interfering with Pennzoil's attempt to buy Getty Oil.[45]

From these examples, it is clear that SBC is a universal phenomenon in any modern market economy based on credit money and that the root is not necessarily state ownership. Given the fractional reserve system, the existence of central banks as lender of last resort, and the Bankruptcy Code, it is impossible to get rid of SBC. The real problem is to control it within an acceptable limit by legal and regulatory means. Privatization itself is not a cure for SBC.

Conclusion

This chapter focuses on two arguments: (1) Privatization in Eastern Europe under the current recessionary macroeconomic condition is not sensible, and (2) privatization is not the solution to the problem of SBC because SBC has the deeper root in any monetary economy.

When we consider monetary factors, we can gain new insights into the strategies of transition (such as stabilization and privatization) beyond the reach of the real-analysis approach of mainstream neoclassical economics. This statement does not imply that real analysis is unimportant, but there is an urgent need to bring monetary factors into the picture. Schumpeter complained that the victory of real analysis in neoclassical economics was so complete that monetary analysis had to "lead a lingering life . . . in an underworld of its own."[46] This situation should be changed today.

The main new idea put forward in this chapter is the monetary perspective on property rights and privatization, but conventional wisdom on these issues is too real to be true. The faith that secured property rights held by real persons will solve the incentive problem (SBC) reflects the narrow view on risks in economic development—the only perceived risk is government confiscation of private property.[47] However, from the monetary perspective, there are more risks (such as bank runs, credit rationing, and inflation). To deal with the risks and imperfections in a monetary economy, governments developed many institutions and regulations governing the credit market (such as the role of the central bank as the lender of last resort and Chapter 11 of the US Bankruptcy Code) because the performance of financial institutions and their client firms is a public good (because of the correlated balance sheets between banks and firms). However, these necessary government involvements also induce SBC on the part of insured (explicitly or implicitly) economic agents.

There is a dilemma. Given the existence of the fractional reserve system and the central bank, we cannot do away with SBC; but without them, we cannot foster economic growth and must run into more serious troubles.[48]

William Black once said: "No contradiction, no progress." While the neoclassical real analysis depicts a harmonious picture of free price and hard budget constraint, the monetary analysis developed in this chapter highlights the paradoxical nature of our modern monetary economy. From this perspective, SBC is not necessarily a bad thing.[49] The main implication is that many institutions and regulations (other than property rights) are needed for a well-functioning market economy because these institutions and regulations are essential to confine SBC within an acceptable limit.[50] The failure of the traditional socialist economy in Eastern Europe and the former Soviet Union is a result of these economies' noninstitutionalized legal and regulatory systems (subject to too much arbitrary behavior of party leaders), as well as many international factors exogenous to this system, rather than to state ownership itself.[51]

From this perspective, the striking feature of the proposed strategies of privatization in Eastern Europe—whether selling off or giving away—is the absence of serious thinking on financial regulation[52] and on those institutions necessary to create a modern market economy based on credit money. To reiterate a central theme in this chapter: In a complex monetary economy with an inevitable role for government, privatization does not solve the problem of SBC simply through change in ownership. Rather than rushing into rapid privatization in an institutional vacuum, reforming the public sector—with the emphasis on institutional building in a broad sense—is a more workable and desirable approach.[53]

Notes

An earlier version of this chapter was presented at the Privatization in Eastern Europe, Asia, and Latin America conference, Brown University, April 24–25, 1992. For comments and discussions I am grateful to Cevdet Denizer, Jon Elster, John Freeman, Jack Knight, Anthony Levitas, Vedat Milor, William Parish, Adam Przeworski, Thomas Rawski, Charles Sabel, David Stark, Lester Telser, Tang Tsou, Eric Olin Wright, and the participants in the conference. However, none of them should be held responsible for any mistakes in this paper. The research is supported in part by a grant from the John D. and Catherine T. MacArthur Foundation to the Project on East-South System Transformations.

1. A fine-tuned classification has to deal with the issues of selling to whom and giving away to whom. Since what I say about these two strategies is valid no matter who the buyers and receivers are, I do not pursue a fine-tuned classification in this chapter. See David Stark, "Path Dependence and Privatization Strategies in East-Central Europe," Chapter 6 of this volume; Branko Milanovic, *Liberalization and Entrepreneurship: Dynamics of Reform in Socialism and Capitalism* (Armonk, N.Y.: M. E. Sharpe, Inc., 1989); and Zhiyuan Cui, "Privatization in Eastern Europe: A Panacea?" East-South System Transformation Project, Working Paper no. 16, University of Chicago (1992), for three detailed classifications of all proposed strategies of privatization in Eastern Europe.

2. My emphasis on monetary factors should not be confused with Milton Friedman's "monetarism." In fact, monetary factors do not play an essential role in his monetarism: "Despite the important role of enterprises and money in our actual

economy, and despite the numerous and complex problems they raise, the central characteristic of the market technique of achieving coordination is fully displayed in the simple exchange economy that contains neither enterprises nor money." See Milton Friedman, *Capitalism and Freedom* (Chicago: The University of Chicago Press, 1982), p. 14. He argues that one may assume that money is dropped from helicopters. See Milton Friedman, *The Optimal Quantity of Money and Other Essays* (Chicago: Aldine, 1969), p. 4. Essentially, Friedman's monetarism is still a theory about the neutrality of money. I emphasize in contrast that monetary factors—money and credit institutions—have real effects.

3. Joseph Schumpeter, *History of Economic Analysis* (Cambridge, Mass.: Harvard University Press, 1954), p. 277.

4. All countries in Eastern Europe, including the former Soviet Union, were in deep recessions in 1990 and 1991, with the average GDP declining more than 12 percent (compared with the 1989 level). The concrete figures for each country can be found in *European Economy,* supplement A (August–September 1991).

5. Jan Winiecki, "The Inevitability of a Fall in Output in the Early Stages of Transition to the Market: Theoretical Underpinnings," *Soviet Studies* 43, 4 (1991): 669.

6. David Lipton and Jeffrey Sachs, "Creating a Market Economy in Eastern Europe: The Case of Poland," *Brookings Papers on Economic Activity* 1 (1990): 75–147.

7. Formally, this cause can be called the firms' "cash-in-advance" constraint. For more on this, see Don Patinkin, *Money, Interest, and Prices: An Integration of Monetary and Value Theory* (Cambridge, Mass.: MIT Press, 1989). Interestingly, Karl Marx can be viewed as a forerunner of the cash-in-advance model because he emphasizes the sequence of money-commodity-money (m-c-m). Presumably, this sequence is one of the main reasons that Schumpeter was always interested in Marx: Both consider money and credit as crucial in the dynamic process of economic development.

8. Don Patinkin's *Money, Interest, and Prices,* which first appeared in 1956, is a modern classic of the neoclassical approach to monetary economics. This approach is often referred to as the "Walras-Hicks-Patinkin tradition" in the literature.

9. Don Patinkin, *Money, Interest, and Prices,* p. 176.

10. Patinkin, *Money, Interest, and Prices,* p. 75.

11. In fact, Michael Bruno ("The Choice of Nominal Anchor and Disinflation," NBER Working Paper no. 3518 [1990]), a major scholar of the stabilization program, explicitly mentioned that Patinkin's theory of neutral money is the foundation of stabilization policy.

12. See Oliver Blanchard et al., *Reform in Eastern Europe* (Cambridge, Mass.: MIT Press, 1991), p. 6. Most countries in Eastern Europe chose the exchange rate as the nominal anchor.

13. Leo Hurwicz, "The Mechanisms of Resource Allocations," *Journal of Asian Economics* 1 (1991): 1–14, another leading figure of competitive general equilibrium theory, observed that even though Arrow's theoretical work is about the efficiency of competitive equilibrium, his applied work is about market failures (such as his study of medical care). Hurwicz suggested that Arrow did this applied work intentionally in order to warn his followers not to misuse the competitive general equilibrium theory (an example of such misuse is Patinkin's integration of monetary theory into value theory).

14. The textbook Keynesian economics (e.g., Hicks's IS-LM paradigm) represents money only as the "store of value" because of its emphasis on money as an

asset to hold. The "overlapping generations model" with an infinite number of periods also justifies people's desire to hold money as an asset. Only Robert Clower's "cash-in-advance" model in "A Reconsideration of the Microeconomic Foundations of Monetary Theory," *Western Economic Journal* 6, 1 (December 1967): 1–8, tries to capture the role of money as a "medium of exchange." However, if we still work within the framework of complete markets, the cash-in-advance model can be criticized as ad hoc. To develop the cash-in-advance constraint, we must resort to the theory of incomplete markets. Moreover, even if the overlapping generation model can justify the existence of money, it does not answer Schumpeter's critique because, as cited in note 3, neoclassical economics sees the role of money only as "a technical devise that has been adopted in order to facilitate transactions . . . it does not affect the economic process, which behaves in the same way as it would in a barter economy."

15. A natural question at this juncture is: What is the alternative, if any, to the standard stabilization program and its built-in recessionary bias? Sebastian Edwards, "Markets and Democracy," *World Economy* 15, 2 (1992): 35–36, discusses four potential ways of solving monetary overhang: (1) a reduction of nominal money balances through some type of monetary reform (blocking or confiscating the existing currency); (2) a once-and-for-all increase in the domestic price level; (3) an increase in domestic real output; and (4) a rise in the real demand for money. He dismisses the last two methods as "impractical and implausible." However, Chinese economic reform applies precisely the last two methods to solve the problem of "monetary overhang" (Zhiyuan Cui, "China's Economic Reform: Beyond Textbook-Microeconomics," unpublished manuscript [1992]). Also, Yoshio Suzuki's study, *Money and Banking in Contemporary Japan* (New Haven: Yale University Press, 1980), of the Japanese monetary policy since 1954 confirmed that the last two methods are plausible.

16. Joseph Stiglitz and A. Weiss, "Credit Rationing in Markets with Imperfect Information," *American Economic Review* 71 (1981): 393–410, prove that optimal behavior of commercial banks in a world of imperfect information is credit rationing, so even without government credit ceiling, interest rates do not clear credit market. Interestingly (and ironically), new established private banks (13 in Hungary, 36 in Poland, and 8 in Czechoslovakia) "lend only to state-owned enterprises, viewing the many small new companies in Eastern Europe as too risky" (David Manasian, "Business in Eastern Europe," *The Economist,* September 21, 1991), pp. 10–14. This is a telling example of nongovernment credit rationing in the credit market.

17. Such an estimate is difficult because it involves counterfactuals: What would be the output level if the credit crunch were not there? Due to the data limitation, I cannot pursue the estimate here and only point out that the correct method for it would be "switching regression model with endogenous criterion function." See G. S. Maddala, *Limited Dependent and Qualitative Variables in Econometrics* (Cambridge: Cambridge University Press, 1983).

18. Ironically, the real analysis of neoclassical economics is correct in the sense that the system of barter exchange expanded after the shock therapy. See Michael Burawoy and Pavel Krotov, "The Soviet Transition from Socialism to Capitalism," *American Sociological Review* 57, 1 (March 1992): 16–38.

19. Hungarian Prime Minister Jozsef Antall complained that privatization has generated too little revenue for the government. See *Report on Eastern Europe,* February 1, 1991. In Poland, only five large state enterprises were sold in 1990.

20. In this respect, what is relevant for the East European reformers is not Fama's and Jensen's "efficient capital market" theory, which is problematic even in

the advanced capitalist countries today, but C. Kindleberger's accounts in *Manias, Panics, and Crashes* (New York: Basic Books, Inc., 1989) of the early financial history of England. In the recent process of implementing vouchers in Czechoslovakia, some investment fund managers made impossible promises to the public in order to attract vouchers to be invested in their funds—a sign of the forthcoming stock bubble.

21. János Kornai, "The Soft Budget Constraint," *Kyklos* 39, 1 (1986): 3.

22. Kornai admits there is SBC under capitalism, too. But he considers it an exceptional phenomenon, whereas under socialism SBC is a normal state of economic life.

23. Harold Demsetz, "Toward a Theory of Property Rights," *American Economic Review* 57, 2 (May 1967): 348.

24. János Kornai, *The Road to a Free Economy: Shifting from a Socialist System* (New York: Norton, 1990), p. 85.

25. Adam Przeworski, "Ideology, Theory, and Reality: A Note of Caution About Neoliberal Policies," *Journal of Democracy* 3, 3 (1992): 4.

26. D. North and R. Thomas, *Rise of the Western World* (Cambridge: Cambridge University Press, 1973).

27. A. Alchian and Harold Demsetz, "Production, Information Costs, and Economic Organization," *American Economic Review* 62 (December 1972): 777–795.

28. In fact, the current reserve requirement on demand deposits in the United States is 3 percent for the first $41.5 million and 12 percent for the total above $41.5 million. For nonpersonal time deposits, the reserve requirement is 3 percent for deposits with a maturity period less than 18 months and no reserve requirement for deposits with a maturity period of more than 18 months. See *Annual Report of the Board of Governors of the Federal Reserve System* (Washington, D.C.: Federal Reserve, 1988), p. 225.

29. If reserves were under control of the bank, one could say that banks are still subject to hard budget constraint. However, both institutional analysis and econometric studies suggest that reserves are not quantity-constrained by the central bank. As Moore points out: "It has only recently been recognized that the conventional view, that the growth of monetary aggregates can be controlled through a quantity-constrained process over the sources of bank reserves, represents a fundamental analytical misunderstanding of the nature of the money supply process. . . . Bank loans are determined by borrow demand for credit, much like debit balances outstanding on consumer credit cards, a total over which banks in the short run have little or no control. More than half of all loans are made under lines of credit arrangements, and the utilization rate of lines of credit is characteristically about 50 percent." See Basil Moore, "Contemporaneous Reserve Accounting: Can Reserves Be Quantity-Constrained?" *Journal of Post Keynesian Economics* 7 (Fall 1984): 106.

30. The three sources of SBC are all monetary sources. For a discussion of real sources of SBC, especially monopoly market structure as a cause of SBC, see Sadoa Nagaoka and Izak Atiyas, "Tightening the Soft Budget Constraint in Reforming Socialist Economies," Industry and Energy Department Working Paper no. 35, The World Bank, Washington, D.C. (1990).

31. Schumpeter, *History of Economic Analysis.*

32. Mainstream macroeconomics textbooks describe the central bank as the controller of aggregate money supply. However, as a matter of historical fact, the central bank developed as the lender of last resort. See Charles Goodhart, *The Evolution of Central Banks* (Cambridge, Mass.: MIT Press, 1990).

33. For example, when the Penn Central Transportation Company defaulted on its commercial paper, the Federal Reserve intervened to protect the commercial paper market by assuring the refinancing by banks of billions of dollars of commercial paper borrowed by companies, including Chrysler Corporation and many small firms. See Albert Wojnilower, "The Central Role of Credit Crunches in Recent Financial History," *Brookings Papers on Economic Activity* 2 (1980): 292–293.

34. *Repurchase agreement* means that banks sell government bonds and agree to repurchase them the next day at a higher price. This system can be used to raise the average reserve holdings of the bank.

35. For example, in order to prevent the collapse of the Continental Illinois Bank of Chicago in 1984 (then the seventh-largest bank in the United States), the FDIC announced that it would guarantee all of Continental's deposits—not just the first $100,000—and all of its nondeposit liabilities. See Meir Kohn, *Money, Banking, and Financial Markets* (Chicago: The Dryden Press, 1991).

36. Randall Wray, *Money and Credit in Capitalist Economies: The Endogenous Money Approach* (Brookfield, Ver.: Edward Elgar, 1990), p. 246.

37. Hyman Minsky, *Stabilizing an Unstable Economy* (New Haven: Yale University Press, 1986), p. 50.

38. See Thomas Stanton, *A State of Risk* (New York: Harper Business, 1991), p. 4.

39. Joseph Stiglitz and A. Weiss, "Banks as Social Accountants and Screening Devices and General Theory of Credit Rationing," NBER Working Paper no. 2710 (1988), p. 58.

40. Stiglitz and Weiss, "Banks as Social Accountants," p. 19.

41. This problem does not contradict the ability of banks to create money, because they may overloan only to their familiar customers. In fact, the birthplace of modern banking—medieval Italy—was characterized by family networks. See Raymond De Roover, *The Rise and Decline of the Medici Bank* (New York: Norton, 1966). In the nineteenth-century United States, the New England banking industry also was characterized by insider lending. See Naomi Lamoreaux, "Information Problems and Banks' Specialization in Short-Term Commercial Lending: New England in the Nineteenth Century," in Peter Temin (ed.), *Inside the Business Enterprise* (Chicago: The University of Chicago Press, 1991), pp. 161–194.

42. Cevdet Denizer suggested to me that a good firm can offer higher interest rates so that it is able to get credits. But I believe credit rationing equilibrium is a "pooling equilibrium" rather than a "separating equilibrium" because the cause of credit rationing is exactly that banks cannot distinguish good and bad firms, so they view the offer of high interest rates as an adverse signal.

43. Remember that "on the morning of Franklin D. Roosevelt's inauguration the governors of New York and Illinois closed the banks of New York City and Chicago," and the first legislation Roosevelt signed was the the Emergency Banking Act. James Olson, *Saving Capitalism* (Princeton: Princeton University Press, 1988), p. 29.

44. Lawrence White, *Competition and Currency* (New York: New York University Press, 1989), p. 138.

45. Keizo Nagatani, *Political Macroeconomics* (Oxford: Clarendon Press, 1989), p. 170.

46. Schumpeter, *History of Economic Analysis,* p. 282.

47. D. North and B. Weingast, "Constitutions and Commitment," Working Paper, Washington University, St. Louis, Mo. (1987).

48. Irving Fisher, *100% Money* (New York: Adelphi Publication, 1935); Milton Friedman, *Capitalism and Freedom* (Chicago: The University of Chicago

Press, 1982); James Tobin, "Financial Innovation and Deregulation in Perspective," *Bank of Japan Monetary and Economic Studies* 3, 2 (1985): 1–25; and Maurice Allais, "The Credit Mechanism and Its Implications," in George R. Feiwel (ed.), *Arrow and the Theory of Economic Policy* (New York: University Press, 1987), pp. 491–529, advocate a 100 percent reserve system; F. A. Hayek, *Denationalization of Money* (London: Institute of Economic Affairs, 1976); and Lawrence White, *Competition and Currency,* propose to eliminate the central bank altogether. However, as Schumpeter recognized long ago, the 100 percent reserve requirement would reduce the incentive of banks and thus retard economic growth. Moreover, Hayek's proposal of eliminating the central bank would repeatedly bring back depressions resembling the Great Depression. Appropriately, Walter Bagehot, the main founder of the theory of central banking in nineteenth century England, said: "Nor would any English statesman propose to 'wind up' the Bank of England [the central bank]. A theorist might put such a suggestion on paper, but no responsible government would think of it." Walter Bagehot, *Lombard Street* (London: John Murray, 1927), p. 105.

49. Even Kornai admitted in his latest book that "any static interpretation would provide a highly simplified picture of the intricate social phenomenon termed here the softness of budget constraint. It depicts a static problem of choice, whereas this is clearly a case of dynamic process in which an expenditure flow is opposed to an income flow." János Kornai, *The Socialist System* (Princeton: Princeton University Press, 1992), p. 143. From a static perspective, SBC is bad, so there are proposals for establishing 100 percent reserve banking. However, from a dynamic perspective, a proper degree of SBC is necessary for economic growth. For a fuller discussion of static versus dynamic perspectives in the context of socialist economic reform, see Zhiyuan Cui, "Market Incompleteness, Innovation, and Reform," *Politics and Society* 1 (March 1991): 59–69.

50. The recent S&L debacle is a telling example of out-of-control SBC. The main reason for this crisis is that deregulation on one side (such as freeing interest rates charged by S&Ls) was not accompanied by proper regulation on the other (such as regulation on "safety and soundness" of investment by S&Ls). As a result, many S&Ls imprudently bought large amounts of junk bonds.

51. SBC is perhaps a matter of degree both in the advanced market economies in the West and in the traditional socialist economies. The degree of softness depends on the institutional arrangement in question. For example, regulation of the bank capital requirement can reduce the degree of moral hazard (SBC). I concede that the degree of budget constraint softness in the traditional socialist economy may be higher than that of the advanced capitalist economy. But what is relevant here is that private ownership is not the direct cause of this difference.

52. This feature certainly paves the way for massive fraud later on. It should be noted here that both British and (especially) French privatization programs devoted much attention to regulation after privatization. See C. Graham and T. Prosser, *Privatizing Public Enterprises: Constitutions, the State, and Regulations in Comparative Perspective* (Oxford: Clarendon Press, 1991).

53. The discussion of details of public sector reform is beyond the scope of this chapter. See Thomas Rawski, Chapter 2, and Andrew Walder, Chapter 3, in this volume for an insightful study of the Chinese experience of public sector reform.

About the Authors

IZAK ATIYAS is an economist at the World Bank, specializing in industrial organization and financial economics. He holds a doctorate in economics from New York University.

ZHIYUAN CUI is an assistant professor at the Department of Political Science at Massachusetts Institute of Technology and research associate at the John Fairbank Center for Chinese Studies, Harvard University. He is the author of "Market Incompleteness, Innovation, and Reform," *Politics and Society* 1 (March 1991); and "Privatization in Eastern Europe: A Panacea?" in Adam Przeworski (ed.), *Transition and Reform: East and South* (forthcoming).

CEVDET DENIZER is a consultant at the World Bank and a Ph.D. candidate in economics at Miami University. He has collaborated on and authored several World Bank publications.

SANTIAGO EDER is an MBA candidate at the London Business School. He holds an M.A. in Soviet studies from Harvard University and a B.A. in economics from Brown University. He has conducted extensive privatization research in Ukraine.

ALAN GELB is chief of the Socialist Economies Unit at the World Bank. He holds a doctorate in economics from Oxford University and is the author of numerous articles and several books, including *The Transformation of Economies in East and Central Europe,* with Cheryl Gray.

SIMON JOHNSON is an assistant professor at Duke University's Fuqua School of Business. He is the author, with Heidi Kroll, of "Managerial Strategies for Spontaneous Privatization," in *Soviet Economy* 7, 4 (1991); and "The Implications of the Polish Economic Reform for Small Business: Evidence from Gdansk," in Acs and Audretsch (eds.), *Entrepreneurship in East and West*

HEIDI KROLL is a Fellow at Harvard University's Russian Research Center. An economist who specializes in the economy of the former Soviet Union, she is currently researching economic reform and monopoly in the Republics. She has taught courses on the economy of the former Soviet Union and comparative economics. Her publications have appeared in a number of journals, including *Soviet Economy and Soviet Studies.*

ANTHONY LEVITAS is a Ph.D. candidate in the Department of Political Science at the Massachusetts Institute of Technology. He is the author, with Janusz Dabroski and Michal Federowicz, of "Polish State Enterprises and the Properties of Performance: Stabilization, Marketization, and Privatization, 1990–1991," in *Politics and Society* (December 1991).

VEDAT MILOR is assistant professor of sociology at Brown University and a former consultant at the World Bank. He is author of two articles, including "Eastern Europe and the International Development Institutions," in *Brown Foreign Affairs Journal* (Winter 1992). He was awarded the Best Dissertation Prize by the American Sociological Association in 1990 for his "Planning and Economic Development in Turkey and France: Bringing the State Back In," which will be published in 1994 by the University of Wisconsin Press. He holds a doctorate in sociology from the University of California–Berkeley.

THOMAS G. RAWSKI is professor of economics and history at the University of Pittsburgh. He is the author of *Chinese History in Economic Perspective* (forthcoming) and *Economic Growth in Prewar China.*

DAVID STARK is associate professor of sociology at Cornell University. He is the author, with Victor Nee, of *Remaking the Economic Institutions of Socialism: China and Eastern Europe.*

ANDREW G. WALDER is professor of sociology at Harvard University. He is the author of "Urban Industrial Workers: Some Observations on the 1980s," in Arthur Rosenbaum (ed.), *State and Society in China: The Consequences of Reform.*

LEILA WEBSTER is an economist, specializing in small and medium industrial development, in the Industry Development Division of the World Bank. She is the author of three World Bank working papers on private sector manufacturing in Poland, Hungary, and the former Czechoslovakia.

Index

Agency of Ownership Change (Poland), 103, 105

Agency problems, 16, 195; external finance, 196–197

Agriculture: collective, 57, 58; household, 58

Aid, 11; conditional, 79; cutoffs, 87, 89–91; external, 79; foreign, 86, 92–93; international, 79

Antall, Jozsef, 130, 224n18

Assets: acquisition of, 119, 120, 121*fig;* income from, 56; institutional holdings, 56; liquidation of, 56; management of, 55, 57; market value, 75; ownership, 93; returns from, 55, 57–59; transfer of, 56, 59–60, 65n10; use restrictions, 56; valuation of, 119, 121*fig,* 122, 126, 130, 133, 142n38

Atiyas, Izak, 15, 18, 195–208

Balcerowicz, Leszek, 128

Banking: centralized, 73*tab,* 73–74; commercial, 72*tab,* 179; in corporate restructuring, 198; creation of, 161–162; German, 199; Japanese, 199; monitoring function, 126; reform, 73; regulation, 17; in restructuring, 205–207; supervision of, 9; system legalization, 72*tab*

Banking Act (United States), 219

Banking Law (Mongolia), 73*tab*

Bankruptcy, 27, 33, 113n21, 198, 203–205, 220–221; costs, 210n27; implementation procedures, 3; legislation, 17

Bankruptcy Code (United States), 198, 219, 220

Bankruptcy Law (Mongolia), 73*tab*

Bargaining, 119, 124, 130, 144n58; financial, 53; flexible, 10; objectives, 61–62; and taxation, 10, 61

Barter, 9, 16, 87, 152, 160, 164, 165, 213, 214, 215, 224n18

Basic Provisions of the Privatization Program (Russia), 153, 155

Behavior: entrepreneurial, 50; market-oriented, 10, 38, 50; monopolistic, 8; risk-taking, 9

Bielecki, Jan, 127, 128, 213

Borrowing. *See* Funding

Budget constraints: flexible, 61–63; hard, 53; soft, 15–16, 20n17, 29, 40–41, 60, 61–63, 213–222

Bulgaria: gross domestic product, 19n4, 84, 96n28; imports, 70*tab*

Capital: accumulation of, 75; domestic, 88; goods, 69; low-capacity utilization, 3; markets, 16, 93, 126, 127, 131; shortage of, 14; stock, 52n21; underutilization of, 88; working, 14

Capitalism, 3, 6, 11, 17, 55, 56, 218; "cookbook," 115–117, 137; creation of, 12; nomenklatura, 128; popular, 130; punter, 7, 15; replication of, 115; resource allocation in, 17; variations, 135

Cartels, 159, 173n59

China: access to credit in, 10; corporate organization in, 53–64; economic growth in, 29; employment in, 30tab, 60; gradualism in, 5, 27; gross national product, 60; industry in, 30–43; investment in, 38; per capita income in, 60; prereform industrial structure, 32; private sector in, 33; privatization in, 10, 27–50, 54; production in, 9; property rights in, 53–64; reform in, 27–50, 54–61

Chinese Academy of Social Sciences, 44

Collectives, workers', 8

Colonialism, 83
Commercialization, 12, 106; of funding, 48; of state-owned enterprises, 102–107; veto power for, 105
Communism, 12, 63, 64, 83, 134, 135
Competition, 28; economic, 8; foreign, 14; import, 179; industrial, 60; market, 123; and profit reduction, 43; role of, 9; in state enterprises, 39–40
Constant elasticity of substitution, 88
Consumer demand, 14
Contracts, 55, 57, 147; economics of, 65n9; form, 167n4; reasonable, 107–109; relational, 119, 130, 131; rewriting, 167; structure of, 150
Cooperatives, 151
Corporatization, 42, 171n38; of ministries, 152; privatization through, 154
Corruption, 64, 66n26, 106
Cost(s): control, 28; production, 116; transaction, 131, 141n33; transition, 116
Council for Mutual Economic Assistance: dissolution of, 77; trade, 3, 68, 71, 82, 87
Credit: appraisal capability, 95n19; bank, 10; institutions, 133; market equilibrium, 220; rationing, 220–221; terms, 62
Cui, Zhiyuan, 16, 213–222
Currency: appreciation, 14; convertible, 1, 14, 74, 84; devaluation, 72tab, 73, 74, 178, 179; exchange, 72tab; hard, 130, 160, 163, 179
Czechoslovakia: business environment, 179–180; distribution of shares in, 21n19; entrepreneurs in, 14, 180, 181; free market approach in, 4; gross national product, 180; imports, 70tab; industrial output, 2; manufacturing firms in, 183, 183tab; private sector in, 177–178; privatization in, 13, 121fig, 124–127; state role in privatization, 101; trade unions in, 145n62

Debt: enterprise, 133; for equity exchange, 144n57; external, 197; financing, 197; foreign, 1; interenterprise, 16, 216; reduction, 197; short-term, 162
Decapitalization, 8
Decentralization, 12; economic, 67
Decision-making, 12
Denizer, Cevdet, 11, 67–93
Development: infrastructure, 40; private sector, 74–75; technical, 28

East Germany: privatization in, 13, 121fig, 122–124; radical reform failure in, 5; renationalization in, 109; state role in privatization, 101; Treuhandanstalt, 122–124, 202–203; westward migration, 123–124
Economic(s): competition, 8; of contracts, 65n9; decentralization, 67; development, 17; institutional, 6–9, 18, 20n18; liberalization, 4, 11; neoclassical, 18, 214, 215; neoinstitutionalist, 15; of organization, 55; policy, 20n13; reform, 5, 67, 71, 72tab; restructuring, 71; stagnation, 11
Economy: administrative controls on, 77; barter, 213, 214, 215; capitalist, 3, 6, 55, 56, 218; centrally planned, 82; industrial, 18; market, 2, 14, 67, 82, 96n28, 102, 118; open, 87; organizational structure, 7; pastoral, 69, 85; planned, 50; rural, 32; second, 118; socialist, 6, 55; stock market-based, 197; transitional, 195–208; wartime, 11, 85
Eder, Santiago, 13, 147–167
Employee councils, 12, 102, 103–104, 105, 106, 107, 108, 109, 142n41, 143n43
Employment: growth in, 60; nonagricultural, 60; preservation of, 3
Enterprise and Bank Restructuring Law (Poland), 206
Enterprises, leased, 160–161
Enterprises, private, 54
Enterprises, republican, 162–164
Enterprises, small, 151, 153–154, 156, 169n17, 169n22, 173n65
Enterprises, spread of the market, 59
Enterprises, state-owned, 15; asset holding, 56; commercialization of, 12, 102–107; competition in, 39–40; conversion into joint stock companies, 13, 75, 102, 132, 151–152; corporatization of, 42; cost pressures, 40–41; distribution systems, 94n8; efficiency in, 29; external control structure, 148; improvement of performance, 29; industrial, 3; as limited liability companies, 132, 133; and market forces, 43; monopoly power of, 39; privatization of, 1, 2, 4; productivity growth, 28, 54; profits and retained earnings in, 44, 45–47tab, 49tab; redistributive nature of, 55; renationalization of, 12, 103, 106, 107–109; subsidies in, 62; supervision of, 150; voucher systems, 75–77, 79,

124–127, 128–130, 140–141*n21,* 142*n36,*
154–155, 171*n39;* worker-led buyouts,
99
Entrepreneurs, 14, 180–182; constraints on,
185–187
Europe, East-Central: gross domestic product, 3, 82; industrial output, 3; path
dependence in, 115–138; political parties
in, 2; private sector manufacturing in,
175–191; private sector reform in, 11–
15; privatization in, 11–15, 115–138;
recession in, 2, 16; transitions in, 115–
117
European Bank for Reconstruction and
Development, 4, 137
Exchange: commodity, 152; foreign, 33, 75,
90–91, 177–178, 179; market, 33; rates,
72*tab,* 215, 216
Export(s), 15, 77, 96*n28;* agricultural, 68,
90; disruption of, 89–91; markets, 160;
rights, 73*tab*

Foreign Investment Law (Mongolia),
72*tab*
Free rider problem, 7, 197, 200
Funding: access to, 46–47, 49*tab,* 50; commercial, 47, 48; for investment, 72*tab;*
noncommercial, 48

Gelb, Alan, 11, 67–93
Generally Accepted Accounted Principles,
219
German Democratic Republic. *See* East
Germany
Germany. *See* East Germany
Glasnost, 67
Gorbachev, Mikhail, 151
Gossnab, 152
Gradualism, 5, 20*n13*

Hierarchies: authority in, 57–58; forcible creation of, 163; new, 13, 150, 159, 172*n57;*
reconstruction of, 13, 150, 158–159,
172*n57;* replacement of, 58
Holding companies, 151, 152, 159
Hungarian Democratic Forum, 130
Hungary: bank credit in, 47; bankruptcy policy, 204; business environment, 179;
entrepreneurs in, 14, 180, 181; foreign
trade, 5; gross domestic product, 19*n4,*
179; imports, 70*tab,* 179; industrial output, 2; interest rates in, 5; manufacturing

firms in, 182, 183*tab;* price controls in,
5; private sector in, 177–178; privatization in, 13, 121*fig,* 130–134, 153; renationalization in, 110; state role in privatization, 101; subsidy policy, 44; tax
policy, 44; trade unions in, 145*n62*

IMF. *See* International Monetary Fund
Import(s), 14, 216; competition, 179; penetration, 179; rationing of, 74; subsidized,
72*tab*
Income: from assets, 11, 56; derivation from
property, 2; distribution, 152; distribution
rights, 55; lost, 1; national, 120; real,
179; redistribution, 92–93; residual, 58;
rights to, 58; rural, 88, 92–93; sharing,
58; urban, 88–89, 92–93
Industrial: competition, 60; economy, 18;
inefficiency, 3; investment, 32, 69; pricing, 32; production, 32; profits,
34–37*tab,* 39; regulation, 56; restructuring, 102, 195–208; subsidies, 15, 40, 62
Industrial Development Agency (Poland),
206
Industry: decentralization of, 32; defense-
related, 38; infant, 47; innovation in,
31–32; routine activities, 31–32; rural,
39, 60
Inflation, 15, 18, 40, 41, 43, 63, 73, 103, 160,
179, 218
Infrastructure development, 40
Insolvency Act (United Kingdom), 198
Institute for Economic Research (China), 44
Institute for Economic System Reform
(China), 44
Institutions: control, 17; credit, 133; economic, 18; market-supporting, 17; reconfiguration of, 118; replacement of, 117; secondary, 142*n34*
Interest rates, 5, 15, 72*tab,* 216
International Monetary Fund, 3, 4, 14,
20*n13,* 79, 106, 137, 215
Intervention, state, 15, 18
Investment: borrowing for, 47; foreign, 33,
41, 128, 153, 177; funding, 72*tab,* 126;
industrial, 32, 69; institutional, 7; international, 131; private, 40; and profitability,
47; public sector, 72*tab;* state funds for,
47

Jaruzelski, Wojciech, 128, 135
Johnson, Simon, 13, 147–167

Kornai, János, 10
Kroll, Heidi, 13, 147–167

Labor: hired, 151; low-capacity utilization, 3; organized, 3, 127; relations, 107
Law on Cooperatives (Mongolia), 72*tab*
Levitas, Anthony, 4, 7, 12, 14, 15, 17, 99–111
Lewandowski, Janusz, 128
Liberalization: economic, 4, 11; market, 74, 78, 82; price, 1, 67, 72*tab,* 74, 78, 79, 95*n17,* 214, 215; trade, 14, 67, 178
Liquidation, 3, 56, 107–109, 124, 128, 152
Living standards, 69, 85, 92; equalization of, 87; and inflation, 41

Management: of assets, 57; profit objectives, 42; rights of, 55
Managers: accountability of, 3–4, 21*n19,* 56; asset, 129; and control, 56; entrenchment of, 152; incentive structures for, 3, 7, 8; monitoring of, 7, 21*n19;* as new owners, 124; problems with owners, 6–7; and rights of control, 13, 147, 148; and spontaneous privatization, 167*n6*
Market(s): allocation mechanisms, 55; barriers, 39; capital, 16, 93, 126, 127, 131; competition, 123; completeness of, 215; credit, 16; discipline, 7; domestic, 74; economy, 2, 14, 67, 82, 96*n28,* 102, 118; exchange, 33; export, 160; failure, 18, 29, 104, 110; free, 4; growth in, 41; infrastructure, 82; liberalization, 74, 78, 82; local, 32; money, 16; reform, 77; regulation, 10; secondary, 59, 60, 75, 77–78; socialism, 3, 5, 7, 8, 102; stock, 9, 17, 73*tab,* 79, 130, 197, 198, 217; transition, 53
Mazowiecki, Tadeusz, 128, 213
Migration: German, 123–124; reverse, 91; rural, 85
Milor, Vedat, 1–18
Monetarism, 16
Mongolia: dependence on Soviet Union, 68, 69, 71, 83, 84, 87; distribution of shares in, 75; dualistic economic structure, 87; early reform, 68–73; economic restructuring, 71, 72*tab;* exports, 68, 69, 70*tab,* 77, 85, 96*n28;* gross domestic product, 68, 69, 71, 77, 84, 85, 89, 96*n28;* imports, 69, 70*tab,* 77, 84; inadequacy of infrastructure, 68; private sector develop-
ment, 74–75; privatization in, 67–93; reform in, 10–11, 72*tab,* 82–86; socioeconomic structure, 69; urbanization in, 69
Mongolian People's Revolutionary Party, 73, 78, 83, 93
Monopolies: break-up of, 3; deregulation in, 32; deverticalization of, 9; private, 9; public vs. private, 29; regulation of, 56; state, 72*tab*

Nationalism, 71, 83

Organization: administration of, 148; corporate, 53–64; network forms, 17; ownership, 9; strategy, 148
Ownership: of assets, 93; collective, 169*n22;* in competitive conditions, 29; control in, 55, 56; definition, 55–56; dilution of, 7, 21*n19,* 127, 129; employee, 128, 142*n41;* institutionalized, 6; mixed, 132; organizations, 9; private, 56, 74, 151; public, 56; reassignment of, 9; rights, 14, 119, 120–122, 153; share, 20*n10,* 79, 126, 132; transfer of, 14, 76, 118

Path dependence, 12, 115–138, 139*n8*
Perestroika, 148, 150, 165
Poland, 70*tab;* bankruptcy policy, 204; business environment, 178–179; distribution of shares in, 21*n19;* domestic demand decline, 3; economic policy in, 20*n13;* entrepreneurs in, 14, 180, 181; gross domestic product, 19*n4,* 179; industrial output, 2; manufacturing firms in, 182, 183*tab;* organizational structure, 15, 18; organized labor in, 3; private sector in, 177–178; privatization in, 11–13, 99–111, 121*fig,* 127–130, 153; property system, 8; reform failure in, 99, 106; renationalization in, 103, 106, 107–109, 110; restructuring in, 205–207; trade unions in, 145*n62*
Policy: antimonopoly, 172*n53;* economic, 20*n13;* fiscal, 1, 41, 102; monetary, 1, 14, 15, 16, 41, 102
Politics: and motivation for reform, 1, 2, 83; multiparty, 73
Price(s): concessional, 41; consumer, 179; controls, 5, 11, 77, 151; deregulation, 73*tab;* distortions in, 48; domestic, 74; formation, 119; free, 1, 102; increases in, 1; liberalization, 1, 67, 72*tab,* 74, 78, 79,

95*n17,* 214, 215; reform, 77; regulation of, 63; setting, 141*n31;* stock, 103
Principal-agent problem, 6–7
Privatization, 1; centralized management of, 133; definition, 118; differing types, 13; domestic savings in, 20*n10;* employee buyouts in, 12, 105–107, 151–152, 153–154; former all-Union enterprises, 157–162; of former republican firms, 162–164; immediate, 9; independent strategies, 159–162; and institutional economics, 6–9; in isolated economies, 67–93; laws, 155; of local enterprises, 164–165; managed, 152–156; nomen-klatura, 153; organizational basis of, 151–152; and path dependence, 115–138; and private sector reform, 11–15; privatization of, 130; rapid, 18; and recession, 214–217; and restructuring, 200–202; sectoral, 113*n14;* slow progress of, 4; and soft budget constraints, 213–222; sponta-neous, 13, 76, 147–167, 179, 184; strate-gies, 115–122, 121*fig;* through corporati-zation, 154
Privatization Law (Mongolia), 73*tab,* 75
Production: commodity, 9; domestic, 14; growth in, 28, 53, 60; industrial, 32; modernization of, 137; reduction in, 214; rural, 88; socially unwanted, 214; subordinated to trade, 9; uncompetitive, 3
Profit sharing, 10, 33, 41
Property: decentralized reorganization, 132; foreign management, 130; positional, 121; private, 104; reform, 128; reprivati-zation of, 140*n20;* rights, 2, 9, 10, 53–64, 100, 104, 120, 124, 127, 130, 133, 147–148, 217; sources of, 183–185; structure, 17; systems, 8; theft of, 148, 170*n32;* transformation of, 149
Protectionism: regional, 39; social, 87

Rationing, 74
Rawski, Thomas, 1, 5, 9, 10, 27–50
Recession, 2, 16, 38, 179, 214–217, 223*n4*
Reform: antitrust, 9; banking, 73; big-bang, 73–77; coherence of, 1; economic, 5, 32, 67, 71, 72*tab;* elements of, 1; enterprise, 151; failure, 5; fiscal, 58, 62; institution-al, 3, 4, 9; legal, 74; long-term process, 18; market, 77; pace of, 1; political, 2, 29, 71, 84; price, 77; profit sharing, 41;

property, 10, 53, 56–57, 128; radical, 82; and resource envelope, 86*fig;* reversal of, 82; shock-therapy, 1, 2, 5, 14, 214; and social disruption, 83; structural, 72*tab;* support for, 83
Regime of bargaining, 10, 61
Regulation: banking, 17; bureaucratic, 10; government, 29; industrial, 56; market, 10; of monopolies, 56; price, 63; stock market, 17
Renationalization, 12, 103, 106, 107–109
Rent seeking, 16, 22*n36,* 40–41, 64
Research Center for Marketization and Property Reform (Poland), 128
Resources: access to, 33; in acquisition of ownership rights, 120–122; allocation of, 17, 41, 148, 215; control of, 6; domestic, 71; industrial, 29; institutional, 117, 118; local, 32; policymakers', 116; positional, 140*n19;* transfer of, 29
Restructuring: bank-led, 205–207; corporate, 198, 199; preprivatization, 4, 20*n9;* and privatization, 200–202; and soft budget constraints, 15–16; in transitional economies, 195–208
Rights: attenuation of, 56–57; exchange, 55; of exclusion, 55; export, 73*tab;* to man-agement, 55; ownership, 9, 14, 119, 120–122; property, 2, 9, 10, 53–64, 100, 104, 120, 124, 127, 130, 133, 147, 217, 218; reassignment, 57–60; residual con-trol, 13, 147, 148, 150, 158, 164, 166, 167*n4,* 168*n7,* 200; transfer of, 55; of use, 57; voting, 4, 171*n41*
Risk-taking, 9
Rural: economy, 32; income, 88, 92–93; industry, 39, 60; migration, 85; produc-ton, 88; taxation, 91
Russia. *See* Soviet Union

Sector, industrial: financial loss in, 38; priva-tization in, 11–12; state-owned, 3
Sector, private: cooperatives in, 72*tab;* cre-ation of, 14, 118, 177; development of, 15, 74–75; guarantees to, 17; manufactur-ing, 175–191; reform in, 11–15; rent seeking in, 22*n36*
Sector, public, 118; investments in, 72*tab;* rent seeking in, 22*n36*
Sector, rural, 59, 85, 90, 92–93; industrial performance in, 63
Sector, self-employed, 177

Sector, service, 3
Sector, urban, 85, 90, 92–93
Shareholding corporations, 151–152
Short-time work, 123, 141*n24*
Socialism, 6, 55; causes of failure, 115; market, 3, 5, 7, 8, 12, 102
Solidarity, 127, 145*n62*, 213
Soviet Union: cessation of trade with, 3; dependence of others on, 68, 71, 83, 87; organized labor in, 3; privatization in, 147–167
Stark, David, 12, 14, 15, 17, 18
State: intervention, 15, 18; ownership of enterprises. *See* Enterprises, state-owned; and reasonable contracts, 107–109; role in privatization, 101
State Planning Committee (Mongolia), 72*tab*
State Privatization Program (Ukraine), 155–156
State Property Agency (Hungary), 130, 131, 132, 133, 144*n54*
Stock: companies, 13; markets, 9, 17, 73*tab*, 79, 130, 197, 198, 217
Structural adjustment, 3, 4, 214
Subcontracting, 59, 143*n50*
Subsidies, 15, 33, 44, 50, 124, 216; cuts in, 73; import, 72*tab*; industrial, 40, 62; removal of, 1; state commitment to, 47; unprofitable, 43
Szomburg, Jan, 128

Taxation, 10; avoidance of, 40; bargaining in, 61; concessions, 151; flexibility in, 53; reduction of revenues from, 43; responsibility contracts of, 58; rural,

91; terms of, 61; and windfall profits, 108
Theories: general equilibrium, 68, 85; neutral money, 215, 216; nominal anchor, 215, 216; property rights, 217–218; rational choice, 21*n19*
Tourism, 41
Trade: barter, 87; controls, 74; Council for Mutual Economic Assistance, 3, 68, 71, 82, 87; disruption, 11, 85, 87, 89–91, 158; foreign, 5, 20*n13*, 33, 60, 73*tab*, 77; liberalization, 14, 67; most-favored-nation, 72*tab*; securities, 93; stock, 80*fig*; terms of, 84, 96*n31*; unions, 127, 136, 145*n62*
Treuhandanstalt (East Germany), 122–124, 202–203

Ukraine, privatization in, 147–167
Unemployment, 1, 73, 124, 141*n24*, 180; compensation, 123; urban, 60, 84, 90*tab*, 92, 92*tab*
Urbanization, 69

Vouchers, 75–77, 79, 124–127, 128–130, 140–141*n21*, 142*n36*, 154–155, 171*n39*

Wages, 50; maintenance of, 3; minimum, 77; real, 180; setting of, 8
Walder, Andrew, 5, 10, 11, 53–64
Walesa, Lech, 127, 128
Webster, Leila, 14, 175–191
World Bank, 3, 4, 19*n4*, 79, 106, 137, 176

Yeltsin, Boris, 145*n65*

About the Book

Since the collapse of communism in Eastern Europe and parts of Asia, two major schools of thought there have wrestled with how the reforming states can best break with the old system and join the West. The dominant school, the so-called "big bangers," has advocated abrupt, sweeping moves toward a Western-style market economy. In contrast, the "gradualist" school has endorsed a slower pace to economic reform.

The economists, political scientists, and sociologists represented in this book question the validity of the "big bang" concept and the wholesale privatization of the industrial sector that serves as the centerpiece of its grand design. Arguing instead in favor of a gradualist program—one less costly economically and more feasible politically—they analyze the diverse strategies for privatization and restructuring being adopted in various states. The cautious approach to economic liberalization successfully implemented in the PRC is suggested as a relevant model for Eastern Europe.

Emerging Global Issues

THOMAS G. WEISS, SERIES EDITOR

Third World Security in the Post–Cold War Era
edited by Thomas G. Weiss and Meryl A. Kessler

The Suffering Grass:
Superpowers and Regional Conflict in Southern Africa and the Caribbean
edited by Thomas G. Weiss and James G. Blight

State and Market in Development: Synergy or Rivalry?
edited by Louis Putterman and Dietrich Rueschemeyer

Collective Security in a Changing World
edited by Thomas G. Weiss

Humantarianism Across Borders: Sustaining Civilians in Times of War
edited by Thomas G. Weiss and Larry Minear

Changing Political Economies:
Privatization in Post-Communist and Reforming Communist States
edited by Vedat Milor